THE COKERS OF CAROLINA

PUBLISHED FOR

THE INSTITUTE FOR RESEARCH
IN SOCIAL SCIENCE

BY

The University of North Carolina Press

THE
COKERS
OF
CAROLINA

*A Social Biography
of a Family*

BY

GEORGE LEE SIMPSON, JR.

CHAPEL HILL
THE UNIVERSITY OF NORTH CAROLINA PRESS

Copyright, 1956, by
The University of North Carolina Press

Manufactured in the United States of America

For

George and Joe

Foreword

THIS SOCIAL biography of the Coker family had its origin with Joseph H. Willits, Director for the Social Sciences in the Rockefeller Foundation. Dr. Willits was acquainted with certain members of the family, both in South Carolina and elsewhere. His feeling that a history of the family should be written was not based upon memorializing a distinguished family. Rather, his primary purpose grew out of the Foundation's long-time interest in the welfare of the South. It was thought that the example of Coker achievements, indigenous to the region, should be available on a broad basis.

The Rockefeller Foundation, therefore, made a grant to the University of North Carolina's Institute for Research in Social Science in 1947. An original suggestion was that Dr. Francis W. Coker, then at the point of retiring from Yale University, might undertake the work. Properly, Dr. Coker declined, though agreeing to act in an advisory capacity. Full freedom was accorded the author, and in all cases he has made the final decisions relative to the manuscript.

Dr. George L. Simpson, Jr., lived for two years in Hartsville, South Carolina, carrying on the research and writing pertaining to the Cokers who had lived their lives, or were living them, in that area. Subsequently at Chapel Hill the work on certain members of the family who had left Darlington County was completed.

The Institute is deeply grateful to the Coker family for the complete freedom allowed in this study and for their unstinted cooperation, and to the Rockefeller Foundation for support of the project.

Gordon W. Blackwell

Acknowledgment

THE AUTHOR is grateful to be able to say that all members of the Coker family rendered the highest sort of cooperation. All questions were answered openly and freely; original source materials were provided without hesitation. No limits of any kind were placed on the study by the family.

Gratitude is also expressed to the Rockefeller Foundation, and especially to Joseph Willets, for both originating and supporting this study, as one in a long line of that Foundation's contributions to the upbuilding of the South.

At Hartsville, Miss Mabel Tatum, deceased, rendered heroic service as secretary, and often as adviser. At Chapel Hill, I wish to express my gratitude to Miss Louise Dalton, Mrs. Hugh F. Rankin, and Miss Isabel Winslette.

As always, the pattern of work in the Institute for Research in Social Science removed many obstacles. Appreciation is expressed to Dr. Gordon W. Blackwell, Director, and to Dr. Katharine Jocher, Assistant Director.

In this work, as in other respects, my debt to Dr. Howard W. Odum is incalculable and continuing.

It is true to say that without the support of my wife, Louise Hartsell Simpson, this book would not have been finished, and the dedication to our children is properly made by both of us.

Author's Note

IN WRITING THE biography of a family across four generations, there is an inherent problem and an inherent unfairness. The descendants of Caleb and Hannah Coker today are numbered in the hundreds. (There were, indeed, ten children of Caleb and Hannah Coker.) Clearly it is impossible to write in a single coherent volume of all those people who, whether they bear the Coker name or not, are members of the family.

The book is primarily about those Cokers who, in the public eye and by common agreement, have been a part of a notable achievement, either as individuals or as a part of a persisting family unit bearing the name Coker. Many who are omitted by these measures have claims to distinction through character and goodness and performance that are fully as worthy as those of any included in this volume.

In so far as the family influence is significantly effective through several generations, then in general in American society that influence is found with the family name, and it is found in a place around which the family members are grouped. There are exceptions, but that is the rule. Families in America tend to send their children out to begin what are, for practical purposes, new family units. So this study for the most part has followed the Cokers in name and place. It begins in Society Hill, South Carolina, where Caleb and Hannah Coker established a new family unit; it ends in Hartsville, South Carolina, where in name and place and achievement, the tide of family life has placed it.

Contents

		PAGE
Foreword		vii
Acknowledgment		ix
Author's Note		xi
Introduction		xv
I	Caleb and Hannah Coker	3
II	At Society Hill	20
III	Family Time	37
IV	The Family in the War	57
V	Restoring Life	84
VI	Piney Woods and Paper: J. L. Coker, Jr. and Paper Making	109
VII	David Coker and Pedigreed Seed	132
VIII	The Major	171
IX	D. R. Coker and the Collapse of Southern Rural Life	190
X	C. W. Coker and Industrial Development at Hartsville	219
XI	Scholars and Scholarship	237
XII	New World at Hartsville	271
XIII	The Family Perspective	295
Bibliography		309
Genealogical Chart		322
Index		323

Illustrations

	Facing page
Hannah Lide Coker	80
Caleb Coker	80
Caleb Coker's store today	81
Camp Marion home at Society Hill	81
James Lide Coker	96
William Caleb Coker	96
Major Coker's first store at Hartsville	97
The Carolina Fiber Company plant	97
James Lide Coker, Jr.	256
David R. Coker	256
Charles W. Coker, Sr.	256
Joseph J. Lawton	256
William Chambers Coker	257
Edward Caleb Coker	257
Robert Ervin Coker	257
Francis William Coker	257
James Harvey Rogers	257
Charles W. Coker, Jr.	272
Richard G. Coker	272
James L. Coker III	272
Edgar H. Lawton	272
Robert R. Coker	272
Sonoco Products Company plant, Hartsville	273
Breeding plots at Coker's Pedigreed Seed Company	273

Introduction

HEREWITH THE STORY of the Coker family of Darlington County, South Carolina; or, more accurately, that part of the Coker family in the United States that has proceeded from the union of Caleb Coker, Jr. and Hannah Lide in 1830.

The beginning was modest, unheralded, like countless other beginnings of the time and place. There followed, and not uncommonly, the development of a generation of children of character and responsibility, whose life was harshly interrupted by the Civil War and more subtly affected by the aftermath. Then, late but matured by hard experience, there began to appear in effective ways those distinctive achievements by which the Cokers are known.

Inured to the cotton economy, the family developed early a realistic view of the net effects of that economy, but without despair. Rather there was first a general searching for ways of change and improvement, and then a climactic focusing in the early 1900's on the pioneer breeding of pedigreed seed for southern agriculture. The seed breeding became a matter of incalculable value for the eastern South.

To improved agriculture, the Cokers sought to join the development of industry, hoping realistically as early as 1869, and beginning in the early 1880's with textiles. Then, again a decisive, daring turn to the abundant southern pine in the 1890's, pulping it chemically and making paper, the first to do so.

In a logical progression, they began to make paper cones and tubes for textile yarns, and as the generations have succeeded, the Cokers have become predominant in this activity, meeting and bettering the terms of mid-twentieth century industry. To meet a local need they established a high school; then when public education appeared, the high school was converted into an excellent college for women to meet the next need. From the family there have come scholars distinguished by national and world standards.

There is no reason in this story to strain at finding the family element—it is there in good measure, and palpable. Therefore, there is no compulsion to crowd out other elements—the individual differences of heredity normal in any family, and the kaleidoscope of infinitely varying experience; nor the powerful influence of community, and of the larger regional setting; nor, even, of grand historical incidence, which is what the Civil War was for an individual or a family.

Yet the family influence may not be taken cheaply, since it was not won without cost. For all that it gives, a family demands something in return. In this relationship, we have in America given the benefit of the doubt to the individual, advising him to take his own happiness by the hand, lest he be oppressed by his family. It has been the genius of the Coker family so far to preserve itself in a real sense, but, in the doing, not to oppress its members—each of whom has made his creative, individual place.

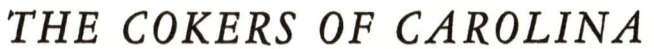

THE COKERS OF CAROLINA

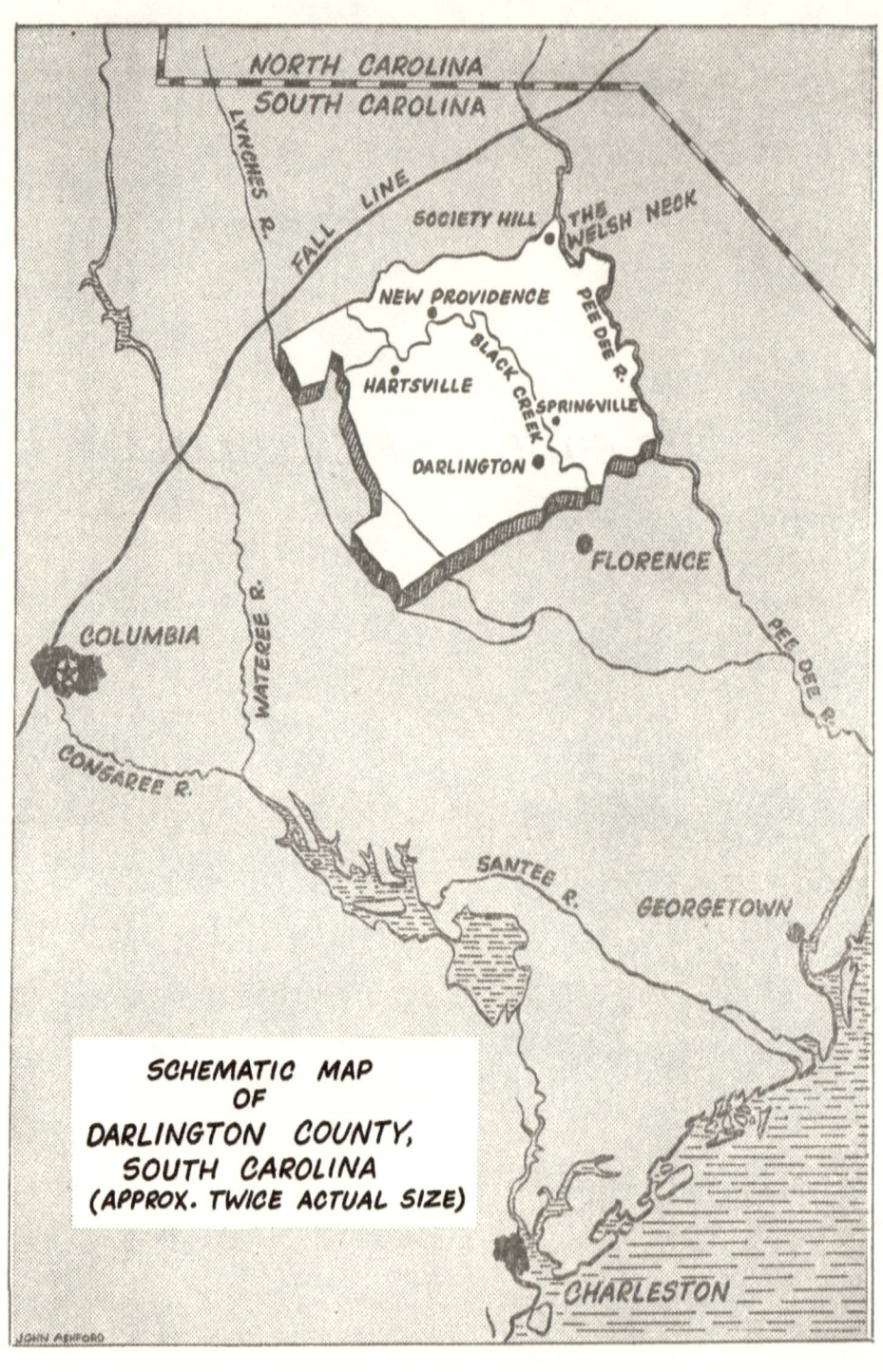

1

Caleb and Hannah Coker

I

CALEB COKER, JR., married Hannah Ann Frances Lide on October 14, 1830,[1] when he was twenty-eight years of age. Hannah was eighteen.

The wedding was in Hannah's home at Springville, South Carolina. All around lay the good cotton lands of the northeastern Coastal Plain—the middle country of South Carolina. For two years past Caleb had been a general merchant to cotton planters (such as the Lides) and to cotton farmers (such as the Cokers). Before that he had been a clerk in a general store, and before that a none too hardy boy on a back country farm. Caleb was of moderate height, well set in the shoulders, and his features were regular and clean shaven. His hair tended slightly to auburn.[2]

Hannah Lide appeared in a simple white wedding gown that she had made herself.[3] She sewed well because her mother had taught her in the natural course of things, and because she had lately learned something more of style and polite needlework at the Misses Ramsey's school for young ladies in Charleston.[4] Finely made herself, she could wear a simple

---

1. Mrs. Furman E. Wilson, "Memories of Society Hill and Some of Its People. Home Life, Written for My Own Children and Brothers and Sisters Alone" (Watson collection), p. 1. Hereafter cited as "For My Own."

2. James Lide Coker, "Short Sketch of the Coker Family of Darlington District, S.C." (Watson collection).

3. Mrs. Emma Edwards Coggeshall, "A Sketch of Hannah L. Coker" (Annie L. Edwards).

4. *Ibid.*

white gown well. Hannah was no beauty in the usual sense. She had the attractiveness of good, almost fragile features, and lively eyes, where, even at eighteen, there were indications of firmness and character. At seventeen she had written this discouraging and apparently final note to a suitor:

As to your honourable motives and your honourable mode of making them known, viz. through the hands of my Father; after acknowledging my obligations for the favourable terms in which you are pleased to speak of me. I can only say, that I am not prepared to receive visits of the kind you propose. Considering my youth and unfinished education, had I not seen you enjoying the confidence of Mr. & Mrs. Morgan, I could not believe you to be sincere.

Respectfully your friend,[5]

Springville can only be described as a way of life. It was not properly a village, but a number of families—at this time about a dozen—living in cottages and houses scattered among high pines. The pines were not unusual, nor were they the best of shade, but they grew on an upthrust of sandy hills. Water did not collect in puddles here, and summer breezes were more frequent. The hills fell off abruptly on the western side to Black Creek, an excellent place for bathing, for the water was clean and cool and sand bars plentiful. There were at least a half-dozen mineral springs in the area, of various tastes and flavors. Whatever their medical value, these springs, as elsewhere in the South, offered a location and an excuse for social gathering.

Hannah's family, the Lides, had a modest cottage at Springville. Their main cotton lands and homeplace lay to the east on the Pee Dee River, about a dozen miles away—richer lands by far, but flat and low. The sandy hills of Springville were cooler, relatively, and by harsh experience there was less sickness and fewer deaths from "fever" than in the lower lands nearer the river. About eight years before the wedding the Lides had built their cottage for summer residence, but well

---

5. Hannah to William Potter, March 17, 1829 (R. E. Coker).

before 1830 they were spending most of the year there. Hannah attended the private academy established by the Springville families before going on to the Misses Ramsey in Charleston. The Lides were not the first to come to Springville, nor the last, though the pattern of their coming was much the same for all. Indeed, by 1830 there were already several handsome permanent houses at Springville—roomy structures with through-running halls, large rooms and wide piazzas, surrounded by great yards and flower gardens.[6]

Though the homes were scattered, and the accession of families unplanned, there was a unity of spirit in Springville and a well-understood way of life. Kinship, close or distant, was common among the families. Almost all, like the Lides, were of families that had lived in the Pee Dee middle country for more than one generation. Hannah's grandfather was Major Robert Lide, one of three brothers who had come down from Pennsylvania to South Carolina in the 1740's. As others were beginning to do, Robert Lide did not stop in the tidewater country of rice, indigo, and Charleston. Inland from the low country was the middle country, a wide swath of coastal plain land lying between the low country and the Piedmont upcountry.

In the 1740's this was unsettled, troublesome back country to the low country, and remained so for several decades. This middle country was undulant rather than flat, and was only occasionally wet and swampy. The soils were of loam and sand, generally fertile, and in wide areas extremely so. This was a land of predominantly high standing pines, though hardwoods grew in the wetter places, and of long hot summers and mild winters.[7] Across the middle country, from North Caro-

[6.] See R. E. Coker, "Springville: A Summer Village of Old Darlington District," *South Carolina Historical Magazine*, LIII (October, 1952), for a detailed description of Springville and its people.

[7.] For a description of the middle country, see South Carolina State Planning Board, *Progress Report on State Planning in South Carolina*, n.p., 1938; Augustine T. Smythe (ed.), *The Carolina Low Country* (New York: The Macmillan Co., 1931), p. 7; R. L. Meriwether, *The Expansion of South Carolina, 1729-1765* (Kingsport, Tenn.: Southern Publishers, Inc., 1940), pp. 3, 7, 9, 10, 182; C. S. Boucher, *The Nullification Controversy in South Carolina* (Chicago: The University of Chicago Press, 1916), map facing p. iii.

lina to Georgia, moved a number of wide, slow moving rivers flowing east and southeast to the sea. Along them there were rich alluvial deposits, and on them was transportation in a country of few and rough roads.

Robert Lide went up one of the rivers—the Pee Dee—to the northeastern part of the colony. He stopped at a place on the river called Mechanicsville, about halfway on the river's course through the middle country, and took up lands. Lide was a man of education and ability. His planting was successful and he became something of a leading figure as this back country took shape and form. He distinguished himself during the Revolution under General Marion, leaving the service a Major.[8] One of his sons was James, father of Hannah, who also went into planting, and who gradually moved his family's residence from near the river to Springville.

Life at Springville was, of course, one of the products of cotton, since virtually all who came there farmed large cotton holdings elsewhere, from which they were able to support residence in a selected place. Springville had come about naturally and yet rather quickly, for the beginning was no more than twenty-five years after Eli Whitney invented the cotton gin. As late as the Revolution, the middle country was still emerging from the relative limbo of back country. Caleb's grandfather had, in fact, received a grant of open land not more than twenty miles northwest of Springville in 1787, and there were unclaimed acres later and even nearer than that. For all of its civility Springville was not far removed in experience from rougher conditions. Hannah, herself, was better educated and turned out than her parents. Had she remained there, she would have known the full flowering of the Springville way of life that came after 1830, in the two decades before the Civil War.

Nevertheless, the pattern was being set in the 1820's, when

8. For information on Robert Lide and others of his family, see Alexander Gregg, *History of the Old Cheraws* (New York: Richardson and Company, 1868), pp. 77-79, 302, 432, 434, 474, 480, 483, 496-98; R. E. Coker, "Coker Forebears" (R. E. Coker); genealogical chart of descendants of Abel Kolb, constructed by T. E. Wilson, C. E., of Darlington, S.C.

Hannah was growing up there. The interests of all the families were common, the seasons of their work the same, the outcomes generally known. All of these elements combined to invite the souls of families—to live well and responsibly; to have care for provision and education; to take time for reading, for conversation and for visiting; to give main energies and prayers for the children; and, for the most part, to have the good sense to thank the Lord and abide by His dispensations.

So, for the times, it was a rather special group of neighbors and kinsmen who attended the wedding at Springville. Relatives of the groom came from their New Providence community twenty miles to the northwest. They were farmers. Caleb's mother could neither read nor write, but they were not abashed.

II

After the wedding Hannah took her seat beside Caleb in his buggy. They drove off northeastward to the small village of Society Hill,[9] twelve miles away on hills overlooking the Pee Dee River from the west. October is a pleasant time in the South Carolina middle country and the road was tolerable. Caleb and Hannah went to a small three room cottage, with piazza, that Caleb had bought and made ready.[10] It was behind and very near the store of Coker and Gregg where two years before Caleb had begun his first venture, in partnership with J. Eli Gregg. The wedding trip, a long trip to the Springs of Virginia, was put off until the following summer since it could not be had now. October was a most critical time in the life of a general store in this southern land of cotton. The new store held all of their hopes, and now was yet the season of the cotton harvest, when farmers and plantation owners who all year long had taken goods and farm supplies—even money—on credit from Coker and Gregg appeared with the harvested bales of the year's work.

9. Coggeshall, "A Sketch of Hannah L. Coker," p. 2.
10. Mrs. Furman E. Wilson, *Memories of Society Hill* (Hartsville, S.C.: The Hartsville Publishing Company, 1909-1910, for the Pee Dee Historical Society), pp. 1-26.

The cotton growers came to pay what they owed with cotton, and, always hopefully, to take away some difference in goods and money. It was not a time to be away from the store, for more than merely meeting customers and selling merchandise was involved. This was the culmination of the entire year, and Caleb and Gregg were accepting the white medium of exchange carefully, not for what it was, but for what it could be sold in Charleston. Only then could they calculate profit and loss. It is not at all unlikely that Gregg was then in Charleston, looking to changes in the market and to the sale of cotton Caleb was accepting many miles away.

If this was so, Hannah understood, for cotton was her way of life also. It is doubtful, even, that she ever considered setting the date of the wedding in the late summer or September, since this would have been inconsiderate of her family and friends at Springville. All of these were completely preoccupied with a capricious weather, and with what it would do to the cotton so near to opening, and then with picking, ginning, and baling. Caleb as always was considerate, and there were kinspeople and warm friends of Hannah and her family in the village to make her feel welcome. There was also in the village challenge for a young bride, as Hannah well knew. It was an entirely remarkable community, with more right than most to set high standards for a newly married couple.

III

Robert Mills, among other things architect of the Washington Monument, described Society Hill at about this time in his *Statistics of South Carolina* as ". . . a group of houses and trees commixed. The houses are built without any regular plan in the woods, according to the fancy of the builder; and so scattered that, as you ramble, you come upon them unawares. . . ." Mills the architect did not neglect an inventory of tangible assets. There were ". . . six stores, a post office, two taverns, a tanyard, and two blacksmith's shops; in all . . . about thirty-five dwelling houses." Mills estimated that there were "about 120 white inhabitants."[11]

If Mills rendered a pastoral, quiet impression of the village, the inhabitants did not object, because they fancied this way of life and were quite up to accepting an understatement as their due, leaving bolder claims to those who needed them. In earlier years, Society Hill had been the center of settlement of the Pee Dee middle country; now, in 1830, it was at a standstill so far as growth was concerned, if not by design then by consent. It remained though, without dissent, the most distinguished settlement in the Pee Dee middle country.

The little village had its beginning in the 1730's when a group of about twenty Welsh Baptists came down from southeastern Pennsylvania (now a part of Delaware) and settled along the Pee Dee River.[12] These Welsh were looking for good general farming lands, and they wanted them well inland from the coastal settlements so that they could follow their ways and establish their Baptistry. Both Charleston and the Crown were desperate for the Welsh to go inland to the unsettled back country, and so gave them a great over-sized grant of land along both sides of the Pee Dee. The southern limit of the grant began about where the middle country merges into the low country, and from there it ran up the river even beyond the present boundaries of North Carolina.

The Welsh found the jewel of their grant in a neck of land about three miles across formed as the Pee Dee, running southeasterly to the sea, makes a great half circle to the southwest. In and around this they settled, just across the river from what ultimately became Society Hill. This neck of land was

---

11. Robert Mills, *Statistics of South Carolina* (Charleston: Hurlbut and Lloyd, 1826), pp. 513-14.

12. For the story of this Welsh settlement, see *The Welsh Tract Baptist Meeting, Records of Pencader Hundred; New Castle County, Delaware, 1701 to 1728, Report of the Historical Society of Delaware, Papers of the Historical Society of Delaware*, XLII (Wilmington, 1904), Parts I and II; Meriwether, *The Expansion of South Carolina*, pp. 90 ff.; Gregg, *History of the Old Cheraws*, pp. 47 ff.; Leah Townsend, *South Carolina Baptists, 1670-1805* (Florence, S.C.: The Florence Printing Company, 1935), pp. 61 ff.; The Welsh Neck Church Book, the Welsh Neck Baptist Church, Society Hill, S.C.

low and swampy in places and thick with growth, but it was alluvial and rich; its half moat seems to have suited their mood, for they were close, communal and self-centered so far as the rest of South Carolina was concerned. Not unnaturally this area quickly came to be known as the Welsh Neck. A Baptist congregation was established, and along with the communal understanding of the Welsh, was for several years the main instrument of order and government; Charleston was glad to leave the new settlers to their own devices. The Welsh Neck Baptist Church became the mother church for the area. It was not long before discomfort and malaria demonstrated the advantages of living on higher ground. Across the river on the west bank there was high ground, a long bluff, where settlement developed, taking the name "Long Bluff."

The first Welsh were few, their grant large and valuable, and within a few years other settlers, the Lides and Cokers among them, began to come in and settle up and down the river, as well as in the Welsh Neck area. In 1747, George Hicks, with a large family and eleven slaves, "'lately arrived from Virginia,'" petitioned for and received over four thousand acres,[13] and in 1748 John Purvis, also from Virginia, was granted one hundred and fifty acres on the Pee Dee for himself, his wife and their one child.[14] Their names were Pouncey, Todd, Pledger, Powell, Kolb, Staples, Singleton, Pegues, Boyakin, M'Iver, Brockington, Sweeney, DuBose and a whole long list that virtually calls the roll of the movement of peoples to the frontier, in nationality, in wealth, and in belief.[15]

These people came to this new country for their own purposes, and so a new way of life was inevitable. Yet, for the most part they came from the seaboard of North Carolina and Virginia and the middle colonies, and from England, Scotland, and Ireland. They had therefore a somewhat common reference to order and government, rule of law, facilities for roads and ferries, the levying of taxes, and a part in

---

13. Gregg, *History of the Old Cheraws*, pp. 79-80.
14. *Ibid.*, pp. 81-82.
15. *Ibid.*, chapter V.

public affairs. All of these the settlers had known in some degree and wanted, but they existed almost exclusively in South Carolina along the coast. For lack of them, and quickly, the people along the middle Pee Dee rose in open, violent defiance of the low country and the Crown in the 1760's. In large part they were successful; the establishment of a courthouse and jail at Long Bluff serving the whole Pee Dee country was both symbol and reality of success, and of the gathering identity of this inland region.[16]

The new judicial tribunals soon became channels for expression of local opinion on political issues of wider importance. In a session of the Circuit Court in Long Bluff, in November, 1774, three formal statements, concerning the rights violated by the royal officers and rights asserted by the colonists, were put forth successively by the judge, petit jury, and grand jury. On November 17, Judge William Drayton (of Charleston), in his charge to the grand jury, reviewed the colonists' grievances, with a long constitutional argument in support of the community's claim of the right to disobey and resist the unconstitutional orders of the British government. "I am servant," the Judge declared, "not to the king, but to the constitution, and I shall best discharge my duty as a good subject of the king, and a trusted officer under the constitution, when I boldly declare the law to the people, and instruct them in their civil rights." On the following day (before the grand jury had acted) the petit jury, in an unusual action for such a body, made its own response to the Judge's charge; they expressed their "great satisfaction and warmest acknowledgements for so constitutional a charge at this alarming crisis, when our liberties are attacked and our properties invaded by the claim and attempt to tax us, and by their edicts to bind us in all cases they deem proper; ... by the constitution of this country, we owe obedience to no human laws but such as are enacted with

---

16. See Rosser H. Taylor, *Ante-Bellum South Carolina*, Vol. 25, No. 2, *The James Sprunt Studies in History and Political Science* (Chapel Hill: The University of North Carolina Press, 1942), pp. 4-5; Gregg, *History of the Old Cheraws*, chapter VII; W. Roy Smith, *South Carolina as a Royal Province, 1719-1776* (New York: The Macmillan Company, 1903), pp. 133-41.

the consent of our representatives in General Assembly." On the next day the grand jury included the following in its report: "We present, as a grievance of the first magnitude, the right claimed by the British Parliament to tax us, and by their acts to bind us in all cases whatsoever . . . if we may be taxed, imprisoned, and deprived of life by the force of edicts to which neither we nor our Constitutional Representatives have ever assented no slavery can be more abject than ours."[17]

Such were the community's official declarations of essential political rights, asserted a year and a half before the adoption of the Declaration of Independence by the Continental Congress. Three years later, in the midst of war, and three years before independence was won, a private group, St. David's Society, looking ahead, set forth its ideas on the need there would be for an educated citizenry, to maintain the sort of independent republic they hoped to have. The following is from the resolution the society adopted on January 17, 1778, explaining its decision to establish a school:

As the enjoying and establishing public schools and other seminaries of learning has ever been attended with the most salutary effects, as well by the cultivating in youth the principles of religion and every social virtue, as by enabling them afterwards to fill with dignity and usefulness the most important departments of the State; who that is a lover of his country, as he looks around him, can fail to deplore the great want of this necessary qualification in our youth, especially in the interior parts of it, at this early period of our flourishing and rising state. In the future, when we shall be at liberty to make our own laws without the control of an arbitrary despot, what heart would not glow with pleasure to see a senate filled with learned, wise, and able men, for want of whom the most flourishing republics have become the tools of arbitrary despots.[18]

The Society built its schoolhouse on a hill about a mile west of Long Bluff, and soon most of the villagers were building on this and adjoining hills, and Long Bluff dissolved into Society Hill. The little village was thus the religious, legal

17. Gregg, *History of the Old Cheraws*, p. 216.
18. Minutes of the St. David's Society (Mrs. A. M. Coker), p. 1.

and educational center of the Pee Dee middle country, and major commercial center also.

The first Welsh were general farmers, as were most of the others who came immediately after them. But after 1747 and before the Revolution, it was profitable to grow indigo along the Pee Dee, and on this basis the outlines of a plantation-slave system appeared.[19] After the Revolution, the Pee Dee middle country fell back almost entirely on general agriculture, though new people continued to come in. Following Eli Whitney's invention of the cotton gin in 1793 the middle country quickly became the land of cotton. There was an increased influx of white settlers during the first decade of cotton, diminishing rapidly and ceasing when the lands were taken up and began to wear out. But always there was a constant accession of Negroes, until by 1830 the latter were nearly half of the population.[20] These developments took away some of Society Hill's more tangible centrality. The division of the middle country into smaller civil units removed all but the court of chancery; other and larger schools were established; and a few offspring of the Welsh Neck Church outgrew their ancestor. In commerce, Society Hill did not secure the fast growing, Piedmont upcountry trade because it was about fifteen miles below the fall line and, as well, lost much of what it had once had.

So the village grew little if any after 1800. Cotton did not enlarge it physically. A core of families took the bounty of cotton grown on still fresh lands and produced over the next generation the Society Hill into which Caleb and Hannah came. The same names appear repeatedly in all records: Evans, Wilds, Witherspoon, Edwards, Williams, Wilson, Sparks, McIver, and others.[21] Some were planters, with out-

19. Meriwether, *The Expansion of South Carolina*, p. 94.
20. *Ibid;* Julian J. Petty, *The Growth and Distribution of Population in South Carolina*, Bulletin No. 11 of the South Carolina State Planning Board (Columbia, July, 1943), Table 12, p. 73.
21. Gregg, *History of the Old Cheraws*, records the movement of a great number of these families into the Pee Dee middle country and the Society Hill area, particularly pp. 52, 56, 59, 64-65, 77-107, 159-60, 199-200. Minutes of the St. David's

lying lands. The Welsh Neck Church pulpit could almost always command a distinguished man. From the community came a governor, a senator, congressmen, state legislators, judges and other officials.[22]

Among these was young Josiah Evans, about Caleb's age, who in 1830 was starting up the ladder to the bench and the United States Senate. Although Evans was described by a colleague in the Senate as being " '... to my mind more fully than any other man it has ever been my fortune to know, the ideal which had formed in my youth of an old Roman Senator,' "[23] he was by no means the most distinguished.

That title belongs to David Rogerson Williams, who was killed the same year that Caleb brought Hannah to Society Hill, crushed by a timber as he built a bridge. By this time, Williams had been a Charleston newspaper editor strong in support of Jefferson; three times had he gone to Congress; during the War of 1812 he was a Major General; and then from 1814 to 1816 Governor of South Carolina.

With aplomb, Society Hill remembered the day in December of 1814 when Williams was notified that the South Carolina Legislature had elected him governor, an office he had not sought. The messenger came from Columbia to Society Hill, and there got his directions for finding Williams' home on the outskirts. On the way he came up with an ox-team wagon and driver. He asked the driver if Williams was home, and the reply was that Williams was likely to be there before long.

Society (Mrs. A. M. Coker) show recurring names over a period of over sixty years of people having direct responsibility for the school in Society Hill. Similarly, the Welsh Neck Church Book, particularly in its list of Deacons, shows these recurring names in responsible positions; Mrs. Wilson's *Memories of Society Hill* gives a detailed account of the families of Society Hill, their history and community functions, during the three decades before the Civil War; Rev. John Stout (ed.), *Historical Sketch of the Welsh Neck Baptist Church* (Greenville, S.C.: Hoyt and Keys, 1889), also records the community functions of the people of Society Hill, pp. 43-45.

22. John Witherspoon DuBose, *The Witherspoons of Society Hill* (Hartsville: The Hartsville Publishing Company, 1910, for the Pee Dee Historical Society), discusses some of these people.

23. E. C. Coker, "Sketch of the Early History of Society Hill and Brief Notes on Some of Its Noteworthy Natives," in Records and Papers of the Darlington County Historical Society, p. 23.

The messenger rode on to Williams' house, and went in to wait. Shortly the wagon driver came in and presented himself as David Rogerson Williams.

There was some humor in the episode, but no pose. Williams' great interest lay in his several thousand acres of land, in their full use and conservation, and in the manufacture at home of the products of this land. Early, well before 1820, he understood the passing fertility of the land under a one crop culture, and he practiced and preached rotation of crops and the use of natural fertilizer, even leaves and pine straw. He urged and demonstrated a more balanced agriculture, giving over some of his best lands to growing corn. More than this, in 1812, he established on his plantation a cotton mill, one of the first in the South, and put it into successful operation with slave labor. It was running when Caleb Coker came in the early 1820's, and when Hannah came, and continued until after most of their children were born, ultimately employing more than a thousand spindles. In 1829 he installed at home a machine built by two Virginia inventors to extract oil from cottonseed. Except for use as fertilizer, the cottonseed was largely going to waste. Governor Williams operated his mill successfully, found the cottonseed oil good, and used it to light the plantation buildings and as a base for paint.[24]

Williams was exceptional but not unrepresentative. These people of Society Hill had a rare poise and self-possession in the use of themselves and their environment. To be sure, they were well read, travelled not infrequently, and many were intimately connected with public affairs. Yet life on the Hill, in their own midst, was the important thing. Naturally, unaffectedly they cultivated this life, neither boorish nor imitative, so it seems. As the care of St. David's Academy fell back mainly on the Society Hill families, it was their pleasure to go at the end of school to examine the scholars rigorously, and the teacher who had not taught the classics and mathematics as well as reading and writing was in a poor way. In 1822,

24. See H. T. Cook, *The Life and Legacy of David Rogerson Williams* (New York: The Garden City Press, 1916).

about the time Caleb came to Society Hill, a group of leading men organized the Society Hill Library Society, each beginning with a contribution of twenty dollars. This was one of the few libraries beyond the seacoast; by 1850 it contained 2,000 good and well used volumes.[25]

They did not hesitate to dip generously into the rich product of their fertile fields and to live well:

I must mention a custom of the planters about Society Hill which contributed greatly to the comforts of life. In summer and winter they maintained a fresh meat "market" so called. By turns in summer, each member of the market club killed a beef on the day designated and all the other members sent to his house for the parts due them. In winter, a mutton market was maintained on like terms.[26]

Not long after Caleb and Hannah were married, one of the ladies of the village wrote a note to the wife of the Welsh Neck pastor:

I could not, when alone, have so little compassion as to ask you to spend a day with me, being fully aware of my own dullness as a companion; but I will venture to ask you today as I have the hope of a visit from my sister Mary . . . so come and make me a sociable visit. If Brother Furman is not afraid to encounter unassisted four female tongues, I shall be very glad to see him too. Mr. McIver's business will detain him till evening. I shall not omit to enumerate amongst my attractions a fine wild turkey.

Or, again, there is a note to the pastor's wife:

Will you have the goodness to loan me one of Brother Furman's shirts? Aunt W. wishes to make a present of the half piece of linen and I want the pleasure of making them. If you wish any alteration made do specify it. Aunt W. unites with me in affectionate regards to Brother F. and yourself. A kiss for little Liz.[27]

25. J. M. Napier, "Society Hill and Some of Its Contributions to State and Nation," privately published pamphlet, 1946.
26. DuBose, *The Witherspoons of Society Hill*, p. 17.
27. Quoted in H. T. Cook, *The Life Work of James Clement Furman* (Greenville: copyright by Alester G. Furman, 1926), pp. 52, 68.

The closely-knit village had its eccentric minority of dogmatics and dissenters. Some members of the church thought that, with increasing prosperity, the church was getting too gay. Charles Fort, local cabinet-maker, wheelwright, and justice of the peace, stopped attending church services for a while because newly installed crimson cushions and curtains reminded him of the "scarlet beast." His wife stopped church attendance altogether because she objected to the "un-Christian pride" shown by the ladies who wore "fine dresses" to church.

Mr. Fort used his workshop not only as a place for both his carpentry and his judicial work but also as a place for discussing various issues of importance in the village. Neighbors reported hearing an argument there between Fort and the local shoemaker on the proper form of baptism: the cabinet-maker upheld the orthodox Baptist version of baptism by immersion; the shoemaker contended that it had been "proved" that the "im" in the "Greek verb" for "immerse" (he probably had in mind the Latin "immergere") means "at" or "to" rather than "into," so that differing ways of using water in the essential sacrament were permissible.[28]

It would be easy to think of this little world of Society Hill as almost at a fruitful standstill, so well did these people have life in hand. This would not quite be accurate. Underneath, the cotton economy was in full course toward some unknown end, massive and overpowering. Each year the lands became a little less fertile, the commitment to cotton stronger. As a Jeffersonian in every sense, David Rogerson Williams was after his time; as a manufacturer he was at least two generations ahead of his time. His examples of making cloth and cottonseed oil were realistic, but they were not even straws in the wind, and eventually were stopped at Society Hill.

Life in the village itself was changing, though slowly and naturally. When Caleb and Hannah set up housekeeping in 1830, Hannah almost immediately delivered her letter of membership to the Reverend Dossey, who had been pastor of the

---

28. Wilson, *Memories of Society Hill*, pp. 43-44.

Welsh Neck Baptist Church since 1814. Mr. Dossey hewed straight to the line of strict, simple living, of literal ceremony and doctrine, and of a frequent evangelism. Church discipline, as far as he was concerned, applied to weekdays as well as Sundays, and was to be administered publicly from the pulpit when necessary, from which duty he apparently never shrank.[29]

In the early years of Mr. Dossey's tenure there was at least acceptance of his stern ministry. But as time passed, as wealth and urbanity grew, and no doubt as Mr. Dossey became more demanding, many members began to take exception. He also served the Episcopalians, who eventually left him in anger.[30] From the pulpit he drew his own conclusions as to the use of a "company room"—a sort of banquet room—on the second story of the home of a leading citizen, who while not a member of the church, sat that day in the congregation. The gentleman walked out and never came back.[31] Even the most pious and venerable came to say ". . . of a particular sermon that she was neither reproved, nor edified, nor comforted by it."[32] Mr. Dossey was of an earlier time that was passing, and he was both too honest and willful to change. Grudgingly and with some bitterness he resigned in 1832.

His successor was James Clement Furman, a highly educated, sincere Baptist who later would found Furman University. One of the strongest reasons for his coming to Society Hill was the community's reputation for learning and culture. The final judgment on his coming and Mr. Dossey's going was that:

> The temperament of the new pastor was adapted to the peculiar condition of the church and congregation. There was no asperity in his speech and manner. A gracious attraction went out from him upon all, and brethren dwelt together in unity. . . .[33]

---

29. Rev. John Stout (ed.), *Historical Sketch of the Welsh Neck Baptist Church*, p. 17.
30. Wilson, *Memories of Society Hill*, p. 20.
31. DuBose, *The Witherspoons of Society Hill*, p. 14.
32. Stout, *Historical Sketch of the Welsh Neck Baptist Church*, p. 17.
33. *Ibid.*, p. 21.

This then was the community where Caleb and Hannah were to begin their life together and where, if all went well, they would raise and nurture their children. Hannah, joining the church choir and the prayer meeting group, was stepping suddenly into a way of life that was only beginning to develop at Springville.

2

At Society Hill

1

WHEN CALEB had come alone to Society Hill in the early 1820's, the change for him had been more abrupt, though he no doubt bore it calmly. He had come from the New Providence community, fifteen miles west of Society Hill, where he was born on September 14, 1802. The New Providence community, like Springville and Society Hill, was part of the South Carolina middle country. It was on the western edge, verging on the sterile sandhills, and was too far removed from river transportation to have been among the first areas settled. In Caleb's lifetime, however, cotton had become the principal crop and preoccupation, rendering at New Providence also the imprint of a way of life.

Caleb's grandfather, Thomas Coker, Sr., had been the first Coker to settle in what was essentially open country. Before the Revolution he had lived near the river in the same area as the Lides, and with them belonged to the Cashaway Baptist Church.[1] During the Revolution he served as Lieutenant under General Marion. For the trouble of this good service he was granted ". . . a tract of one thousand acres originally surveyed & granted for Thomas Coker the fifth day of February one thousand seven hundred and eighty seven by His Excellency William Moultrie Governor. . . ."[2] Thomas Coker

1. Meriwether, *The Expansion of South Carolina*, p. 88.
2. Record Book F (Register of Deeds, Darlington, S.C.), p. 183.

helped mightily to establish the community, to give it shape and identity out of the raw shapelessness of new lands. He persevered in the establishment of a Baptist church, succeeding finally in 1804.³ He became venerable in the lusty, democratic congregation, where preaching on Sunday was normally supplemented by lay exhortation and leading in prayer, and where church concern with personal conduct was not unusual. From the latter the Cokers, important members of the church and community though they were, were not exempt. On November 23, 1811, James Coker—son of Thomas and uncle of the then nine year old Caleb, Jr.—". . . came forward (and admitted) his disorder in taking spirits and getting angry and gave signs of repentance and was continued in fellowship."⁴

Caleb, Jr.'s father, brother of the repentant James and son of Thomas, Sr., was a substantial farmer and land owner in the community, though he was not a member of the church. This senior Caleb liked the open country life—to live well as this went in New Providence, but informally, to hunt and fish. One of the few records remaining of him shows that at a store in Society Hill he ". . . bought hunting knives, powder and shot, and occasionally Jamaica rum."⁵ He liked to own land; just as well, he liked to buy and sell and trade land. Having only one slave, a houseservant, he always held title to more acres than he could cultivate, even with a large family. In 1817 he sold to one Samuel Crossland five hundred acres "whereon the said Coquer now resides,"⁶ for $1,600. Land was worth then about one dollar an acre, so the sale price indicates that the Coker homestead was of considerable value for the time and place. In 1821, having in the meantime sold the original Thomas Coker tract (less about twenty-five acres), he repurchased the tract he had sold Crossland, paying $1,150.⁷

3. Church Book of the New Providence Baptist Church, Darlington County, S.C.; also Townsend, *South Carolina Baptists*, pp. 102-3.
4. Church Book of the New Providence Baptist Church, Darlington County, S.C., under entry of November 23, 1811.
5. Cook, "The Coker Family" (R. G. Coker).
6. Record Book F (Register of Deeds, Darlington, S.C.).
7. Record Book H (Register of Deeds, Darlington, S.C.), pp. 118, 79.

When he died in 1833 he left almost seven hundred acres[8] to his wife and to several of their children, having previously given land to other children. Yet this land was the ultimate measure of his wealth; he was "land poor," a not uncommon thing in the South. He was too restless, too convivial, to consolidate his gains.

The center and heart of his household was Ann McLendon, whom he married in 1798. Ann McLendon, called Nancy, was one of the many Scotch-Irish women whose families had come to the interior parts of North and South Carolina before and after the Revolution. In 1859, when she died at New Providence, a Baptist church publication carried some two hundred words of special tribute to this unlettered woman. It was mournful and overdone for present tastes, but in the middle of the tribute is a sentence that rings utterly real: ". . . during all that time, her unobtrusive, mild, consistent Christian course won the confidence and esteem of her brethren, and of all who knew her." The tribute closed with the comment that it ". . . may be profitable to the living, to record her worth and meditate on her example."[9]

The example was not set without cost, for Nancy Coker, religious, resilient, and tender, worked long and hard, and the tribute spoke accurately of her long "labors on earth." Hers was the household to run through the several rhythms of the crop years; the daily work of cooking, washing and cleaning; the seasonal work of feeding cotton pickers and harvesters, of spinning and sewing, slaughtering and preserving, of holidays and family gatherings—and always, for her, the Sabbath at worship. Nancy Coker's life, though she had one Negro woman to help, was a different existence from that of Hannah Lide's mother.

In the custom of the time, Nancy carried on the detailed care of the children, nine boys and one girl surviving of the original eleven. Young Caleb grew up in a way that was much

---

8. Will of Caleb Coker, Sr. (Judge of Probate, Darlington, S.C.).

9. "A Tribute of Respect," published in a Baptist periodical, probably in 1859. The clipping is in the possession of T. E. Goodson, Hartsville, S.C., and bears neither date nor name of publication.

closer to his mother than that of his brothers. For Caleb as a child was not hardy, and he could not do a full boy's work in the fields.[10] He remained much around the house, cutting fire wood and carrying water, working in the barnyard and garden. During two or three months each year there were rough, uncertain schools in the neighborhood, and Caleb and his brothers and sister went to these.[11] Because he was at the house so much, it is likely that Caleb spent more time than the others on his lessons, and in reading, for by the time he was grown he was adequately educated for business.

There was some hazard in this situation, since a none too hardy boy in this rough and ready community might well have grown up dependent and clinging. Nancy Coker did not have it so; Caleb moved out even more decisively on his own than did his brothers when the time came. Yet, the pattern of the young Caleb's growing up was not without consequence for the man he became. His brothers all went into farming, either at New Providence or elsewhere, and several went on westward to newer lands. Caleb was not beguiled by land, new or old, and he was not robust enough to love the work of farming. There is also a reliable hint that the Cokers, at about the time Caleb was coming to maturity, were in need of cash money help, though there was no shortage of land. If not farming, the possibilities were limited. He had neither the funds, nor, really, the education for the professions. Given the inclination and opportunity, he was qualified to go as a clerk in a general store; indeed, he could learn much as he worked. So it was that he walked eastward to Society Hill.

II

Caleb moved quickly and accurately in Alexander Sparks' dark, cavernous store. Mr. Sparks was well established in the village and his store was, among other things, a public forum, where issues great and small were discussed, valuable for a young man's education. Into this forum came the ordinary

10. James Lide Coker, "Short Sketch of the Coker Family of Darlington District, S.C." (Watson collection).
11. *Ibid.*

lore of the countryside, of the plain average people. Here came talk and news and judgment of people up and down the river, and back from it on both sides. There was registered a knowledge of individuals and of families, their history, idiosyncrasies, their toughness in a bad crop year, their humor, their wisdom and their faults.

Caleb did not dawdle in his listening. Within two or three years after his arrival, Mr. Sparks' bookkeeper left the store. Unasked, Caleb began to do the work after hours. He did his book work well enough for Sparks to give him the job of office man and the top clerk's pay of about $500.00 a year.[12] Some of the money, it seems, was sent home to New Providence. For the rest, he must have lived rather closely, because by 1828 he had saved at least $1,400.

It was in 1828 that Caleb joined with J. Eli Gregg to open Coker and Gregg. Together they bought $2,800 worth of goods and set them up for sale in a vacant building on the other side of the street from Sparks' store.[13]

In the first years Coker and Gregg received the trade of small farmers, as was to be expected, and most of the yearly accounts were well under five hundred dollars.[14] Over a year the needs of a family were written on the debit pages: twist tobacco, nails, lace, bacon, coffee, saddle and stirrup, lead, crackers, homespun and fine dresses, whiskey, wine and rum, fine bootees and buttons, raisins, books and letter paper, harness and oil, needles and thimbles, hats and fertilizers and Negro shoes. Then, usually in October, November and December, there was entered on the credit page the record of payment:[15]

297 lb. Pork @ 5	14.95
11½ bu. Corn @ 50	5.75
1 Bale Cotton 363 lb. @ 9½	34.48
Cash	17.32
	72.50

12. *Ibid;* also Cook, "The Coker Family" (R. G. Coker).
13. James Lide Coker, "Short Sketch of the Coker Family of Darlington District, S.C." (Watson collection).
14. The earliest ledger book remaining is for the year 1832 (South Caroliniana Library).
15. Coker and Gregg Cash Book, p. 125 (South Caroliniana Library).

It was slow, often tedious, business. It required all energies, for this was a highly personalized economy. As often as not, families favored stores out of attachment and habit, and out of respect for the storekeeper. In the same way, credit was expected, services asked, and sharp dealing severely objected to. Goods were bought on periodic trips to New York, and though the buying was exacting, there was some pleasure in the trips. He may have gone earlier, but the first record remaining of such a trip by Caleb is in a letter to Hannah written from New York on July 25, 1831. He wrote, in part, that

> I went over to Newark on Saturday as I anticipated and done what business I had there and returned the same evening. Today I have made a smart beginning with my business here. In looking round I find the assortment of Goods very good and prices if anything higher than last fall, but as there are but few merchants here now buying and a great many wanting to sell, I hope to get some stock. The dunstable shaped bonnets are still the go. I have not yet look'd among the milliners for Sister Mary. Miss Eliza Evans will get the New Fashion first "I expect" this fall. The trimming or flounce is beautiful on the Dress that I am having made for her. She will no doubt feel a year or two younger when she gets in it. This however must be kept secret from her as you know she is not *very old*.[16]

Caleb obviously was not above taking pains. This, together with good judgment by him and Mr. Gregg in buying and selling cotton, produced moderate but steady and increasing profits from the store. Whatever the total of profits, Caleb's withdrawals for personal and family use between 1832 and 1835 fell between $2,000 and $2,500 a year.[17] These sums did not provide for luxurious living, nor did Caleb consider spending all the profits. They were sufficient, though, to live well and to build an attractive, larger house.[18] After the pattern of Mr. Sparks and others, the new two storied house was set well behind the store, which itself was expanded before long. Han-

16. Caleb to Hannah, July 25, 1831 (R. E. Coker).
17. Store Books (South Caroliniana Library).
18. Wilson, "For My Own" (Watson collection), p. 1.

nah commissioned Caleb on his summer trip to New York in 1833 to buy additional furniture for the new house. He wrote her on August 6 from his room in the " 'Great Emporium' Holt's Hotel" that

I have not yet bought any part of your bill of Furniture; am almost ashamed to commence till Mr. Lacoste leaves as he buys articles so very different from what I can afford. He bought a carpet for $135, a hearth rug for $27, another carpet for a bed room for about $65, (a splendid pinafort for his wife who must have learned to play long since she was married), three splendid lamps at about $16 each, etc., etc., etc.[19]

Whatever he could not afford in the way of furniture, Caleb had already bought, on the stopover at Philadelphia, "... a beautiful china *toy* flour pot for Jane," and he instructed Hannah to "Kiss Jane and tell her, Father will bring her some pretty books and a baby...."[20] Jane had been born in the small cottage on August 16, 1831, the first child, who wrote in later years of "Dim recollections of my parents, especially Father's coming in after the day's work almost always with some little thing for me and a frolic of some sort with me...."[21] During the summer trip of Caleb in August 1833, when he was buying furniture for the new house, Hannah wrote Caleb that Jane was ill. Caleb had planned as a sort of holiday to return home by way of Saratoga. But because "I have not received any letter from you since I last wrote, have concluded to decline my trip to Saratoga as Jane is sick and I am anxious to get home to see you and her."[22]

Caleb's concern was as much for Hannah as for the child, and it was not altogether new. As early as July of 1831, not long before Jane was born, Caleb had thought it necessary to urge Hannah "... not to give way to the Melancholy feelings which my absence occasions...."[23] Hannah's melancholy was not brought on merely by Caleb's absence, and it did not pass

19. Caleb to Hannah, August 6, 1833 (R. E. Coker).
20. *Ibid.*
21. Mrs. Wilson, "For My Own" (Watson collection).
22. Caleb to Hannah, August 14, 1833 (R. E. Coker).
23. Caleb to Hannah, July 25, 1831 (R. E. Coker).

off easily. Caleb was sympathetic, and earnest, and his devotion no doubt was a great help to Hannah. He may have been something less than inspired with his advice. In this same August of 1833, he wrote that "... I am glad to hear that you ride horse back every day—it will certainly be of great service to you."[24] Four days later he wrote: "I hope you have resumed your horse back riding; it will no doubt be of service to you. If you can get to riding in a fast pace or canter you will find it a good way to wear off some of your dull feelings. I hope you may cheer up and keep in good spirits."[25]

Hannah was not physically strong. She had a persistent cough. She was very young—eighteen in 1830, twenty-one in 1833—and had come to live in a village community of local distinction and tradition, where her husband was seeking to make his way. If she was welcomed warmly because of her family, then also a great deal was expected of her. Caleb was immersed in the store, where he spent most of the daylight hours, and many at night, it being his custom to complete all book entries before quitting work. Unknowingly, perhaps, he brought home much of the tension of buying and selling cotton. Caleb had learned to control his impatience and to live with the inevitable. Held up for a day at Fayetteville on the uncomfortable trip to New York in 1836, he wrote Hannah that "I assure you that the detention here and day of rest will not set well with me but I found it impossible to get off and have submitted to it with the appearance of patience, as usual."[26]

Hannah took her duties seriously. Life in her parents' home had been good, but the religious emphasis was pervasive and literal, and at times doleful. As late as when she was at school in Charleston, her father had written her, "O my dear Child look to that Blessed Savior who suffered and died to redeem you from sin. Be often at the throne of grace, pleading with him to support, protect and guard you from the temptations and vanities of the world."[27] In the letter writing habits

---

24. Caleb to Hannah, August 6, 1833 (R. E. Coker).
25. Caleb to Hannah, August 10, 1833 (R. E. Coker).
26. Caleb to Hannah, July 16, 1836 (R. E. Coker).
27. James Lide to Hannah, December 31, 1829 (R. E. Coker).

of the times, religious reference and exhortation were not unusual. As it happens, though, there remains a large body of letters and other materials written by the Lides. The cumulative effect of these writings points to an unusual amount of preoccupation with literal religion and the troubles of the world. For all of his sympathy and understanding, Caleb may not have understood all of Hannah's problems.

Hannah's attachment to her family brought another problem during these years. The Lides were having hard going in their cotton raising; they were beginning to talk of going west to the new cotton lands of Alabama, and did go in 1835.[28] Hannah was disturbed, for her parents were both in their sixties, her mother was not well, and there were still young children at home. The Lides urged Caleb and Hannah to join them. Caleb was not tempted, and there is no reason to think that Hannah wanted to go. Yet she could not have been altogether easy about the prospect, in view of the age and health of her parents, and of the capabilities of her older brother Eli, who was to lead the migration.

Hannah had her gay, vivacious side, and a sense of humor that eventually appeared in time to lighten moods and troublous times. Her brother David had these qualities in even fuller measure, to which Hannah responded gaily. Their letters were full of joking and nonsense, though the affection was near the surface. Once David abruptly ended a short letter to Hannah because "I can't think of anything that would be funny."[29] Caleb was part of this interplay, for he liked David immensely. At times David was also a merchant; he and Caleb sometimes travelled to New York together. In August of 1833, Caleb wrote Hannah to "Tell Sister Fanny not to grieve about Brother David as he gains about a pound a day in weight and looks much better than when he left home and I keep strict eye on him that he may not get into mischief."[30]

28. Fletcher M. Green, *The Lides Go South . . . And West: The Record of a Planter Migration in 1835* (Columbia: The University of South Carolina Press, 1952).
29. David Lide to Hannah, August 13, 1835 (R. E. Coker).
30. Caleb to Hannah, August 10, 1833 (R. E. Coker).

Hannah would not have Caleb forget her on his trips, though she reminded him with humor. In 1835 she was on her way to the Sulphur Springs in Virginia, in company with her uncle and others, while Caleb was again buying in New York. She wrote him en route from Salem, North Carolina that ". . . there is quite a party of young ladies here to-day and a few young gentlemen also, the ladies are mostly from the 'Institution.' A blooming, healthy looking group, Uncle John admires them very much, he says he is ashamed of us tallow-faced things, and we expected from his representations, to have to drop our heads when we got among them, but on the contrary, we were vain enough to think we were as good looking as the most of them. . . . Uncle says he intends to put Cousins J and M under Dr. Dargan and Mr. Law, and me under old Mr. Dargan, that he may be at liberty to ride about and see the young ladies. Now won't I be fixed. But this is a joke."[31]

Hannah was on her way to the Springs to rest. The second child, Anna, was born in May of 1834, and Hannah did not recover her strength and her cough worsened. As the hot summer months of 1835 approached it was decided that she should go to the Sulphur Springs of Virginia for a month or more, leaving the two little girls with the Lides. Since Caleb's business affairs were in a critical time, she went with a small group of relatives and close friends. Now twenty-three, and after almost five years of marriage, this was a short interval of retreat, with Caleb's sympathy and understanding. Her pastor, Rev. James C. Furman, had himself spent half of the preceding year at the Springs recuperating from overwork and worry imposed on a frail body. He wrote her a long letter from Society Hill, with news of the village community and the hope that ". . . before this you have reaped sensible benefit from the travelling, the change of air, and the use of the mineral water." He went on to warn her that such places as "the Springs" are ". . . very unfriendly to that spiritual health which

31. Hannah to Caleb, July 25, 1835 (R. E. Coker).

with the child of God is the grand consideration." He then gave her this prescription:

One means I find serviceable in endeavouring to excite gratitude to God is a comparison of what I enjoy not only with what I deserve, but what is allotted to others. Whilst therefore you are enjoying the means you are using for restoration, it may be profitable to think how many even of God's own people, who may be borne down with disease, are yet necessitated to groan away the remnant of a wretched life in a scanty hovel, without any alleviation from the kindness of friends and the thousand circumstances which make our afflictions so tolerable—so comparatively light. This grateful thought may enable you the better to sustain the painful absence from your children. But I must stop. Commending you to God and to the world of His grace I remain, my dear sister, with sentiments of Christian love.[32]

Hannah replied in some humility, confessing to ". . . levity and vanity of mind, self-will and many, many other unholy tempers of mind." Her intent in going to the Springs was plain: "When I left home, I thought I shall be clear of the troubles and perplexities of my family, and would be able unmolested to attend to serious reading and meditation. . . ." Characteristically, she did not feel that she was doing enough serious reading and meditation at the Springs, ". . . there is so much to divert the attention that the mind is forced from its object."[33] But the Rev. Mr. Furman, older and wiser, had anticipated her: "The benefit, however, of the Spring is not always felt *immediately,* it is often times after a return home that the valetudinarian sees most evidently the good which he has received."[34]

Mr. Furman was both wise and correct. The time at the Springs helped, her cough improved, though temporarily. But her object was greater than mere rest or reading and meditation. In these years the young, frail Hannah was, with integrity and courage, ordering her qualities of sincerity, religious

---

32. Quoted in Cook, *The Life Work of James Clement Furman,* pp. 44-46.
33. *Ibid.,* p. 47.
34. *Ibid.,* p. 45.

feelings, hard work, devotion to her family, and saving humor into a pattern and perspective with which she could live in spiritual comfort and physical health. It was not easy, but she was eminently successful. She held tightly to her tested faith. Yet she became neither doctrinal nor morbid, and only on occasion articulate. She found the physical strength, and the emotional satisfaction, to become the center of a large, intimate family, bearing and rearing ten children.

If in these first, young years she drew on Caleb's greater maturity and calm purpose, she paid him back many-fold. For she was the other side of his dispassionate, business self. It was Hannah who entered most completely into the life of Society Hill, finding meaning and substance for her family in the daily and yearly round of community life. Later, as Caleb came to travel from home only reluctantly, Hannah maintained her taste for different people and new sights, about which she wrote home to her children with delight and detail.

III

It was these years of the mid-thirties that were most critical for Caleb in business. Coker and Gregg had opened their store in the relatively stable money and credit situation of 1828, a situation established and controlled by Nicholas Biddle's Bank of the United States. Money was expensive, and the credit on the store books was in terms of this expensive money. Andrew Jackson's ultimately successful effort to disestablish the Bank had the first effect of cheapening money. The consequence was that when the farmers paid their bills to Caleb, the amount of money was accurate, but it would not replace goods on which the credit was originally extended. A later phase of these unsettled economic conditions appeared with the issuance of the Specie Circular in 1836, which in effect cut the supply of money drastically. This embarrassed Caleb in paying for goods from his New York and Charleston suppliers. This crisis was soon followed by the Panic of 1837, when the price of cotton dropped suddenly and far.

Two other events added to the importance of these years. Sometimes, apparently in 1835, Mr. Gregg reached a decision to leave Society Hill and establish a store some twenty miles down river at Mars Bluff, where he owned lands. Caleb agreed to buy Gregg's share. At the summing up, late in 1835 or early in 1836, the net worth of Coker and Gregg was set at $45,000, a satisfactory growth on the original investment of $2,800. For the larger part of Gregg's $22,500, Caleb gave him notes due in one, two and three years, all of which were paid when due.[35] This was a strain on Caleb's resources of these years. But there was yet another. Caleb and several other men of the area had invested in a steamboat on which goods could be brought up the river, and cotton and produce taken down the river. In 1836 this boat, fully loaded, struck a snag on its way up the river and sank. The question of liability was taken to court. The owners were cleared of blame, but this was a serious financial threat for many months.[36]

Caleb talked very little about himself, or of what was past. He did, however, look back with some quiet pride to the fact that when, during these years, he was forced to ask for more than the usual amount of credit from his suppliers, there was never any hesitation or quibble. This meant that he had become known as a good and reliable merchant. He took the trouble to point this out to his eldest son, James, as a matter of instruction.[37]

Credit was the life blood of the cotton economy. In literal truth, cotton grew on credit—the larger part of the stalks growing in the fields at any given time were mortgaged. The farmer, to plant his crop and to live to harvest it, had taken goods on credit from the storekeepers, who in turn were in greater or lesser debt to the suppliers in Charleston, Philadelphia, New York, and elsewhere. These suppliers were often in debt to banks, cotton brokers, and manufacturers. The object, and

---

35. James Lide Coker, "Short Sketch of the Coker Family of Darlington District, S.C." (Watson collection), p. 5.
36. R. E. Coker, "Coker Forebears," manuscript, pp. 32-35.
37. James Lide Coker, "Short Sketch of the Coker Family of Darlington District, S.C." (Watson collection), pp. 6-7.

the collateral of all this credit, was cotton—this was usable, negotiable and profitable. In general, to a merchant like Caleb, land, chattels and slaves were embarrassments as security, assuming foreclosure, for they required further trouble and expense either to use or to liquidate, and the customs of the economy looked upon foreclosure as a last resort. In actual practice, therefore, Caleb extended credit on his judgment as to a farmer's ability to grow cotton and his integrity in paying up. Knowing this, Caleb knew that he stood in the same relationship to his creditors, and was grateful for the confidence they showed in him during the 1830's.

The cotton economy was colonial and crude. It was a simple operation of growing cotton and shipping it out raw to the mills of New and Old England in exchange for manufactured and processed goods of the world. From his vantage point at one of the main crossroads of the economy, Caleb, with his usual clarity, knew this well. In 1836, on his way to buy in New York, he wrote Hannah that

The Steam Boats and Railroads are crowded to overflowing and I expect to find New York fill'd up with Southern and Western merch'ts. In fact it appears to me that the whole South and West have turned fools, or they would import goods to their Southern Towns and not be so dependent on the North for their supplies. The money they pay for their traveling expences in one year would, if divided equally among 100 persons, make them independently rich. But who can turn the current. If I with my present experience was only 20 years old and as rich as the Rothchilds and something more of a Book man, perhaps I would make an effort. But these *ifs* makes this all foolishness. I only set down to let you know that I was here and well and that in the midst of all those crowds I remember my Hannah and children, and shall waste no time in getting my business done and returning to them, where if I enjoy any happiness at all, *it is with them*. Kiss the dear little *ones* for me.[38]

What was left unwritten, Hannah knew well: that, like the system or not, Caleb would make the best of it. In this same

38. Caleb to Hannah, July 16, 1836 (R. E. Coker).

year of 1836 he became postmaster at Society Hill,[39] willing to have the trouble of the mail in order to locate the post office in the store. Increasingly, Caleb began to receive calls to act as a general business agent for friends and customers in Charleston and other places. In an area where banks were few and far between, the store advanced cash money, and often received cash deposits against which goods would later be drawn. For many customers, the store would pay bills for such things as lumber, blacksmithing, stage fares and shoe repairs. Collections for public and private enterprises—road money, postage, taxes, school fees for St. David's Academy—were made in the ordinary course of the day's work. Caleb was named frequently as an administrator of estates, at times because he was the largest creditor and in other cases through choice of the deceased. His accountings as administrator were detailed, neat and accurate to the last cent.[40]

In the matter of credit, Caleb deviated from the general practice. As a rule merchants in the South charged interest on credit extended cotton growers at rates ranging between 10 and 20 per cent. Caleb's standard rate to all customers was 7 per cent, during all of the years of his storekeeping.[41] No doubt this was good business, but perhaps he was also setting a challenge for his ability in buying and selling. If this was so, then he did not underrate himself. The store prospered increasingly.

So much so that not later than 1838 he was beginning to branch out into cotton planting. That year he spent slightly over $5,000 for slaves, and bought almost $7,000 worth of land near Society Hill,[42] the latter on notes payable in one, two and three years. In succeeding years there were further additions of land and slaves. These were natural developments; planting was the best and highest way of life, and storekeepers, in company with doctors, lawyers, and ministers, more often

39. Caleb to Hannah, July 16, 1836 (R. E. Coker).
40. Estate Papers, Packet Numbers 596, 643, 910, 861, 352, 326, 901, 920 (Judge of Probate, Darlington, S.C.).
41. Store books (South Caroliniana Library).
42. Store books (South Caroliniana Library).

than not became heavily involved in growing cotton, owning slaves, and building fine residences. But amidst it all, Caleb held firmly in mind that his main interest was the store, and he became no part-time leisurely storekeeper. He once wrote Hannah from Alabama, where he saw the rich prairie lands, that "If I was young and expected to get my living by planting, I have never seen lands that would suit me as well, but perhaps before getting to the end of my journey I may see better."[43] There was in him this remarkable consistency, and partial independence of status and fashion—to remain what he was without explanation or immature show of difference.

The implications of this quality of Caleb's are considerable. He was maintaining not only his identity, but his clearheaded view of the cotton economy. In this economy, there was little net profit in raising cotton. This was so for many reasons—because the cotton lands were wearing out, because of crop failures, because of high interest charges, because cotton was a raw material traded for finished goods, because slave labor ultimately became unprofitable. Despite all of the hazards of storekeeping, and perhaps a majority of the storekeepers succumbed over a lifetime, this was one of the few places where a substantial increment of money could be achieved in the cotton economy. If these funds were put back into growing cotton, and into ostentatious living, then they were not available to establish banks and southern supply houses, to build railroads, or to establish industries. In personal terms, many able, vigorous men turned to this area, where there was already a surfeit, and identified their interests with the survival of the cotton economy as a way of life. Caleb went into planting, and he built a handsome home. But the store was always the first order of business. Nor did he put all of the store profits into growing cotton; some went into a railroad that was built into Society Hill, and another part into stock of a bank in nearby Cheraw.[44]

43. Caleb to Hannah, July 5, 1856 (R. E. Coker).
44. R. E. Coker, "Coker Forebears" (R. E. Coker), p. 30; Caleb to Hannah, June 7, 1856 (R. E. Coker).

The home that Caleb built for Hannah and their children was begun in the early 1840's, on the lands he had begun to buy in 1838. It was built about two miles south of the village, on high ground, and took the name Camp Marion from the fact that adjoining was the field where an annual militia encampment was held. It was a large, roughly square house, two storied, high ceilinged and divided by a wide middle hallway. It was raised on high foundations amid oak trees. The kitchen was detached, and scattered about were such outbuildings as barns, carriage house and well house. There were eight rooms, all about twenty feet square. The proportions were excellent, and remains a notable structure.

This was Hannah's natural habitat. Here was room and scope for all the activities and intermingling of a large family. Here was space for work, and when time could be taken, a place for pause and renewal. It was perhaps a physical burden, but spiritually and emotionally she thrived. The family moved in 1844. Camp Marion was not merely a symbol of success, but of family identity achieved.

3

Family Time

I

IN ALL THERE WERE ten children. Jane Lide, the oldest, was born in 1831; then came Anna Maria in 1833. Four years went by before the next child, James Lide, the first son, was born in 1837. Then followed William Caleb in 1839, Charles Westfield in 1841, Frances Elizabeth Pugh in 1844, Mary Lide in 1847, Edward Thomas in 1850, Emma Sarah in 1852, and Florence in 1854.

Caleb and Hannah agreed from the first that the children were the sum and substance of their living. Their letters over the years revolved around the children.[1] They dealt sensibly with each other in this as in other things. The home and children were Hannah's first responsibility, but their training and the atmosphere of the home was a matter of effective cooperation between Caleb and Hannah. In none of the contemporary letters of the children is there any hint of private speaking to one parent, except in such things as the girls writing their mother about clothes and beaux, and the boys their father about crops. Sometimes Hannah gave

us little tasks to finish before going to our play. One well remembered day, I had a small wash-towel to hem which I could have finished in a half-hour, but I was lazy that day, hemmed two or three inches perhaps, idled over my task and spent a great deal of time holding my work in my hands and pitying myself for having

---

1. See, for instance, letters in the possession of R. E. Coker.

such a hard task: Of course I laid it aside for lunch and then dinner, thinking I had plenty of time to finish when I should feel more like sewing. The day wore on until father came home and the other children ran to meet him. "Why, where is Jane," he asked, "why doesn't she come?" Sister told him I hadn't finished my work. He came in, sat down by me, asked me to show him my task, and asked why I couldn't do it. I felt very much ashamed, but handed it to him. He took it and carefully hemmed it while I stood by and looked on in deep humiliation, then told me to "show it to mother and ask her if it would do."

She accepted the work of my substitute and told me to thank father for helping me out of my trouble. She saw that I was sufficiently penitent of my disobedience and idleness. I never needed such a lesson again.[2]

The Coker children went to school and church, formed friendships with other children and brushed against the varying personalities of adults of the village, as the natural extension of their family life. Community and family merged closely and the cleavage point was often not clear. Their performance in the morning was community knowledge by nightfall, when it was often translated tacitly and unconsciously into family performance.

Hannah began the instruction of her children at home, before they started to school, and sent them to St. David's with the framework of home still much about them. Jane, the eldest child, did not begin school until she was eight years old, so as to wait for her younger sister Anna, six, because "we were such constant companions and so dependent on each other . . . Mother had taught me at home and I was fully as advanced in my studies as the children of my age."[3]

James, the next oldest, could read a little also when he began school, and his first school experience was essentially a family experience, though he felt quite early the testing and trying that was also a part of family-community life: "When I first went to school, being such a little boy, I took my seat on the girls' side with my two sisters where the teacher permitted me

2. Wilson, "For My Own" (Watson collection), p. 8.
3. Wilson, *Memories of Society Hill*, p. 22.

to stay for two days. At the end of that time he told me that I must either wear petticoats or sit on the boys' side, so I moved my seat."[4]

St. David's was "their" school, as much a part of their life as their father's store or the road running through the village. Caleb often collected tuition fees at the store, and as a member of the Society was active in its administration.[5] The teacher, always male and usually a bachelor, boarded in the various homes of the village. James was surprised to find, when a certain teacher came to stay at the Coker house, that he was friendly and capable of going fishing and duck shooting with the boys. This particular teacher was from the North, and he amazed all the children by skating over a small pond that had frozen during an unusual cold spell.[6] James could have spared himself some surprise at this teacher's affability and attraction if he had consulted his older sisters more. The girls had already found this man from over the horizon interesting. "He would tell us about his sisters or entertain us with stories, and sometimes sing comic songs."[7]

The schoolhouse was a large square building, divided into a large and a small room by a platform on which the teacher sat. As a rule the smaller room was used for the younger students. In each room the girls sat on one side and the boys on the other. Discipline varied somewhat with the teacher, but thorough recitation in the three R's was never neglected. Spelling was taught from the blue-back Webster and once a week a spelling contest was held.[8]

About all of the larger pupils were required to recite daily in Latin grammar, and exercise, and the the course led on to reading Caesar, Virgil, Cicero and Sallust. All intending to go to the South Carolina college or other literary institutions were well drilled in Greek but this study was optional with the other students.

Arithmetic and algebra were thoroughly taught and studies in

---

4. James Lide Coker, "Schools" (Watson collection), p. 1.
5. Coker and Gregg receipt book (R. G. Coker).
6. James Lide Coker, "Schools" (Watson collection), p. 14.
7. Wilson, *Memories of Society Hill*, p. 23.
8. James Lide Coker, "Schools" (Watson collection), pp. 2-3.

English were not neglected. Every Friday the boys far enough advanced were required, one half of them to declaim speeches and the other half had to write original compositions. The girl pupils wrote compositions.[9]

The church, almost as much as the school, extended from the home. This was Hannah's province primarily. Caleb did not join the church though he supported it freely and was in regular attendance. He told his son James' wife, when she first came to Society Hill as a bride, that he was not good enough to join the church.[10] For the children, church activities were important. In Sunday school, catechism and question books were used and scriptural passages were memorized. Just before the closing of Sunday school each pupil was required to quote one verse of the Bible, the verse selected either by the pupil or by his or her parents.[11] The Cokers were always close to the Welsh Neck pastors and their families. As they grew older the Coker children, particularly the girls, were much occupied with church activities.

Nature was all about. Nature was the tall, heavy oak and hickory trees, and their summer shade and falling leaves in the long southern autumn, and their buds and greening again in the spring. Nature was paths across the river bottoms, the droning of insects around the mudflats and sink holes in the hot suns of August. Nature was the fearful, hopeful rhythm of the crop season that the children absorbed from the tenseness and worry of their parents. Nature was in the songs of the Negro boat crews as they poled and pulled the boats up the river. Nature was the carriage driver, the Negro Dembo, as he taught the Coker children about the animals, and lived to become "Uncle Dembo."

Most deeply, perhaps, nature was the strong feeling for family that underlay the home. Caleb and Hannah and their children were always conscious of their larger family of inti-

9. *Ibid.*, p. 4.
10. As told to Dr. W. C. Coker by his mother.
11. Wilson, *Memories of Society Hill*, p. 5.

mate relatives. Nature was the older Lides, long away and far off, but always symbol and reality of an organic continuity of life. Jane, the eldest child, remembered good and gay times at Springville with her grandparents,[12] before the Lides went to the southwestern cotton lands. She also remembered the family westering:

Grandpa lifted me up to look into the large covered wagon which was to take their baggage, tents, etc., and in which he and the boys would sometimes ride and sleep, but it looked most dark and gloomy and I did not like it. . . . A carriage was to take our sick grandma and our aunts, and other wagons were provided for the servants. I remember the weeping at that sad leavetaking in the early autumn of 1835.[13]

Hannah's younger sister, Maria Lide, was a special favorite. She spent her vacations while in school at Charleston with Caleb and Hannah. In the mid-forties she stayed a year with the Cokers, nursed the children through measles, and helped them move to Camp Marion.[14] In 1846, after she had returned to Alabama, she wrote James, then almost ten, this letter:

Your grandparents are both very old, your grandpa will soon be 76 years old!! There are not many people who live as long as he has. His head is nearly as white as snow; but he is very cheerful and takes great delight in playing with and amusing children. He is right mischievous too sometimes. . . . He talks about you a great deal, wishes very often that he could see you. If he felt like he could stand such a journey I believe he would go to see you all again but he is so feeble he seldom ever leaves the house because it fatigues him so much to ride and the weather has been so cold he could hardly keep warm by the fire.

Your grandma's health is better than it has been in a very long time. She walked to church last Sunday for the first time in several years. I believe she does not feel any worse today from it. She has been busy in her garden today, tell your mother it is coming on finely. She will have radishes in a day or two large enough to use. Ask your mother how her garden comes on? Ask her if she ever

12. Wilson, "For My Own" (Watson collection), p. 3.
13. *Ibid.*
14. *Ibid.*, p. 10.

brags on it now-a-days? Your Aunt Mary's garden looks quite gay now.[15]

She knew a great deal about small boys, and how to teach them about doing what must be done:

James, your grandpa has a colt and the other day it was running and playing about in the lot and it ran to the gate to jump over and the pailings were so sharp they caught it in its breast and tore two great holes in it. Your Uncle Joseph washed it with No. 6 and then took a large needle and thread and sewed it up. The colt stood perfectly still until he was done, it seemed to feel very grateful to him for doing something for it.[16]

Maria's husband died not long after their marriage, and she and her three daughters came back to Society Hill to live.[17]

Venerable Nancy Coker seldom left the home of her daughter Ann Hudson at New Province. She made occasional visits to Society Hill. Nancy and Hannah were fundamentally alike, but the life of Society Hill may well have been strange to her. She was no stranger to her grandchildren, though. Jane remembered her visits, and remembered going with Hannah to see her. Hannah wrote James at The Arsenal in 1853 that "I went out to see your grandmother & Aunt Ann Tuesday. They were all in usual health. Your grandma is very feeble & blind but can get about the house very well."[18]

The stewardship of his family fell on Caleb. He was an executor of his father's estate, and, with her power of attorney, managed Ann Hudson's affairs after the death of her husband. His brother Thomas came into the store in a partnership that was cut short by Thomas' early death. The younger twin brothers, Josiah and Lewis, came to live at Society Hill where they worked in the store and attended St. David's, Caleb paying them for the work as well as their school fees and furnishing room and board. Josiah returned to farming, but Lewis remained a lifetime as Caleb's partner.

15. Maria Lide to James, March 9, 1846 (R. E. Coker).
16. *Ibid.*
17. Wilson, "For My Own" (Watson collection), p. 11.
18. Hannah to James, Sept. 9, 1853 (R. E. Coker).

FAMILY TIME

The maturity of the children, as they passed from one stage of physical and mental development to another, was matched with appropriate activities. Nature and the village community furnished many of these activities. There were wide spaces for play; opossums, rabbits, and squirrels to hunt and to capture and raise; there were all the interests of plantation animals and work, of barn and yard lots. Maria Lide, in her letter to young James, told him to write her ". . . about the garden and chickens and turkeys and everything else."[19]

Caleb and Hannah took a direct hand. "During vacations mother would have us spend part of each day in reading with her, writing letters, and doing some easy sewing, selecting such books as would cultivate our taste and give some instruction in an entertaining way."[20] Caleb taught the two oldest children, Jane and Anna, to ride, and rode with them himself until James was old enough to go with them.[21] The boys had horses more or less of their own. Charles wrote James at The Arsenal that Dembo ". . . says your horse is as good as ever. He says he can take him and go to Columbia in a day and a half."[22]

The boys, as they became old enough, were given small plots of cotton to tend and work themselves, and they had their troubles.[23] Family life for the children as they moved into their teens was probably as it appears from the following letter from Charles, aged twelve, to James, sixteen, at school in Columbia.

Our peaches are not gone yet. We have two or three quite nice trees of nice big yellow press that are not quite ripe yet. Our water melons are all most gone. They are hardly fit to eat. Father is having some of the vines cut up. Well Jimmie one month of our vacation is gone and I think it has gone very quick. I have not begun to get tired of staying at home. I hope it will not be long be-

19. Maria Lide to James, March 9, 1846 (R. E. Coker).
20. Wilson, "For My Own" (Watson collection), pp. 7-8.
21. *Ibid.*, p. 6.
22. Charles to James, September 9, 1853 (R. E. Coker).
23. Hannah to James, September 9, 1853, and James to Hannah, September 2, 1846 (R. E. Coker).

fore yours will come so that you can come home. Ben has made Willie a nice desk to keep up here in our room and he and I are setting up here writing on it and I have been down to ask mother what else to say and she told me to tell you that the snake bit Mary on the heel and that it swelled up the leg and foot, that it bit her right in the open yard by the swing. It pained her very much yesterday. It is a little better today, but it still pains her a great deal. Dembo killed the snake, it was about nine o'clock in the night when it bit her. Willie and I was gone to bed and did not know any thing about it until next morning. I told you in my last letter that your horse had run away, but did not tell you why he did so, both times that he ran away, loose horses ran by him and started him but as soon as the buggy was mended we put him in again and put a curb bit on him and he seems as gentle as ever. Willie has commenced to press some cider and has pressed about three gallons and it is very nice he intends to press some more there are a great many apples this season. Father says if we had proper things to press with we might make about half barrel. Fanny and Mary are in the kitchen trying to make muscadine jelly. Anna has not learned to walk yet. When mother told Eddie what you said about the peaches he said that he would send Willie with some to you. When I asked Eddie what to tell you for him he told me to tell you howdy for him. Well Jemmie I must close. All the family join me in love to you.[24]

Early training for maturity was a little more serious for the girls, and probably Hannah had more patience with them in the house than Caleb had with the boys in the fields. In 1846, Caleb and Hannah went north on a trip together, leaving Jane, Anna, James, Willie, Charles and Frances at home. Several adult relatives were in charge, but Hannah wrote Jane, then fifteen, in adult fashion about the trip, and about matters of the home. She admonished Jane and Anna not to neglect their music, and asked, "... how do you come on reading and housekeeping?"[25] In 1856 Hannah visited her relatives in Alabama. Jane by now was married, but Anna, twenty-two, was at home to keep house for her father. Caleb wrote Hannah

24. Charles to James, September 2, 1853 (R. E. Coker).
25. Hannah to James, August 8, 1846 (R. E. Coker).

that Anna filled her place as mistress of the dinner table well, "... although the young ladies accused her of looking careworn and matronly."[26]

The children themselves were aware of each other's growth, and often offered each other gratuitous advice on the proper behavior in the new estate.[27] Throughout the family there was good-natured amusement at growing pains. Anna wrote her mother to tell Caleb that Charles, then a baby, "... woke up early yesterday morning and made the house ring with old dan tucker before he was dressed."[28] Hannah wrote James that fourteen year old Willie had received an invitation to a party addressed to *"Mr."* William Coker, and added, "Don't you think he is rising?"[29]

Camp Marion was always remembered as home. It was a teeming, busy place, yet quiet, shaded, encompassing. Here Hannah held sway in the intermingling of her large family, bearing, teaching, training, taking to church, and, finally, sending off to school. Nor was this the end of her responsibilities. There was help in the kitchen and for the housework, but the supervision of cooking and cleaning, canning and gardening, making sausage and churning butter and a thousand other details was a large job, and though it taxed her strength she did it well.

Caleb contributed a peculiar, personal element to life at Camp Marion, one that was of considerable effect in the training of the children. He carried over to planting the mind and methods of a business man; he maintained his concern that the credit and debit side of the ledger book of any activity remain in balance, or at least be complete as to entries so that a clear estimate of success or failure could be made. He was not alone in this approach in the South, but he was unusual.[30]

This approach was not just a method of bookkeeping; it

26. Caleb to Hannah, May 30, 1856 (R. E. Coker).
27. Anna to James, November 16, 1853 (R. E. Coker).
28. Anna to Caleb, August 29, 1846 (R. E. Coker).
29. Hannah to James, February 24, 1853 (R. E. Coker).
30. Rosser H. Taylor, *Ante-Bellum South Carolina*, Vol. 25, No. 2, *The James Sprunt Studies in History and Political Science* (Chapel Hill: The University of North Carolina Press), pp. 17-19.

was a habit of life and exerted great influence within the family. Camp Marion itself bore Caleb's mark. It was built on the plantation lands where supervision would be easier and constant. More than this, it brought to an end the delightful but expensive movement to a summer home in the nearby sandhills every year. The family lived the year round at Camp Marion, which, on its hills and removed several miles from the river, was as cool and as healthy as the sandhills.

Life was good at Camp Marion. The children were indulged in education, horses and travel. Yet the establishment was orderly and not wasteful, and in this the cue was given by Caleb. He rose early and went to the store. He came home to lunch about two o'clock, taking a toddy before eating. After lunch he took a short nap and saw to the work of the plantation, and then to the work of the store. He retired early.[31]

It is a matter of frequent remark in the Coker family that no one remembered in later years anything that Caleb had said. He was not formal or aggressive; perhaps he never laid down the law. But his orderly, precise habit of life permeated the family—if not as much as did Hannah's constant influence, then significantly. He was not altogether at ease in writing to his children, not very chatty or informative, but his main influence on the family appears in a letter to James at school in Columbia: "I believe your Mother wrote you the first of this week, and I would not now attempt it but pay day is at hand and I do not like to be unpunctual."[32]

II

In the late 1840's and through the 1850's, the older children, as their time came, went off to school. The two oldest, Jane and Anna, one year separated in grades, went first. They attended Limestone Springs Female High School in Gaffney County for two years, and then each spent two years at Mrs.

---

31. Conversation with W. C. Wilson, grandson of Caleb and Hannah, who spent several of his early years in their home.
32. Caleb to James, March 31, 1853 (R. E. Coker).

FAMILY TIME 47

Dupre's school for young ladies in Charleston.[33] Jane was married to Dr. F. W. Wilson in 1850, soon after her schooling was finished.

James went to the South Carolina Military Academy, composed of The Arsenal at Columbia, in 1853, and then to The Citadel in Charleston. Willie went to South Carolina College in 1856.[34] James did not find life at The Citadel very congenial, writing to his mother in June of 1856 that "The Citadel looks as dull as ever.... We are overladen with studies. So we finish the session tho' at the right time I don't care what they give us to do in the mean time."[35] Hannah gave him some sympathy, but let him understand that he was expected to do his work. Neither James nor Willie cared for the limelight at college. James wrote from The Citadel that he did not like being a student officer, because this required him to give orders and report his classmates.[36] Willie came home after graduation to teach at St. David's for the two years that remained of peace.[37]

As it turned out, James did not graduate from The Citadel. He was expelled during his final year. On Monday, September 15, 1856, young Cadet Tom Law, friend and confidant of James, wrote in his diary that

A circumstance took place today, which from its consequences has become a matter of some moment. While reciting to Major Capers, Jim Coker was called up to the board. When he went to demonstrate, Major Capers insinuated that he suspected him of taking his figure from the book. This being quite offensive to sensitive gentlemanly feeling, J. L. C. was somewhat touched by it, and told Major Capers that he did not think that he had any reason to think him guilty of such a thing, which led on to some pretty sharp words. What was said I have not fully ascertained, but it seems to have been of quite a plain nature.

33. Wilson, "For My Own" (Watson collection), pp. 11-12.
34. R. E. Coker, "William Caleb Coker" (R. E. Coker), p. 58.
35. James to Hannah, June 2, 1856 (R. E. Coker).
36. James to Jane, January 15, 1856 (R. E. Coker).
37. R. E. Coker, "William Caleb Coker" (R. E. Coker), p. 41.

The plain talk was not done with. On the seventeenth, Cadet Law recorded that "This morning for some purpose he [James] went into Major Capers' office. The latter told him he had been waiting for him to apologize for what he had said on Monday. J. L. C. told him (I believe) that he had not intended to apologize, that he would never get an apology from him, and walked out of the office." By Retreat that evening ". . . sure enough, here came an order which read (as near as I can recollect), as follows, 'Cadet J. L. Coker, for repeated acts of insubordination and violation of the regulations is hereby suspended,' etc."

The matter dragged on for a week or more, with Superintendent Jones conducting an investigation. The upshot was that "Gen. Jones tells him [James] that Major Capers disclaims all intention of insulting him in the section room. He (J. L. C.) therefore agreed to retract what he had said provided that it be mentioned in the order what Major Capers had said—(as above). This, however Gen'l Jones would not consent to do, & as J. L. C. is unwilling to retract without it, he was determined to bid them adieu."

James bid them adieu with a parting shot, and, so it seems, the last word. As a suspended cadet his going and coming was severely restricted. Nevertheless, on the twenty-sixth, "Jim Coker came up today to tell us good-bye as he was going to start at 4 p.m. While standing in the passage-way Capt. Stevens went up & desired to know if he had heard of that order, etc., & told him if he did not take care he would involve his friends in a difficulty, etc. Jim told him to shut his mouth—that he wished no more of his gab (to that amount) & the bold Capt. (??) left him."

All this was bold and prideful, but when James ". . . came up from dinner he told us good-bye & I think there were few hearts that were not filled with regret. Jim, himself, I think would have cried for a little."

Cry or not, he went home. This was a critical point in the family time. During the affair at The Citadel, Cadet Law had written in his diary that "J. L. C. seemed quite mortified at it, tho' he did not appear to care very much on his own account, principally that of his parents." Several days later he recorded that "He (J. C.) told me today that he had written home about it, & that his Mother was so shocked at it, that she had to take her bed—said he was ready to do almost anything just for the folks at home."[38] Beyond this account of distress, there is no record of what Caleb and Hannah thought of James' action. Perhaps they thought him justified in principle, but, also, that the price was rather high. After the first emotions had passed, counsel no doubt was taken as to what the erstwhile Cadet, who had not lost, and never would lose, his military bearing, would do next. There remains no record, but it seems certain that it was decided then that James would take over a plantation which Caleb had bought several years previously at public auction at Hartsville, a crossroads about three miles from his old home at New Providence and seventeen miles west of Society Hill. Undaunted, James proposed that he spend a year at Harvard before going to Hartsville, taking at Harvard such courses as seemed most appropriate and helpful for his not yet begun career of agriculture. It is to the everlasting credit of Caleb and Hannah that they approved.

James, then, went on to Harvard in 1857.

Most of my time at Harvard was spent in practical analytical work in the chemical laboratory under Professor Horsford. Near me worked in the same laboratory Alexander Agassiz, afterwards well known as Professor at Harvard University, the son of the great Louis Agassiz the most distinguished naturalist of his day. In Botany I received practical instruction from the distinguished botanist, Asa Gray, whose lectures in the University I also attended. At his home twice a week, under this charming teacher, with only two others in the class (Barnwell of South Carolina and Jenness of Maine), the lessons were occasions of greatest delight. . . . At this time Professor Louis Agassiz was a Professor at Harvard and I was privileged to attend his lectures in Zoology. . . .[39]

38. Tom Law, *Citadel Cadets, the Journal of Cadet Tom Law* (Clinton, S.C.: Presbyterian College Press, 1941), pp. 50-56, for account of James' difficulties.
39. James Lide Coker, "Schools" (Watson collection), p. 7.

Whatever James may have learned of specific information, he learned about science at Harvard, about that state of mind which science implies. From the laboratory he learned about method: he learned to lay off a measured field, and in the field to lay off equal plots; to draw a sketch and to label the plots; to record what was planted in each plot and how; to keep accurate and continuous records of the growth in each plot; and to measure carefully at the end.[40] In these years of the 1850's there was only scattered allegiance to this way of doing things, especially in the South. This kind of work required then, as now, money and time as well as conviction, good seasons, plenty of labor, and encouragement. Such work knew nothing and cared less for profit and loss, for sick field hands, for drought or for energies soon to be consumed by sectional conflict and war. James, on his return from Harvard in 1858 to take up his work at Hartsville, began almost immediately to set up some experiments.[41] Within three years this work begun so hopefully would be stopped cold by a nation's catastrophe. Forty years later this work would appear again, as his sons began, in that strange organic continuity of family, community and region, to breed pedigreed seed for the South's crops.

In between these years, though, the South and the nation were to determine the terms of this development, determine them without regard to youthful high hopes. The basic question, then, was the quality of this young man who came back from Harvard in 1858, and how he would persevere. He brought home a box full of scientific equipment,[42] and a burden on his mind. The family ought to hear of his enlightment. He gathered them around, his mother and father, brothers and sisters, and quite likely some of the Negroes were in the background. He delivered himself of a speech, on chemistry. The group was tolerant but only mildly interested, a rather shocking thing no doubt to the young man from

---

40. James Lide Coker's farm journal (W. C. Coker).
41. *Ibid.*
42. Conversation with Dr. W. C. Coker.

Harvard. Only his sister Fanny asked penetrating questions.[43] Not his father, or his brothers, but his sister. So began a hard education.

James learned first out of some inner confusion. He had been raised under the pervasive religion of his mother and in what must be called a devout community. He had a religious experience at The Citadel which was strong enough to cause him to join the church and to discuss this experience with his close friend. All of this background contributed to a compelling personal sense of God and tied him quite closely to literal Christianity.

But he had gone to Harvard to study science. This in itself, as well as the new worlds of travel and friendships, put a heavy strain on his earlier religious teachings. More particularly, these were the times when evolution, despite Professor Agassiz's opposition, was in the scientific air. All of these things in the year at Harvard wrought on the young man. Perhaps he felt some guilt when he returned home about the things he had learned and heard at Harvard. Certainly, placed against the nearness of home and family, they set up a conflict which had to be resolved.

So in his farm journal that he began so confidently in the interests of a new world of science he wrote one last and unsuccessful affirmation of the older faith. His subject was the doctrine of special providence. He did not deny his science and he had the simple loyalty to try and affirm the religion of his mother.[44] But he had gone too far. Hannah believed. But James, in his tract, attempted to *prove* the special providence of God. That was the word that stood between two eras. Special providence can be believed in with the whole being, but it cannot be proved. Deep in himself James must have known this, because the whole tract has a hollow sound of circular reasoning, totally out of tone with anything he wrote before or after. He was a good many years working this

43. *Ibid.*
44. James Lide Coker's farm journal (W. C. Coker).

problem out, but in the end it was to be science and the church, rather than Hannah's intuitional religion.

Most of all, perhaps, he moved into man's estate learning from nature. Nature is rich in the middle country of South Carolina, but it is a hard nature. The crop season of cotton is long and delicate. Beginning in April, too little rain and too much sun can kill the young stalks; or, far the greater hazard, too much rain can sprout out the evergrowing grass that will choke off the cotton.

If all goes well in the early months, then in June there will be a fine, healthy, even stand of cotton in the fields; good enough for a young man making his first crop to be proud. But August and September are killing months, if some rain does not come. These times, there seems to be nothing in the world but high, hot sun and sky, and the tall pines shout down that this is so. In his first crop year at Hartsville, James ran into five weeks of drought in August and September, turning great hopes to dry brown leaves and poor cotton.[45]

When rain comes, it is often part of a storm, when wind and rain beat down the crops, and muddy water runs off the exposed land. A great storm came in 1861, leaving the Negroes wonder-eyed, and James thankful for the chance that saved him from a falling limb. Work hands were a week or more clearing limbs and debris from the fields, while the grass grew.[46] Much of the Hartsville lands were new grounds to be cleared, and this was rough, stubborn work that broke plows and was seldom finished on time.[47] There was the great responsibility of the Negroes, of providing food and clothes, of sending for the doctor, and of keeping them at work. Almost in desperation, he recorded in his journal on May 18, 1861: "Sick children—sick children."[48]

Caleb and Hannah watched developments at Hartsville closely, aware that here was one testing, and one conclusion of the family time. Caleb had given James outright a half interest

45. *Ibid.*, entries of October, 1858.
46. *Ibid.*, entries of May, 1861.
47. *Ibid.*, throughout journal.
48. *Ibid.*, entry of May 18, 1861.

in the Hartsville plantation; he had agreed to the experiments, and had given advice freely. But beyond that he insisted that businesslike arrangements be maintained. He and James scrupulously divided the profits, half and half. For the crop of 1858 they each received $659.16 in cash settlement; $631.91 in 1859; and $850.55 in 1860. When additional Negroes were brought in to take care of the expanded operations at Hartsville Caleb paid the bill, but James gave his father a note for $3,350, this being half of the purchase price. The note drew interest from January 1, 1859.[49]

James' experiments went well, although his journal entries were often interrupted by more pressing affairs. As a thoroughgoing scientific record the journal probably would not have passed either Professor Horsford's or Asa Gray's inspection. He had, however, grown crops of cotton and corn on measured tracts, under specific applications of various types of fertilizers. By the end of the crop year of 1860 he was drawing definite, though negative, conclusions as to the efficiency of commercial fertilizers. For 1861 he had laid out new tracts to test home fertilizers.[50] On April 12, 1861, while South Carolina guns were firing in Charleston on Fort Sumter, opening the war years, he recorded that he was "planting cotton just as yesterday" in "cloudy and showery" weather.

III

Secession and state's rights, slavery and war, do not appear in the surviving family letters and journals of the 1850's, partly, perhaps, because the Cokers were vigorously intent on their own affairs. As, in the forties and fifties sectional differences and emotions crystallized, Caleb, in his quiet, dry way had set a course that did not provide much scope for colorful action or phrases. It was a moderate, but firm course of seeking to prevent a final break. In 1852 he belonged to the "Coopera-

---

49. Store books, ledger marked C. Coker and Brother, 1857-60, pp. 95, 103, 126, and ledger marked C. Coker and Brother, 1859-63, p. 472 (South Caroliniana Library).
50. James Lide Coker's farm journal, entries of 1861 (W. C. Coker).

tion Party" in Darlington County.[51] He took young James and Willie down to Darlington for a day-long meeting of the Secession and Cooperation parties. Willie began to cheer Caleb's side, and James, at a proper fifteen, tried to quiet Willie. Caleb told James to let Willie "holler" as much as he pleased.[52] In 1856 he went to Columbia as a delegate to the state convention of the Democratic moderates under the leadership of James Orr. James attended a Union meeting in the town of Darlington in 1858,[53] and he and Caleb may well have attended other such meetings.

Caleb continued to think of himself as a storekeeper, but he had a large equity in the cotton economy, in planting and slave owning. As late as 1858 he paid $14,000 for an entire estate of Negroes.[54] When the last prewar Census was taken in 1860, Caleb owned 113 slaves;[55] he was thus one of sixteen men in Darlington County owning more than 100 slaves. The home plantation at Camp Marion was large. In the 1850's he produced on the average one hundred bales of cotton every year. In 1859 he harvested 146 wagon loads and 42 ox loads of corn, and on January 7 of that year he owned 9 mules, 4 horses, 3 mares, 27 head of dry cattle, 7 milk cows, 7 calves, 2 oxen, 11 sows, 72 shoats and pigs, 10 head of sheep and uncounted poultry, and in the same year he slaughtered 9,655 pounds of hog meat.[56]

The extent of the reluctance, throughout the South, to go the full way to secession, or to be irreconcilable to compromise and eventual adjustment of differences, has been somewhat obscured by later bitterness, and by facile romancing about the ante-bellum South. Caleb's position was not uncommon. His reasoning must be deduced, though, since there is no record of his argument on the subject. Basically, change through up-

---

51. Cook, "The Coker Family" (R. G. Coker), p. 6.
52. From W. D. Woods to Major Coker, dated only July 19 (Watson collection).
53. James Lide Coker's plantation journal, under entry of May 28, 1858 (W. C. Coker).
54. Cook, "The Coker Family" (R. G. Coker), p. 5.
55. Census of 1860, Slave Schedule for Darlington County, S.C.
56. Caleb Coker's plantation journal (South Caroliniana Library).

FAMILY TIME 55

heaval went against his grain. For all of the warmth of his personal feelings, his analysis was always objective and realistic. He had no illusions about the cotton economy, and even a successful war would not solve its problems. There was no gain for storekeeping in a divided nation, and in separation the same factors of the trading situation would remain. Caleb laid heavy emphasis upon individual effort and community responsibility. He was by now a leading citizen making his views known, plainly but quietly. Arriving in Columbia for the moderate Democratic convention in 1856, he wrote Hannah a letter in which there was no mention of the political issues or of the expectations of the Convention.[57]

Yet, once the issue was joined, there was no question as to his course—he would remain with the South and support it with all of his energies and resources. This was not so much a loyalty to southern government, nor to slavery, nor to any of the other usual symbols of the ante-bellum South. This loyalty was to the compelling web of family, community, and region, to neighbors and kinsmen, to emotions and feelings learned he knew not how or where.

To Caleb and Hannah was given slightly more than thirty years of family time, before April 12, 1861. They had been full years, some of them hard years, but, in all truth, fortunate years. Caleb and Hannah had made them so, and all of the children lived. Caleb was now fifty-eight, still erect and calm faced. Hannah was forty-eight, the ceaseless center of the household. What she had done so well was not without effort and cost, for at mid-life she was "grayhaired and careworn ..." with "a slight cough and hoarseness...."[58]

Despite the three decades of rich family life, Caleb and Hannah may well have felt that the family was caught up in war too soon, that their job was half finished, that perhaps the children were not ready. On a physical accounting there was

---

57. Caleb to Hannah, May 4, 1856 (R. E. Coker).
58. Edwin Charles Dargan, *Harmony Hall, Recollections of an Old Southern Home, 1852-1882* (Columbia: The State Company, for the Pee Dee Historical Society), p. 107.

good reason for their concern. Family identity and closeness had been achieved, but only two, possibly three, of the children were fully mature. Jane and Anna were married and established in their own homes. James was becoming established at Hartsville, with his wife Sue Stout Coker whom he had married in 1860, and there was a young daughter. Willie was living at home and teaching at St. David's, not quite certain of his future course. The other six children straggled out behind, in various stages of schooling. Frances and Charles were away at school and the others were at home. Florence, the youngest, was eight and a half.

4

The Family in the War

I

THE THREE BOYS who were old enough—James, William, and Charles—were in the war from the beginning. On the day the guns were fired on Fort Sumter, in the early morning of April twelfth, William was recuperating from an illness at Camp Marion, where Hannah was nursing him, and was still too weak to ride a horse.[1] The local infantry company which he had joined the preceding January as a private was called up by the Governor on the thirteenth.[2] Sick or not, William left with the company on the fifteenth for Charleston and slept that night in the stands of the Charleston race track.[3]

Charles was in Columbia at South Carolina College, where he belonged to the cadet corps.[4] The excitement of the preceding months had made him restless at school. To be a cadet was not enough when his two brothers belonged to regularly organized companies, and he had talked and written of joining William's company. As Hannah helped William make his preparations for leaving, her thoughts strayed worriedly to Charles. With James and William already committed, her main hope necessarily had to be that Charles would not have to go.[5] On the thirteenth she wrote to quiet him; it was

---

1. Hannah to Charles, April 13, 1861 (R. E. Coker).
2. William Caleb Coker, "Partial History of Companies F and M, 8th Regiment of South Carolina Volunteers" (R. E. Coker).
3. *Ibid.*
4. Hannah Lide Coker, *A Story of the Late War* (Privately printed), p. 2.
5. Hannah to Charles, April 13, 1861 (R. E. Coker).

too late. Caught up in the excitement, Charles and his fellow cadets made their way to Charleston.[6]

At Hartsville James, the captain of an infantry company which he had organized in 1859, was ready.[7] The company had been at the disposal of the Governor for some time prior to Fort Sumter, but June[8] came before it was called up as Company G, 9th Regiment, South Carolina Volunteers. The departure from Hartsville, long expected, was an event. There was a procession of buggies and wagons from Hartsville to the train at Darlington. Fathers and mothers, wives, sisters, brothers and friends saw the company off. Old Union men, now that the issue was joined, gave their benediction. Every man, not yet acquainted with war, was laden with personal equipment; James and others took body servants. The roll was called and the men boarded the train. Unfurled on the staff of the color bearer was the company flag that Jane had embroidered with golden silk floss on a blue silk banner: on one side a palmetto tree and crescent; on the other a bugle and the words, "Valiant for the Truth."[9]

After the first alarm there was a short lull. The Governor told Charles and the cadets to go back to school.[10] William's unit moved up to Florence for a few weeks,[11] while James' company was put in training at Ridgeville.[12] William's company was sent to Virginia in the first part of June and reached the front on the twenty-second. On July twenty-first he saw action at First Manassas.[13] At noon on that day he and his company were moved from the right to the heavy fighting on

---

6. Hannah Lide Coker, *A Story of the Late War*, p. 2.
7. James Lide Coker, *History of Co. E. 6th S.C.V. Inf. Co. G. 9th S.C.V. Inf. C.S.A.* (Charleston: Press of Walker, Evans & Cogswell Co., 1899), p. 14. Hereafter cited as *History of Company G*.
8. Wilson, "For My Own" (Watson collection), pp. 14-15.
9. James Lide Coker, *History of Company G*, pp. 18-19.
10. Hannah Lide Coker, *A Story of the Late War*, p. 2.
11. R. E. Coker, "William Caleb Coker" (R. E. Coker), pp. 41-42.
12. James Lide Coker, *History of Company G*, pp. 20-21.
13. R. E. Coker, "William Caleb Coker" (R. E. Coker), p. 42; also W. C. Coker, "Partial History of Companies F and M, 8th Regiment of South Carolina Volunteers" (R. E. Coker), pp. 5-7.

the Confederate left in time to fire several rounds before the Federals broke and ran. James' company arrived just at the close of the battle while the dead and wounded were still on the field.[14] Both saw here, beginning to emerge harshly, the image of war.

The family, intent on its own purposes, was thus forced to open its plans and its personal relations for the war to enter in. The first reactions were naturally those of habit and peace. Caleb, after the war had begun but before communications were cut off, paid his northern creditors in full, conforming to the bookkeeping of a lifetime.[15] Hannah looked about for ways to carry through the education of Frances, already in college, and of Mary soon to go. She attempted to set up a measure of what the family could give, and of what might properly be held back. With James and William gone she wrote Charles to say that he must not think of going to war, "as we do not think it would be right."[16] In May, Caleb went to Florence to see William at camp there,[17] and doubtless there were many other such visits of which no record remains. Letters were of the familiar, and James even found time to come home and look at his crop.[18]

Hannah and Caleb knew that war was more than inconvenience. Even as she fended off the war with everyday work and the constant hope that it would be over quickly, Hannah felt that ahead was something bursting and irrational, some tragedy that would test the family to the limit, or beyond. This feeling was held down, unspoken, until vexation uncovered it briefly: "I told Manie that she wrote about the boys going to the war as if they were going on a pleasure trip somewhere. But it was a sad day with us all, when they left,

---

14. James Lide Coker, *History of Company G*, pp. 29-31.
15. James Lide Coker, "Short Sketch of the Coker Family of Darlington District, South Carolina" (Watson collection), p. 7.
16. Hannah to Charles, April 13, 1861, and Hannah to Frances, May 12, 1861 (R. E. Coker).
17. Hannah to Frances, May 12, 1861 (R. E. Coker).
18. James Lide Coker's farm journal (W. C. Coker).

and our hearts are full of sadness and anxiety all the time. I live in dread...."[19]

Whatever Hannah's foreboding she did not know of the several climactic tragedies that lay ahead, nor of the four years of attrition and worry to be lived through. In a war that involved all America as none other has ever done, the Cokers were to have a full part. The complete story is too long for this work. What is important, in the history of the family, is the reaction to the first full measure of war, a measure that held fighting and death as well as loneliness and sickness. This first full measure was embodied in the experience of the family that began when James and William went into camp around Centreville, Virginia, in August of 1861. The experience ended in the fall of 1862 when James and William camped again in Virginia after the battle of Sharpsburg. During this interval of time—the winter of 1861-62, and the spring and summer that followed—the Cokers were to learn about war, about how to live in war, how to fight, how to die, and how to grieve.

II

Food was scarce and poor in the winter camps around Centreville, Virginia, in the fall and winter of 1861-62; its cooking was worse. There was no lard or butter, or eggs, and no soda to leaven the flour. Beef, fried or boiled, grew monotonous. The cold winds blew down from the Bull Run Mountains, and the troops were sheltered in crude log huts with tent canvas for roofs. Disease moved in on an ill-equipped army. "First measles, followed by lung and bowel diseases, and after a while the dreaded camp fever." Seventeen men from about ninety in James' company died during this winter, leaving him forever puzzled that it was the strong, outdoor farm boys who most frequently fell sick.[20] Writing to Hannah, he believed that a change in diet would improve the health of the men, though he did not tell her the full story of the company's sickness.[21] The brothers saw each other at least

19. Hannah to Frances, May 12, 1861 (R. E. Coker).
20. James Lide Coker, *History of Company G*, pp. 32-35.
21. James to Hannah, August 3, 1861 (R. E. Coker).

THE FAMILY IN THE WAR

once, and James reported home that William had stood the battle of First Manassas and the rigors of camp life well. James' servant was sick and William loaned him "Alex," whom William "could spare easily."[22]

That winter there were no battles but there was skirmishing along the picket line, James' company moving up for picket duty several times. A big blue-eyed New Hampshire Yankee was the first man that he saw shot down. James never forgot this simplest equation of war; it was a stark and gray experience: "He was given a decent burial in rear of our lines."[23] Both boys escaped serious illness during the winter, and in the spring William, his year's enlistment almost up, came home to help recruit a new company.[24]

In the spring, armies moved into position. McClellan brought his Union army by water to the Peninsula country east of Richmond, so as to flank the city from that direction. Johnston moved his Army of Northern Virginia southward to interpose between McClellan and Richmond.[25] James' company was part of the rear guard for Johnston's movement southward;[26] here, sideslipping cautiously, he and his men began to learn the primer lesson of southern resources: to fight on the move and to move fast and light. Trunks and boxes that had been loaded on the train in Darlington not a year before were discarded. They learned ". . . to cook with hardly any utensils, and to make coffee in tin cups often heating it up with the end of a ramrod. We learned that good dough can be made up on an oil cloth, that wound around a stick it bakes beautifully, and that eaten with broiled fat meat or even with raw bacon, it furnishes an excellent meal."[27] This movement made a field soldier out of James. There was a reorganization

---

22. *Ibid.*
23. James Lide Coker, *History of Company G*, pp. 36-37.
24. R. E. Coker, "William Caleb Coker" (R. E. Coker), p. 42.
25. Douglas Southall Freeman, *Lee's Lieutenants*, I (New York: Charles Scribner's Sons, 1942), chapters XI, XII.
26. James Lide Coker, *History of Company G*, pp. 37-38.
27. *Ibid.*, p. 37. See also Freeman, *Lee's Lieutenants*, I, pp. 137, 140.

of the company on the Peninsula and James was re-elected captain by the men in the ranks.[28]

The Peninsula Campaign of May, June, and July, 1862, was a confused, costly lesson in warfare, fought over swampy, disease-ridden ground. On neither side at the beginning was there the organized leadership that could win a war, or even a battle, decisively. In the ranks, the men wrought out their own personal lessons of death and survival, and paid also for the higher education.[29]

James' turn came first, in the delaying action fought at Williamsburg, on May 5, where Johnston sought to slow down McClellan's advance toward Richmond.[30] James, with his company, was in a fortified position on the left, near Fort Magrudger, from where he saw Union forces occupy a redoubt left vacant by poor planning and reconnaissance.[31] The Federals proceeded to make the most of this excellent gun position. Before long, after more poor reconnaissance, two gray-wearing regiments charged across an open miry field toward the strong Federal position. A charge of such small numbers was folly. This was obvious to James and all those around him. There was a heady enthusiasm, almost a dare, to the charge; an excited staff officer rode up to call them on, "reminding us that we were South Carolinians, who, as he said, 'began the war.'" So Company E moved out of its protected position into the charge. By good fortune James and his men escaped damage and were able to retire.[32]

Throughout most of the battle the men of Company E were crouched away from the Federal sharpshooters, whose guns outranged Company E's muskets and Mississippi rifles, and whose accuracy showed much practice. James got the point: afterwards he asked permission to hold long-range target prac-

---

28. James Lide Coker, *History of Company G*, p. 43.
29. For account of campaign see Freeman, *Lee's Lieutenants*, Vol. I, Chapters XII-XIV, XVI, XVIII-XX, XXX-XXXII, XXXIV-XXXVII.
30. James Lide Coker, *History of Company G*, p. 53. For detailed account of battle see Freeman, *Lee's Lieutenants*, Vol. I, pp. 176 ff.
31. James Lide Coker, *History of Company G*, p. 53.
32. *Ibid.*, p. 53.

tice—not granted because "not one cartridge could be spared for practice firing."[33]

The battle of Williamsburg was fought in early May. On the thirty-first of that month Johnston attacked McClellan at Seven Pines.[34] Company E was part of the attack in the center and as James remembered it they charged through at least four fresh lines of Federal troops.[35] Long afterward there remained vivid pictures of this first fighting charge—pictures caught on his receptive youth with clarity for a lifetime:

The first man killed in Company E was Corporal J. L. Kilgore, a shot passing through his brain. His brother Peter, was his file leader. Peter stopped one moment to see his brother's condition, and to remove from his pockets what they contained. Quickly coming up with us again, he continued bravely his duties in the fight. It was only a few minutes before he, too, fell mortally wounded, and the two brothers together as they marched to serve their country, were not parted in their death.

Caleb Tiner was loading and firing where the regiment was lying down in line of battle. He was observing the exact order of drill, and when he rolled over on his back to "tear" and "ram cartridge," a cruel bullet crashed into his forehead and left him stark, the butt of his gun between his feet, and the cartridge in his hand and between his teeth as he was tearing it to load.[36]

About half of the committed company were casualties at Seven Pines—nine killed, thirteen wounded and four taken prisoner.[37] After the battle the survivors outfitted themselves with captured supplies and ate Yankee food. They traded their short-shooting Mississippi rifles for the better Enfields, and James saw, with surprise, that "the people with whom we were fighting lived in luxury, even while in camp."[38]

Johnston was wounded at Seven Pines and Lee eventually took command of the army.[39] By the twenty-sixth of June he

---

33. *Ibid.*, pp. 59-60.
34. Freeman, *Lee's Lieutenants*, Vol. I, chapter XVII.
35. James Lide Coker, *History of Company G*, p. 67.
36. *Ibid.*, p. 67.
37. *Ibid.*, pp. 65-66.
38. *Ibid.*, p. 69.
39. Freeman, *Lee's Lieutenants*, Vol. I, pp. 262-63.

was ready to move out against McClellan. There followed the Seven Days Battle—Mechanicsville, Beaver Dam, Gaines' Mill, Savage Station, Frayser's Farm, Malvern Hill.[40] Company E was in reserve on the first day. On the second day, the twenty-seventh, it was part of the attack at Gaines' Mill. "Over the hill we went, and down the slope to the creek, passing over hundreds of poor fellows lying dead or wounded upon the field, until striking a double quick and raising the 'Rebel Yell,'[41] we dashed into the enemy's position." One man from the company was killed and three were wounded.[42] The next day the June sun shown hot on a piece of oil cloth that shaded James' fever-ridden body. In the afternoon the regimental surgeon sent him to the rear.[43] On the thirtieth the company fought without him at Frayser's Farm where two were killed and eight wounded.[44] Only about twenty men remained on their feet after Frayser's Farm, and these fought no more during the Seven Days.[45] The battle moved on down the Peninsula, McClellan retreating slowly and stubbornly, coming finally to a stand to protect his evacuation at Malvern Hill, on the first of July.

William had returned just before the opening of the Peninsula campaign. He was elected first lieutenant in a company organized from a core of veterans and the recruits secured at home.[46] One of the new recruits was Charles,[47] a private attached to the ordnance supply, who had refused to stay longer at college. This company, part of Kershaw's Brigade, had seen limited action at Williamsburg, but during the later fighting had been held in reserve. It was thrown into the abortive attack on Malvern Hill in the evening twilight of July 1.[48]

William and the company went into the charge, up a wide, cleared slope dominated by Federal artillery. Charles was sup-

40. See note 29.
41. James Lide Coker, *History of Company G*, p. 67.
42. *Ibid.*, p. 74.   43. *Ibid.*, p. 75.
44. *Ibid.*, p. 93.   45. *Ibid.*, p. 94.
46. W. C. Coker, "Partial History of Companies F and M, 8th Regiment of South Carolina Volunteers" (R. E. Coker), p. 11.
47. *Ibid.*, p. 11.
48. *Ibid.*, p. 2.

posed to remain in the rear with the ammunition. Instead he picked up a rifle and went in too. He was shot down immediately. William saw him fall but went on.

Afterwards, William, wounded himself, hunted among the dead and wounded through a dark night for Charles. In the morning he found him, lying in the rain, dead. William carried his brother from the field and made a coffin from rough boards and buried him.[49] Then he sent home the news.

James was still sick with fever, receiving his nursing from Sue who had come to Richmond. They sent for word of William and Charles after the battle and got the bare fact that Charles was dead. On the fourth William came to tell them, and on the fifth James wrote his mother:

Richmond July 5th 1862

My Dearest Mother:

My first impulse after hearing that God had stricken us, by taking from us our Noble Charlie, was to write to you. My thoughts naturally reverted to you after the first shock of grief was over and I longed to do something which would afford you some satisfaction, even if it could afford you no consolation. I thought of the terrible blow which the sudden tidings would inflict, and then of your bursting heart after the realization of the awful truth, and I was apprehensive that your nature would give way and you *could* not bear up under it. Oh! What will Mother do! was our exclamation. How can she bear the loss of her *best* treasure! But the sweet promises of One, who is good even while He afflicts, presented themselves to me, and I felt sure that you would have grace *sufficient* & could even give unto our Father, praise & thanksgiving. For have we not Mother, many causes for thankfulness? First we know that Charles was a Christian, he professed to be one & he lived as a follower of the Lamb. Then as a Son—you & Father know how respectful & obedient and how affectionate he was in all his conduct. As a brother we know him to be so *lovely*, to his sisters tender & gentle, to his brothers all that a brother could be in love & oh how closely are the hearts of brothers knit together....

My sickness, which was slight, saved me from participation in the last battle of my company and I was here with my dear Sue

---

49. *Ibid.*, p. 3.

after the Friday's fight in which I was engaged. After the army followed up McClellan's I was very anxious about Willie and Charlie & told Alex (who came to see me) to bring us word whenever he heard from them. I had not heard a word up to Thursday morning. Wednesday afternoon I told Tom he must go over & inquire at their camp & let us know the next morning. The news he brought us was crushing— Charlie was *killed* and Willie wounded. . . . Such noble sacrifices does God require of us, and now that we are so much afflicted, that so many hearts are bleeding, that we are brought *so low,* may we not hope for deliverance & pray with more confidence for the cessation of this cruel & unjust war, waged upon us by our enemies. Oh, Cruel, Horrible War! Would that all could view it as we do.

In connection with dear Charlie, what a crowd of memories come up. *All* of them pleasant. I think of him when he was a little boy—of his habits and manners & peculiarities & as he grew up his conduct to the children & servants—his many pleasing ways— the little things he used to make for Eddie & the little girls. His conduct towards Fannie & Manie—So many little things which will tell us of him at home. . . . I wish we that are left could fill our brother's place, not in your affections, but in doing all for you that he would have done. I pray constantly that I may be a better son to you & not give you any more pain by my conduct. But we all must miss him. Brothers and sisters, Father & Mother, the little children and the servants all will miss our Charlie.

Your most affectionate Son
James[50]

Charles' death ran through the family, tearing away the hope that the ultimate in war could be avoided. It was a bitter time;[51] acceptance did not come easily.[52] The following winter Anna's husband, Colonel Berryman Edwards, went to Virginia in horse and wagon and brought Charles' body home to the Welsh Neck cemetery.[53]

Whatever the shock, there was little time for stopping to grieve. Either move on or fall out, for the summer fighting

---

50. James to Hannah, July 5, 1862 (C. W. Coker).
51. Hannah Lide Coker, *A Story of the Late War*, p. 19.
52. *Ibid.,* p. 3.
53. *Ibid.*

was just begun and James and William moved northward with Lee on the offensive. Between them they missed very little of that summer's hard fighting: Second Manassas, Maryland Heights, Harper's Ferry, South Mountain[54] and the dreadful flowing of blood into Antietam Creek at Sharpsburg[55] where Willie was wounded again,[56] and where he became captain of his company.

After Sharpsburg Lee moved his army back across the Potomac, to bind its wounds and to rest in temporary winter quarters.[57] The preceding year, from winter quarters, James had written his mother with confidence that he was "more than ever convinced ... that God has been with our forces to protect them from harm & to give them the victory & I trust I feel truly grateful that all our dear friends ... were saved from the hatred of our enemies. May such all ways be the happy result of our battles, if more battles we must have."[58] This year, in the autumn of 1862, Charles and many friends were gone. William had been twice wounded. The attrition of war had set in: James had diarrhea from a diet of fresh beef and musty flour; William, too, was sick. James worried about his wife and child, and about the reports of Negro insurrections.[59] He wrote soberly to Hannah: "I hope there will be no more fighting now & that this winter God will answer all our prayers and give us once more the sweet blessings of peace. I don't know by what means it may come but the Omnipotent can perform whatever he designeth."[60]

James was rounding out the full circle from unknowing hope to sober and tragic reality. The whole family had been around. They knew war now, in all its variety of demands.

54. James Lide Coker, *History of Company G*, pp. 94-113; also W. C. Coker, "Partial History of Companies F and M, 8th Regiment of South Carolina Volunteers" (R. E. Coker).
55. James Lide Coker, *History of Company G*.
56. R. E. Coker, "William Caleb Coker" (R. E. Coker), p. 43.
57. Douglas Southall Freeman, *R. E. Lee* (New York: Charles Scribner's Sons, 1934), Vol. II, pp. 406, 415-19.
58. James to Hannah, August 3, 1861 (R. E. Coker).
59. James to Hannah, October 25, 1862 (R. E. Coker).
60. *Ibid.*

Not just for the world's eye, but in their own counsel they accepted war for what it was. The structure of family morale, whereby difficulties were met and wholesome life affirmed, held steady. James gave the cue when, in that same letter of 1862, he wrote that he could see no value in the prevailing sentiment to have the South Carolina troops come home for the winter, as much as the prospect appealed to him.[61] Later crises had the benefit of this first test successfully met.

III

In December both James and William were at Fredericksburg when the Union Army made its costly attack against Lee's entrenched positions. James' company was not committed; he could view the battle with a professional detachment that was not shared by William who viewed it from heavy fighting on Marye's Hill.[62]

The next spring, 1863, William moved out with Lee's army in the last invasion of the North, while James' company was part of the protection left for Richmond.[63] William's regiment screened Jackson's magnificent march to the left at Chancellorsville and then marched northward into Pennsylvania. He was wounded again, for the third time, in the second day's fighting at Gettysburg. He was being carried to the rear on a stretcher when he was captured.[64]

North and South, military prisons were as much a threat to the health and life as the battlefield and William suffered a great deal. He was taken first to Johnsons' Island in Lake Erie, where the cold was intense during the first winter. He managed by a ruse to hold on to his Confederate blanket, thus having two instead of the usual one per prisoner, but his clothes were almost useless and he was without personal supplies of any kind.[65] He wrote to the merchants William Bryce

---

61. *Ibid.*
62. R. E. Coker, "William Caleb Coker" (R. E. Coker), p. 43. Also James Lide Coker, *History of Company G.*, pp. 116-18.
63. R. E. Coker, "William Caleb Coker" (R. E. Coker), p. 43.
64. *Ibid.*
65. *Ibid.*, pp. 45-46.

& Co. in New York who sent him fifty dollars. Caleb had traded with this firm for many years; theirs was one of the accounts that he had settled when the war began.[66] William was later sent to Point Lookout and to Port Delaware. For him the isolation and the lack of reading matter were as unpleasant as the physical hardships. He had, at least, a mathematics book which he read to pass the time and keep his mind alive.[67]

There was nothing hopeful about the approach of autumn in 1863. Charles was dead, William was a prisoner. In September, James and his company went to Tennessee, around Chattanooga, as part of the force detached from the Army of Northern Virginia and sent to the West under Longstreet. They arrived just after the Battle of Chickamauga, and took up positions along the Tennessee River, on the southern approaches to Chattanooga under Lookout Mountain.[68]

On the night of October 28 there was a small engagement in Lookout Valley, a fight in tangled woods, a small, tactical battle of no great significance. The Confederates were attacking, but they were soon in danger of being cut off in the rear. James, recently attached to the brigade staff, was sent in to give the orders to break off the fight and retire. He was shot down, and carried from the field after the battle.[69] All this now becomes Hannah's story,[70] which she wrote some years later:

". . . On the morning of October 30, 1863, as was our custom, we sent early for the mail, for we always waited for news with eager anxiety. Oh! the sad news of that morning! A telegram from James, saying, 'I am severely wounded; thigh fractured near the hip joint. Sue and mother please come, and ask Dr. Griffin to come with you.' Poor Sue was in delicate health, and was not yet up. We consulted together

---

66. James Lide Coker, "Short Sketch of the Coker Family of Darlington District, S.C." (Watson collection), p. 7.
67. R. E. Coker, "William Caleb Coker" (R. E. Coker), p. 46.
68. James Lide Coker, *History of Company G*, pp. 126-29.
69. *Ibid.*, p. 132.
70. The following account is taken from Hannah Lide Coker's *A Story of the Late War*.

as to whether we should show her the telegram, or simply tell her James was wounded, and that I would go to him—(for it was impossible for her to go). We decided it was better to let her know the worst at once. . . .

"I had no time to sit down and give way to my feelings, for in about three hours after the dispatch came, I had to leave home in order to meet the eleven o'clock train. Arrangements were to be made for leaving at home a large family, some of them little children, and my trunk was to be packed, mostly with such things as we thought my wounded boy would need. . . . At the depot I found Dr. Griffin, our good friend and physician, waiting for me, and we set out on our journey.

". . . At Chickamauga station, we left the cars. An ambulance had been sent there to meet us . . . Hours before we came to the spot, the ambulance driver pointed out the house in which James was lying. It was a neat little white cottage on an elevation near the foot of Lookout Mountain.

"The enemy's camp in front of Chattanooga was also in full view. The idea of being so near them was appalling to me; for we were in easy range of their shells. Dr. Griffin and the driver, however, assured me that there was no danger.

"The painful journey came to an end at last. As we drove up to the house we were met by our good friend, Captain E. M. Griffin, who was on a visit to James. He assured me that the surgeons, who had just left pronounced James to be in good condition.

"I found him, however, in a high fever. His right thigh was shattered an inch and a half below the hip joint, a minnieball having passed through flesh and bone, and lodged in his pants. The surgeons had delayed for several days performing any operation, for they were sure the wound was mortal and wished to spare him unnecessary suffering; but, when they found his strength kept up so well, they decided there was some hope of his recovery, and so they proceeded to operate. On the morning of the day I arrived, most of the surgeons of the brigade had assembled, and, keeping James under the influence of chloroform for two hours, probed his wound, removed the many pieces of broken bone, and bound him fast in splints extending from his foot to his arm-pit. . . .

"It was pitiful to see him lying there on some dirty ragged quilts, which partially covered a mattress of bagging, stuffed with hay, on a rough bedstead of pine boards improvised by the surgeons, and the best they could do under the circumstances.

"I took from my trunk a clean night-gown, tore it open in the back and put it on him—under his head put a comfortable pillow I had brought and spread a clean linen sheet over him. . . .

"Dr. Griffin stayed a week, doing all that a kind friend and physician could do to relieve James, and make him comfortable. He would never consent to receive any compensation for his services.

"As he was returning home, he met 'father' coming to see us, bringing with him our servant Polly, and a large box of provisions.

"Father stayed only two days. His visit was a great comfort to us, but so short. . . .

"By this time James was more comfortable. His fever had subsided, his spirits were good and he enjoyed his food. All the surgeons had told us that it was absolutely necessary for him to have nourishing food. The two armies had left no provisions in the country around us, so we had to depend on our home box.

"About three weeks after James was wounded, the battle of Missionary Ridge was fought and our army defeated. We were left in the enemy lines. Of course, our servants, Tom and Polly, had to be sent home. . . .

"For three weeks . . . we were left without any attention from the authorities. Our provisions were nearly all gone; worse still, James was suffering for surgical attention. The splints had slipped, and the limb was twisted, and we could do nothing for the bed-sore, which was very painful, without some strong men to raise him. Sam and I could not do that . . . I tried to get some of the people in the house to take a note to the Medical Director in Chattanooga, but they were afraid to do anything to assist Confederates. [Finally, Hannah was able to get a soldier to take a letter to the Medical Director. As a result, men were sent to bring James to the hospital; but they found he could not be moved. The next day Hannah walked to Chattanooga.]

"After a five mile walk I reached Chattanooga, and fortunately met with the orderly who had been sent out for James. I asked him to show me the Medical Director's office, which he did. I was invited in and politely offered a seat. I told him at once why I had come; that my son needed surgical attention and provisions; that he had a bad bed-sore, and that Sergeant Nettles and I could not lift him to dress it.... He treated me respectfully, sent for an ambulance to take me back, and for a surgeon, Dr. Stillwell, to go with me, and gave me some provisions. He said the hospital stores were almost out, but he gave me as good as they had on hand.

"While I was waiting for the ambulance, Dr. Huger, a Federal surgeon, came in and talked with me, and asked where I was from. He said he was from Charleston, S. C., told me his name, and asked about his relatives, who were refugees at Society Hill. I asked him how he happened to be on the wrong side in this war. He said he did not think he was on the wrong side. I, as politely as possible, insisted that he was.

"It was nine o'clock at night when I got back to James. He and Sam were exceedingly anxious about me, and were overjoyed to see me safely back. Dr. Stillwell examined James carefully, and, when he went back, reported to Dr. Byrne, the surgeon in charge of the Field Hospital, that he could not be moved, and when he had made this report, thought that he had done all that was expected of him. Dr. Byrne intended that he should attend James regularly. For two weeks after this we had no surgeon. No surgeon and no rations furnished....

"After waiting two weeks for a surgeon to come, I wrote again to Dr. Perrin (the Medical Director), telling him James still had no surgical attention and no rations. He explained that he thought Dr. Stillwell, of the Field Hospital, was attending him and supplying us with rations, and sent Dr. Taylor, of Indiana, who proved to be not only a good and attentive physician, but a kind friend. He came every few days for two months, and brought rations, taking great interest in James and doing everything he could to relieve him. Under his treatment the bed-sore was much relieved. . . .

"The sun went down so early behind the mountain that our days were very short, and we were as busy as could be. That was one reason why we were so cheerful—we had no time to get low-spirited. For some time after the servants left, I washed my own clothes, and ironed them on the floor. Sam washed for himself and James, except the bandages and clothes used about J.'s wound. Those I washed every day. . . .

"With such pieces of board and boxes as Sam could pick up around, he made a little table, which served as dining-table, side-board, cupboard, &c. We had two or three country made chairs which Colonel Bratton had kindly sent us. Having very few conveniences for our housekeeping and cooking, we had many merry laughs over our amusing mishaps. We had no andirons and not infrequently our pots were overturned by rolling logs of wood, just in the midst of preparing our dinner. I prepared the food, Sam cooked it, and James lay in bed and made the jokes. . . .

"Generally, James was cheerful and comparatively free from pain, but sometimes suffered excruciatingly from cramps in the foot and leg of his wounded limb. . . . He sang a great deal. A favorite hymn was:

> From every stormy wind that blows,
> From every swelling tide of woes,
> There is a calm, a sure retreat,
> 'Tis found before the mercy seat.

. . . Christmas was a dark and gloomy day, but was made bright to us by a great and rare treat, Dr. Taylor came and brought us two letters. I said to him 'You could not have brought us a more acceptable Christmas gift,' and begged him to excuse us until we had read them, for they were the first we had received since we had been left in the Federal lines. James saw they were not directed in Sue's handwriting, for one was from Colonel Bratton, and the other Sue had gotten father to direct. So he gave them to me, saying, 'Read them mother, and let me know the worst,' and covered up his head. I opened one and seeing Sue's signature, returned it to him to read first. She told him of the birth of his son on the 23rd of November, and said she would come to him as soon as she was well enough. . . .

"After the days got a little longer and warmer, James amused himself making, with his pocketknife, a set of chessmen of red and white cedar, and occasionally, he and Sam would play a game. Sam made the board. Some pamphlets were sent us from the Hospital, and James had a copy of 'Nicholas Nickleby.' We read these together. We had no reading for Sundays, except our Bible. This we enjoyed greatly, and the chapter we read together every night was very comforting and strengthening to us.

"After six months it was decided that James was far enough along towards recovery to be taken home. Locations of the occupying armies made necessary a somewhat round-about-trip home: by train to Nashville and to Louisville, by boat to Parkersburg, W. Va., by train again to Ft. McHenry near Baltimore [where they were left for several days] and to Fort Monroe near Richmond, and on home. [Hannah's account of the trip reveals some further troubles, but also instances of sympathy and kindness, from foes as well as friends.]

"After leaving Parkersburg, our journey was without special incident until we reached Grafton, where we changed cars. While we were waiting there, a Federal surgeon came up, and inquired with interest about my son's wound and the circumstances which brought us there. He had James carefully put in an express car, and sent to the hotel for a nice meal for him. Early next morning, the express agent came and talked kindly with James, telling him he had obtained his position to keep from being drafted into the Northern army. He cooked his own breakfast, and brought James some coffee, which refreshed him greatly. He also offered him money, which was declined; and when we arrived in Baltimore, got four citizens to move him carefully to the ambulance which was to carry him to Fort McHenry.

"While we were waiting in the depot for the ambulance, the Irish women who had fruit to sell, and several men, seemed much interested in us. They offered us fruit, and the women said they would pray for my son. They were Roman Catholics.

"I mention these little incidents to show how, all along our journey, there was evidence of a protecting Power, watching over us, securing us from disaster and supplying our wants, both great and small.

"James and Sam were taken to Fort McHenry. I hired a carriage, and drove through the gates just behind the ambulance. Taking it for granted that I was to stay, I had my trunk put on the piazza, and sent the carriage off. What was my disappointment to be told I could not stay there! James was carried to the prison hospital, and Sam Nettles to the common prison.

"... Then I went to the Commandant of the Fort, and begged him to let me stay, or, at any rate, that Sam might be left with him. He was polite, and spoke kindly, but said he would have to leave the whole matter to the surgeon in charge. I went back and reported my failure to James. I sat by him for a while, and while I was there, one of the nurses, an Englishman, came to me, and asked if I was a stranger in Baltimore. On my replying that I was, he gave me the address of a lady, Mrs. Berry, with his card, saying: 'Go there. She is one of your sort of people (meaning a Southern sympathizer), and will be kind to you.'

"... Baltimore was two miles off. I was a perfect stranger, and knew not how I was to get there. Near the gate I saw a man sitting, and as I came near him, he arose and asked me if I wanted to go to the city. He was a boatman, and offered to take me across the bay. I waited in the rain while he went in to get my trunk. He handed me his umbrella, but the wind blew so, and the walk to the water was so rough that it was of little use to me. I did not care at all about being wet, I was so tired and miserable, nor was I afraid to go alone to what part of the city I wished to go. I found Mrs. Berry lived on Camden street, and told him I would go there; so he took me to the foot of that street, which lengthened his trip very much. His charge was very moderate. He called up two negro boys, when I left the boat, and said to them: 'Take that trunk and follow behind the lady, and carry it right where she wants it.'

"I told Mrs. Berry why I was there, and asked her to direct me to where I could find a respectable boarding-place in a private family. She looked distrustfully at me; and no wonder, for I was wet and draggled and haggard.... After some hesitation, she said I might stay there that night....

"Next morning Mrs. Berry told me I might stay there, and gave me a small room.

"I was not allowed to see James during the time we were in Baltimore, but we corresponded frequently—our letters, of course, being subject to inspection.

"I had made application, while in Chattanooga, to the Commissary General of Prisoners, to be sent through the lines, and my application was endorsed by the surgeons and General Thomas. As I had not heard from this, I determined to go on to Washington and see about it.

"A lady in Baltimore gave me the address of a friend of hers in Washington, and a letter of introduction to her, and said she would go with me to the Commissary General. Dr. Fuller advised me to go to Mr. Chase, Secretary of War. He said Mr. Chase was a gentleman, and a personal friend of his, and would be polite to me. If I did not get what I wanted from him, Dr. F. said, I should go to President Lincoln himself, who would certainly 'respect my gray hairs,' and treat me kindly. It was, however, unnecessary for me to go to either the Secretary or the President. I found the lady to whom I had been directed ready to show me any kindness. She went with me to the Commissary General's office. He was not in. I asked his clerk if my application sent from Chattanooga, had been received. He replied: "If it has been received, it has been answered; for we answer all communications." I gave him the date of the application, and told him my name. After he had been looking in the book for some time, without finding it, I happened to see that he was looking under the letter K, and told him how the name was spelled; when he soon found it. It was marked 'approved.' I did not know how much that 'approved' meant, and was afraid to be too much elated. At best, I feared it would be a long time before an order, which must pass through so many hands, could be carried into effect, and that we might still be detained for some time. We were detained two months.

"I asked permission to visit Willie at Fort Delaware. The clerk told me to write to the Commissary General of Prisoners about that. I did so, but we were ordered to Fort Monroe before an answer was received.

"I had been given a state-room just opposite a large one which had been assigned to James, because his stretcher could be carried into it; but, after the boat started, the Lieutenant told James he must stay in the cabin. He kept a guard, with fixed bayonet, standing by his stretcher all night long—to keep him from running away, perhaps. A lady came up and entered into conversation with me. The Lieutenant said if I talked with the passengers on board, I should not speak to my son; so, if any one spoke to me, I laid my finger on my lips. The passengers were as indignant as I was at this pitiful tyranny. This man, and General Whipple, at Chattanooga, were the only Federal officers who spoke rudely to me during all my long stay in the enemy's lines.

"At General Butler's headquarters at Fort Monroe, we were paroled, and we then went to the Hygeia Hotel. Some kind ladies in Baltimore had supplied us with some money, and that, with some that James had borrowed from business friends of his father's in New York, enabled us all to board at this hotel for a week. After that, James thought best for Sam and himself to go to the hospital, as it was uncertain how long we might have to stay, and it was necessary to reserve enough to pay my board. I had no other resource.

"We strained our eyes every day watching for the flag of the truce boat. One day, to our great delight, it came steaming in; but our joy was soon turned to disappointment, for it went off—as we heard afterwards—for repairs, and we had another tedious week of waiting.

"At last our weary waiting-time was really over, and we were off on the boat. There was on board a Miss Gunby, from Maryland, who was banished to the Confederacy on account of her strong Southern sympathies. She traveled with us to Richmond, and we found her a pleasant companion. While at Fort Monroe, though under close guard, she obtained information of great importance to the Confederate army, which she gave to President Davis on her arrival in Richmond. At her request, I went with her to the President's Mansion, where Mr. Davis was pleased to receive me kindly, and express his wishes for the speedy recovery of my son.... On Friday, the 17th July, we reached Richmond, and stopped at the Spotswood Hotel.

"James and Sam were obliged to stay through Saturday, to report and get transportation papers. We decided not to start for home on Sunday, so we rested in Richmond till Monday. ... I sent a dispatch home from Richmond, announcing our safe arrival there, and that we would leave for home on Monday. Arriving at Florence on the 21st, we found father, Sue, and Sam's friends waiting to meet us. We reached home about eleven o'clock that night, and found all the family gathered to welcome us."

IV

Wars are not over easily. They end in stages, as war's experience is made part of a lifetime. For the Cokers, part of the war was over on July 1, 1862, when Charles was killed at Malvern Hill, in Virginia. After Charles, there remained two names on the board: James and William. Capture at Gettysburg marked off William's name. When Hannah brought James home, alive but crippled for life, the third main cost had been paid, for James was both under parole and unfit for battle duty.

All of the main returns were in; on a strict accounting of blood and flesh the war was thus over for the Cokers in the summer of 1864. They could not yet live in a world of peace: the attrition of war wore every day at the ordinary vital lineaments of life, building to the climax of Sherman's coming and the disintegration of defeat. But they could resume a bare framework of living, hold on to the contours of life that remained, and catch their breath now the war was over.

Life had gone on. Children were born to both Jane and Anna during the war.[71] James' first child, a girl named Margaret, was born just as the war broke out, to take some of Hannah's interest. "The baby grows finely, notices a great deal and is very bright and sweet."[72] A second child, named for its father, was born in 1863, at Society Hill where Sue had the family's care and attention.[73] Church and school, modified, were carried on; the mails came and went at the store. The seasons passed over, the sun and rains, and crops grew—less cotton now and more foodstuffs.

These were measures of the fact that provision for living fell back on the home and community. In an effective isolation—from goods normally imported, from travel and travelers, from many sources of amusement and reading, and above all from the making of usual plans—life was reduced to the essentials of providing food for subsistence and clothing to keep warm.[74] All decisions were primary, personal, immediate, and vital. Considerable embroidery on living had grown on the favored part of life in Society Hill, and a somewhat lesser

71. Wilson, "For My Own" (Watson collection).
72. Hannah to Frances, May 12, 1861 (R. E. Coker).
73. Hannah Lide Coker, *A Story of the Late War*, pp. 4-5.
74. Edwin Charles Dargan, *Harmony Hall, Recollections of an Old Southern Home* (Columbia: The State Company, 1912, for the Pee Dee Historical Society), p. 33.

amount at Camp Marion. Caleb, with his usual acceptance of fact, no doubt officiated calmly at the shearing of frills.

Goods on the shelves of the store grew scarce, but there was no real privation.[75] The land was good, a large number of field hands remained available, and good management could provide food and clothing. Flour mills remained in operation and there was wheat for grinding. More than the usual amount of corn, vegetables, and meat was raised. Sugar was cut off and syrup from sorghum cane was substituted; chicory, rye, parched potatoes and other articles were used for coffee. Camping parties went to the coast to distill sea water for salt; the salt-saturated floors of smokehouses, and the ground underneath, were cleaned and the salt reclaimed. Out of skills still remembered, sheep were shorn and cotton picked, the fibers carded and spun and woven, the cloth fashioned and sewn. Summer hats were made from such fibers as palmetto leaves, wire grass, and wheat straw; beeves hides were tanned, and local shoemakers trained plantation Negroes to make rough shoes.[76] Thus Caleb and Hannah maintained the homeplace.

James continued to improve through the summer and fall of 1864. By the end of winter he could get around fairly well on crutches,[77] well enough to resume life at Hartsville and draw up plans for planting a crop to grow through the spring and summer of 1865. Within the limits of the fourth year of war, which meant using worn equipment, doing without commercial fertilizers, using deteriorated stock and working every day under the strain of a losing war, prospects for the crop were not disheartening.[78] The land remained in good shape, almost all of the Negroes remained, and there was ample seed for planting. That fall and winter James represented Darlington County in the State House of Representatives at Columbia.

75. *Ibid.*
76. *Ibid.*, pp. 33-35.
77. James Lide Coker, A Short MS dictated by Major Coker to his daughter Susie, undated (Watson collection).
78. *Ibid.*

Above, Hannah Lide Coker (courtesy of Mrs. D. R. Coker). *Below*, Caleb Coker (from a portrait in the possession of C. W. Coker).

Above, Caleb Coker's store today, Society Hill (Ashcraft Studio, Hartsville). *Below,* The Camp Marion home at Society Hill (Ashcraft Studio, Hartsville).

He introduced a bill to establish a system of free public schools, but the bill was defeated in the Senate because ". . . it was thought by that conservative body that the time was inopportune for enlargements of any kind causing additional expense to the state."[79]

There remained, though, one more journey. Company E was back now around Richmond, dug in for the final, half-starved fight that was to end in April at Appomattox. The men were in wretched condition for want of food and clothing. In March, James packed a large box with corn meal and molasses and set out for Richmond. Taking with him "Maum Rachel's York," he went first to Columbia to take the train for Richmond.

Columbia was full of word that Sherman, having reached Savannah and the sea, was preparing to turn his swath northward into South Carolina. There had been heavy rains during the winter; the clay Piedmont soils would stop Sherman's wagons where there was no army to do so. James reasoned correctly that Sherman would choose his route over the fast-drying sandy loams of the middle country and that he would therefore pass through or close to Hartsville and Society Hill. His first reaction was to return home. To scurry back would be to act in panic, and war's first hard lesson for young officers is to take a cool second look at any situation. He wrote home, asking his wife Sue to have the cotton taken from the bales and scattered through the woods, to prevent its being burned, and to have the horses sent away, to forestall their being confiscated. Then he went on to Richmond.

Returning in a week or two, he found Sherman's army between him and home. He rode a crowded train to Concord, North Carolina, and from there sent the Negro, York, across country to Society Hill with word to send a buggy along the Bost Mill-Wadesboro-Chesterfield Court House route, to meet him as he came along as best he could. James made some progress by catching rides and using the open hospitality that prevailed in the broken country. Finally he met Caleb's rocka-

---
79. Major Coker to D. L. Lewis, May 20, 1914 (Watson collection).

way "pulled by two old rips of mules." Within several days he was home.

He found virtual desolation. All the stock—horses, mules, oxen, cattle—had been either driven off or butchered. Almost all the corn and bacon had been loaded into the buggy, the rockaway and the wagons and carts and hauled off. Sue had consulted with Caleb about the cotton after receiving James' letter from Columbia telling her to scatter it through the woods. News from Georgia indicated that attempts to hide property angered Sherman's men and brought greater destruction. They decided to leave the cotton baled and in plain sight, except for a few bales that were scattered through the woods. The soldiers made a great pile of cotton—78 bales—and had the Negroes set fire to it. "The house had been turned upside down, everything of value carried away. They had taken all the silver, the clothing, the pictures out of the parlor, . . . (Sue's) watch."[80]

All this was at Hartsville, but this and more James had seen at Society Hill. Whatever had been preserved through the war was gone now, leaving only the lineaments of life that were in the people and the land, and in the people's living together.

The war ended in April. Soon after, William was released from prison weak and almost unable to travel. He started home, but fell sick in North Carolina, where he was nursed in a private home to the point of being able to travel again. He bought an old, ill-favored horse and took up his journey across the broken country.[81]

We were living at Hartsville then—I was just a little boy. My mother was Jane Coker before marrying my father, Dr. Furman Wilson. One night after we had gone to bed—I remember it was raining—we heard a knock at the front door. Those times we didn't like to open the door at night, but finally my father took a

---

80. See note 77 for the preceding account of James' trip and the results of Sherman's passage.

81. R. E. Coker, "William Caleb Coker" (R. E. Coker), pp. 46-47.

lamp and went to the door. I trailed along behind him. He opened the door a little and the light shone out.

The first thing I saw was two trouser legs. They were ragged and frayed at the bottom, and the water dripped from the frayed ends to the porch. It was Uncle Willie, come home.[82]

82. Conversation with W. C. Wilson, grandson of Hannah and Caleb, Darlington, S.C.

5

Restoring Life

I

THE LAND REMAINED, and if cotton could be grown during the first summer of defeat a cotton hungry world would, for a while at least, buy it at a good price. Nor did Caleb give up the store, having, in fact, fought for it as the war drew to its close. One day, as Sherman's men tarried in the area around Society Hill, a group of Negroes entered the store and began to take goods from the shelves. Caleb appealed to a Federal officer present, who, with the inevitable gesture of conquerors in a strange land, indicated his neutrality. Caleb then grabbed up an axe helve and laid about him with vigor and success.[1] His credit, after the war, was still good with the northern merchants who had supplied him before. Thus he restocked his shelves, in his turn extended credit to the farmers, and began again to move slowly upward.

Certain debts were paid with some of the first money that came to hand. There was the debt owed the merchants who had supplied William with clothing and money while he was in prison, and this was repaid. In February of 1866 Hannah was ill, but she had James' wife Sue send a draft for two hundred and fifty dollars to Margaret Donaldson in Baltimore, asking that lady to distribute the money among the several people who had befriended Hannah when she and James had stopped in Baltimore on the painful trip home in 1864. Margaret Donaldson knew what this money had cost: "If I was

---

1. R. E. Coker, "Coker Forebears" (R. E. Coker), p. 42.

glad to receive your draft for $250 it was because it showed us you were able to send it."[2] Only a part of the money was retained, and the rest sent back to Hannah, the people in Baltimore "desiring you to apply it to the relief of sufferers in your section."

William, who for the rest of his days would be known as Captain Coker, did not get well quickly. To his already weakened condition there was added malaria contracted after he came home. Caleb and Hannah sent him to the mountains of Virginia, with his sister Frances as nurse, where it was hoped that his health would improve. When their money gave out, the Captain and Frances started home by train, sending no word ahead of them. They were surprised, therefore, to find Caleb waiting for them at the depot in Darlington. Caleb's explanation was simple: "I knew how much money you had, and the cost of your room and board. It was not difficult to know when you would be home."[3] The times were that close. They were also disorganized. Not long after the end of the war the President of Furman University wrote William offering a professorship. But the letter never reached Society Hill, and William learned of it several years later in a conversation with the sender. This was work for which he was well suited; loss of the letter was the missing of a major opportunity that he might well have accepted. For a while after his return from Virginia, William worked as a surveyor, and then began to read law in the office of his brother-in-law, Berryman Edwards.[4]

At Hartsville, Major James, who like his brother had acquired lifetime military title, and his wife, Sue, were working their way out of the wreckage that Sherman's men had left. The young Major was still confined to crutches and unable to do any work himself in the fields. Of consuming importance was the fact that here, as throughout the countryside, Sherman's men in their passage had left no work stock. There was

---

2. Margaret Donaldson to Hannah, February 25, 1866 (R. E. Coker).
3. R. E. Coker, "William Caleb Coker" (R. E. Coker), 47.
4. *Ibid.*

cotton seed to plant, and seed corn, but no animals to pull the plows. An old sore back mule, turned out by Union soldiers to die, had been stabled and kept alive, and to this beast was added a pair of oxen that James obtained from an uncle. With these animals a hundred acres were put in cultivation, sixty of cotton and forty of corn. Five Negroes, no longer slaves but living on the plantation, worked the crop, along with one white laborer. James was in the fields ceaselessly, watching carefully, for this first crop meant much. The result was twenty-five bales of cotton and three hundred bushels of corn. Sale of twenty-four of the bales of cotton brought seventeen hundred dollars at the prevailing good prices.

With no precedent, but under the necessity for all to live, a new pattern of work was emerging. Each of the Negro laborers received one hundred dollars for working the crop, in addition to housing and such food as was available on the plantation. The white laborer received one-fifth of the net proceeds from the sale of the cotton, amounting to two hundred and seventy-four dollars. All told, James made about eight hundred dollars cash money from this cotton crop, if no deductions are made for rent of land and equipment.[5] This was not much, but it loomed large where nothing had been before.

Sometime during the summer or fall of 1865 James decided to open a store at Hartsville. Actually he was converting the old plantation commissary into a store. Caleb joined him as partner, and James later wrote that it was Caleb's credit and good name that secured a sufficient stock of goods to begin business in a small way. The Major proceeded cautiously. His brother-in-law, John Stout, proposed to come and work in the store, and James was glad to have him, but there were

... misgivings in my mind as to whether you were to be benefited by coming here. Sue is always so sanguine of my success & has so exalted & I must say exaggerated, an opinion of my capacity for business, that, I fear she communicated to you in her letter something of her own feelings & expectations. I hope your expectations

5. James Lide Coker's farm journal (W. C. Coker).

may be all realized but must beg not to be too sanguine, but not to be on the other hand too much discouraged when you come & find out what you are to do. A country store is at best a poor looking place. My little affair is not so inviting as many you see.[6]

II

This was a strange time, these first months after the end of the war. For all the stark reality of defeat, there seems to have been more than a little of the unreal. Whatever else was true, the four terrible war years were over, and this summer and fall of 1865 were peaceful.

When our soldiers returned from the war they found it hard at first, particularly the younger ones, to adjust themselves to the new conditions and to get down to work. And it didn't seem then generally necessary to go to work. The slaves had, up to this time, to their credit, be it said, for the most part remained upon the plantations. The Confederate government had restricted the planting of cotton, and directed the planting of large crops of corn.... So that provisions were then plentiful; cattle and hogs roamed in the woods; and many of the younger men gave themselves up to such enjoyments as they could find.

There were tournaments at Darlington and tournaments at Florence, at which queens of love and beauty were crowned....

Among the younger people it did not then appear so bad at all, so far as their relations with the government and the negroes were concerned. Liberal grants of surrender had been granted by Grant and Sherman to Lee and Johnston; but they did not see on the political horizon the dark cloud that was arising.[7]

Military defeat had been accepted, which was taken to mean freeing the slaves. This done, the white people assumed that they were to go ahead and work out solutions to the several remaining problems. In August, when the crops had been laid by, the Darlington County Agricultural Society held its first meeting since the early days of the war to consider the "distracted sloth" into which agriculture had fallen. Almost

---

6. Major Coker to John Stout, November 26, 1865 (W. C. Coker).
7. W. A. Brunson, *Reminiscences of Reconstruction in Darlington* (Hartsville: Hartsville Publishing Co., 1910, for the Pee Dee Historical Society), p. 6.

immediately the meeting was turned into a citizens' forum for consideration of general problems. Characteristically, it was James who made the motion by which the meeting was "resolved into that of the agriculture society again."[8]

The Major was anxious to propose that a committee be appointed to draw up "rules of plantation discipline & of wages which if generally adhered to would, in their opinion, promote the interest of the land owners & also secure full compensation & proper treatment of the laborers employed."[9] James was named chairman of the new committee. A report was submitted to the September meeting, "amended and adopted," but to little use in a land becoming increasingly strife torn. This again was part of the unreality, that these matters could be worked out directly by the white people, unhindered by outside interference. In the end, of course, arrangements such as James had made for that year's crop at Hartsville were the real forerunners of the pattern of sharecropping that would eventually emerge.

By 1866 the full turbulence of Reconstruction was apparent. As Andrew Johnson's moderate policy evolved into Congressional reconstruction a great unrest spread among the Negroes, and a matching resentment grew among the whites. Carpetbaggers, scalawags and Negroes took over the governmental machinery, supported by Federal troops. There was a considerable amount of outlawry, bushwhacking and general violence. Something of the complete reversal of affairs is found in a listing of certain county officials in later years by a white man who lived through the period. His terse descriptions are indicative of the implacable resentment this state of affairs aroused in the great majority of white people: "Senator: B. F. Whittemore, white, carpet-bagger; Magistrates at Darlington C. H.: J. G. Gatlin, native scalawag; I. P. Brockington, negro, densely ignorant; J. S. Fillbrown, carpetbagger; L. Lewenthal, white radical."[10] (Isaac Brockington was later pastor of the

8. Minute Book of the Darlington County Agricultural Society (J. M. Napier), p. 54.
9. *Ibid.*, p. 55.
10. Brunson, *Reminiscences of Reconstruction in Darlington*, pp. 14-15.

Negro Baptist Church in Darlington. He came to be widely respected by both Negroes and white. For a number of years he was a member of the Darlington school board, his service overlapping that of Captain Coker.)

The Cokers rode no night roads during these times. They were, however, "white folks," and did not forsake their heritage. Nor did they escape trouble. At Hartsville, the story goes, a group of Negroes came into the Major's front yard, demanding their "rights." James came on the porch and heard their demands, then went inside the house and returned with his gun. At sight of this, and with nothing said, the group dispersed. At Society Hill, the rather infamous Negro sheriff of Darlington County, Edmund Deas, came to the store with a document purporting to show that Caleb's brother and partner, Lewis Coker, owed five hundred dollars as endorser of a defaulted note. William was in the store alone and told Deas that his Uncle Lewis was out of town. Deas then said that he would take that amount of goods from the store. William pointed out the illegality of the step, but Deas, armed, persisted. William then picked up a hatchet nearby and ran the Sheriff off. The next day he went to Darlington and surrendered himself to the authorities. He was charged with assault, but successive postponements of the trial lasted through Reconstruction, and of course the charge was dropped afterwards.[11]

The Cokers were willing to admit facts. As the massive poverty and the equally massive control of the radicals made more plain every day, there was no immediate way out. In principle, at least, a great many white people came to feel that the only course open was to seek to find a middle ground somewhere between the extreme radicals who were then controlling and impoverishing the state and the great number of white people who would not give an inch to the new conditions that defeat in war had brought. To this end the Union Reform Party was organized in 1870.[12] Backed by all the conservative

11. R. E. Coker, "William Caleb Coker" (R. E. Coker), pp. 54-56.
12. Francis B. Simkins and Robert Hilliard Woody, *South Carolina During Reconstruction* (Chapel Hill: The University of North Carolina Press, 1932), p. 448.

newspapers, it aimed to induce the white voters to go along with moderate changes, while at the same time capturing enough Negro voters to win. It was not a particularly popular course, perhaps, but James, along with four other white men and five Negroes, was a delegate from Darlington to the state convention of this party,[13] where a platform was adopted calling for, among other things, full recognition of the legal and political rights of the Negro. The effort was a failure, as many white people stood aside from such concessions, while the Negroes were unwilling to accept less than they were receiving from the Radicals; and of course the Radicals controlled the election machinery. The Union Reform Party used no intimidation or force in this campaign.

Caleb lived to see the family on the upward road again, but he did not see the end of Reconstruction. On July 16, 1869, he drove the thirteen miles to Bennettsville, across the Pee Dee in Marlboro County, to pay taxes for several customers and for an estate that was in his charge. The sun shone bright and hot that day, and by the time he arrived home in Society Hill in the afternoon he was exhausted and depressed. Nevertheless, he stopped at the store, and, as was his invariable habit, made the day's entries in the store books. He was unwell during the night, but the next morning went as usual to the store. There he became ill and, finally, unconscious. That evening about nine o'clock, at the age of sixty-seven, he died at Camp Marion.[14]

Caleb's going left a gap. Three children were yet under twenty, and there was needed good and daily management of store and plantation. Several months previously the Captain, as his father had done almost forty years before, had gone to Springville for a bride, Mary McIver. He was living in Springville and practicing law in Darlington. The Captain was an able lawyer, but the constant pulling and shoving for legal advantage in general practice was distasteful to him.

13. Brunson, *Reminiscences of Reconstruction in Darlington*, p. 17.
14. R. E. Coker, "Coker Forebears, (R. E. Coker), p. 38.

With the need apparent at Society Hill, he was willing therefore to return as the main steward of the estate, in close consultation with James who also was an executor. William moved for a while to Camp Marion, where he took charge of the farming operations, before building his own residence nearby. He joined Caleb's brother Lewis as a partner in the store.[15]

Hannah, who had done and seen much since the October day of her marriage to Caleb in 1830, remained at Camp Marion for a while, until the youngest boy, Edward, married and began his family. Then, in wisdom, she turned Camp Marion over to him and moved into the village, first to the house near the store that Caleb had built soon after they were married, and then later to a small cottage built for her diminished needs.[16] In many large rural families in the South, a daughter, unmarried, is that special person who helps the others in times of sickness and emergency, who is an extra parent for nieces and nephews, and who cares for the widowed mother. This was Mary Lide Coker, "Manie," who remained with Hannah in Society Hill until her mother's death in 1900.[17]

III

Individual and family affairs were taken in hand as life went on. Underneath, always and forever, was the question of profit and loss in southern agriculture. The South was almost totally agricultural; Darlington County completely so. Captain Coker, in 1871, stated the situation clearly: "In our country and under our present system of agriculture, the question 'what is the cost of producing cotton' involves nothing more than 'what is the possibility of remunerative farming?'"[18]

We have no other crop which experience has shown to be adapted to our soil and climate and which we can grow profitably for market. In isolated cases a farmer profiting by the neglect or

15. R. E. Coker, "William Caleb Coker" (R. E. Coker), p. 48.
16. R. E. Coker, "Coker Forebears" (R. E. Coker), p. 22.
17. Wilson, "For My Own" (Watson collection), pp. 17-18.
18. William Caleb Coker, "Remunerative Farming," *The Southern Cultivator*, XXIX, No. 5 (May, 1871), pp. 174-76, for this and following quotations.

improvidence of his neighbors may increase the sales from his farm by producing in excess of his own supply, a limited quantity of fruit, vegetables or even grain forage, and find a market with less thrifty farmers or with nonproducers. But to bring money into the country, or to increase the aggregate wealth of the community, we are at present entirely dependent upon the successful cultivation of cotton.

These were the Captain's opening remarks in a paper read before the Pomological and Farmer's Club of Society Hill in 1871, an organization for agricultural betterment that he had helped form shortly after the war. He then went on and asked the important question: "'At what cost per pound can it be produced'; or what would be more practical to say, 'at what cost has it been produced.'" He was not encouraged by what he found:

I have found that the hire of labor, cost of fertilizers, expenses of maintaining plantation and implements in good working order, and a very moderate allowance from rent of land and use of capital, have amounted to fully fourteen cents for each pound of cotton I have sold in the year 1870, and about sixteen cents in 1869. In this estimate the whole of the plantation expenses have been charged to cotton for what ever else was produced, was consumed by men and animals engaged in making cotton, and was, in fact, produced for that purpose.

These figures on the cost of cotton production the Captain had derived from careful records kept on the plantation at Society Hill for the years 1869 and 1870. Referring to 1869, "I kept a record of all the operations of the farm, showing each day the amount of labor performed in every department of the plantation." Here, again, was the rational summing up of costs that had appeared first with Caleb, and then with James on the Hartsville plantation. Even so, Captain Coker had to confess ". . . that nothing astonished me more in the study of the farm journal, than the extraordinary proportion of labor that appeared to have been bestowed upon cotton."

His records showed that ". . . three hundred days of effective labor, assisted by one-third of the labor of one mule are sufficient for the proper cultivation of twelve acres of cotton." But this was not a straightaway proposition: "This is equal to the labor of one man working efficiently through the different years, but it is not distributed through the seasons of the year, so that one man can do it with ease. From January to April he would have some idle time on his hands; from May to August he would require some assistance and during the picking season still more." In fact, his astonishment at the amount of labor required for cotton was ". . . lessened when I remembered that during the months of May, June, July and part of August, the entire hoeing force was rarely absent from the cotton field—and during the months of September, October, and November, the whole labor of the plantation with all the extra help that could be hired was devoted to picking and ginning, with the exception of perhaps two weeks gathering corn and sowing grain."

For 1869, he found that "The cost of a full day's labor with all incidental expense, furnishing the laborers with tools, etc., with me has been 66-2/3 cents, or if one third of the cost of feeding the mule is added, 80 cents. This gives me $20 per acre as the bare cost of cultivation. Putting the natural production of the land at 130 pounds per acre, which is fully up to the average of our uplands; and we have about 15-1/2 cents as the cost of a pound of cotton in the one item of labor."

This was the cost of one hand's labor when applied to the limit on cotton production. However, as noted, there were times when the hand was idle, and times when he could not work his twelve acres of cotton by himself. Was there not then some better way of distributing labor? The Captain thought so. "I will take that proportion which seems to me to give the best distribution of labor and the best rotation of crops, and say that three hundred days of effective labor assisted by one half the labor of a mule, will cultivate eight acres in cotton, eight in corn and eight in small grain." Anticipating the reaction of his listeners that "It may seem that this is much heavier cropping than the former . . . ," he went on to say that "I am satisfied that to cultivate this twenty-four acres thus divided, is really less work than the twelve acres in cotton alone. The several crops thus proportioned, while they are not entirely complementary to each other, yet give a much more perfect distribution of labor through the different seasons of the year."

Thus with all cotton each plowman has 36 acres to plow in the spring, and each hoe hand has 18 acres to hoe—while under the latter estimate, there are only 32 acres of cotton and corn to plow, and 16 acres of cotton to the hoe hand.—This reduction will make room for the time required to harvest small grain in June. Again, under the former estimate there is the produce of 12 acres of cotton to be picked and ginned, under the latter, only 8 acres; which will amply compensate for the labor of gathering corn and sowing grain.

However this all added up, the Captain, talking to a group of neighbors and fellow farmers, had to be realistic, which meant recurring to his introductory remark that ". . . we are at present entirely dependent upon the successful cultivation of cotton." As the men who heard him well knew:

The product of these 16 acres of corn and grain, are only profitable to diminish the cost of paying the laborer. It is impossible to enter into an exact calculation of the extent to which it will do this—so much depends upon the capacity of the soil and the success which attends the cultivation of these crops, that any calculation would be mere guess work. I can only say, that I believe the corn and grain so made ought to pay the entire cost of feeding the mule, and furnish the laborer with provisions for consumption equal to fully one half his wages; besides providing against the depreciation of mules, by feeding a sufficient number of colts to keep the stock up to standard. If this is so, it is easy to see that the actual expenses of cultivating the eight acres of cotton, are less than the twelve in the former case.

To move in the direction indicated by the Captain's remarks required the positive action of the several main elements of the southern agricultural situation. None of these, by their nature, was able to move in this new direction. The farmers, white and black, were not conditioned to this sort of thinking

RESTORING LIFE 95

or planning. Most were in debt, wherein they required all the money a cash crop could bring in, and in this they were encouraged by their creditors. The mere statement of the possibility whereby a people can eke out an existence for a while, and then in some uncertain future enter the land of milk and honey, has never penetrated very far from the top downward. Indeed, ". . . the corn and grain so made ought to pay the entire cost of feeding the mule. . . ." and presumably the mule would object no more to this than he did to everything else. But for several million newly freed slaves, and several other million poor white farmers, to take this corn and grain as ". . . provisions for consumption equal to fully one half . . ." their wages was asking a lot, sound as it was. As long as cotton brought in some cash money, and as long as next year held out its promise of a crop the like of which had never been seen before, then cotton would be planted to the limit.

All this Captain Coker knew; unfortunately for his peace of mind, he also knew that the old ways were no longer profitable, if they ever had been. The prospect was not heartening. Even at the relatively high prices that prevailed in the years of which Captain Coker was speaking, there was little or no margin of profit in raising cotton, and as prices continued to fall in the seventies, eighties and nineties, cotton was raised at a loss.[19] This loss was to be made up by what was taken from the soil, and by the schools and health facilities that were never obtained, by the roads that were never built, by the goods that were never bought.

James, at Hartsville, was more impatient than his brother. No doubt they talked at length of these matters, for they were always close, having a high regard for one another. The Major was farming with as much success as could be had through careful management, and the store, though still modest, was not entirely disappointing. But there was little increment, and he looked for a new day. It was industry that

[19.] Francis B. Simkins, *A History of the South* (New York: Alfred A. Knopf, 1953), p. 344.

beckoned him. On August 10, 1869, at a meeting of the Darlington County Agricultural Society he "discussed the matter at length, urging the necessity and propriety of manufacturing our own cotton."[20] No one dissented on principle, perhaps, but neither was there any one who had money to put into such a venture. Least of all James.

Yet he did not miss the first opportunity to make a start. In 1874 a friend somewhat older than James, George Norwood, proposed that James join him in a factorage and commission merchant business in Charleston. Their dealings would be primarily in cotton and naval stores. James assented. Norwood furnished twenty-five thousand dollars of the initial capital, and James, by mortgaging some land, scraped together five thousand dollars.[21] He did not propose to leave Hartsville completely; the family spent the summers there and James continued, through tenants and a manager, to operate the plantation and store.

IV

The year of redemption in South Carolina was 1876. The Radicals were voted out and the incomparable and symbolic Wade Hampton became Governor. Without pretensions to compromise, a revivified Democratic Party came "straight out" for white rule. Since the Radicals controlled the election machinery and were supported by Federal troops the election was not primarily a debate but became a matter of opposing intimidation to intimidation.[22]

Captain Coker was the Democratic nominee in Darlington County for the State Senate. His opponent was B. F. Whittemore, a man possessed of an interesting history. By profession he was a Methodist minister; by birth a native of Massachusetts. The Freedmen's Bureau had sent him to South Carolina after the war to organize schools among the Negroes. Becoming

20. Minute Book of the Darlington County Agricultural Society (J. M. Napier), p. 66.
21. Copy of agreement between Major Coker and George A. Norwood (Watson collection).
22. Simkins and Woody, *South Carolina During Reconstruction*, chapters XVIII and XIX.

Above, James Lide Coker—the Major (Bradley Studios, New York).
Below, William Caleb Coker—the Captain (courtesy of R. E. Coker).

Above, Major Coker's first store, opened in 1865, at Hartsville (courtesy of J. L. Coker and Co., Hartsville). *Below,* The Carolina Fiber Company plant, about 1900, where the first paper was chemically made from southern pine.

active in politics as a man who could influence the colored voters, he was sent to Congress in 1868. He was soon expelled from that body for being "influenced by improper pecuniary considerations." His constituents returned him to Congress despite this, but he was again refused a seat. He then secured election to the State Senate from Darlington County.[23]

In addition to getting out their own vote in larger number than had been possible since the war, the Democrats proposed to diminish severely the Negro vote. As the campaign progressed a great deal of pressure was exerted to keep the Negroes from going to the polls. Part of this pressure was the so-called rifle clubs. These mounted clubs, by parades, by attendance at Radical meetings, no doubt by visits to individual Negroes, and most of all by their very existence, operated to keep many Negro voters at home. At Hartsville, in February of 1876, Major Coker was chairman of a meeting whose purpose was to ". . . form a social club for the object of cultivating sociability, pleasure & improvement in horsemanship, & protection of life & property if necessary."[24]

Despite all these efforts, the Radicals carried the election in Darlington County, Whittemore being sent to the Senate. However, after much confusion, Hampton was inaugurated Governor, the General Assembly came into Democratic hands, and Whittemore decided that his course had been run. He left the state and Captain Coker was sent to the State Senate in 1877.[25]

The Captain was a big man, six feet one inch tall, and weighed about 220 pounds, which he carried well. His hair was silky black, his eyes brown, and, in the newer style of the times, he grew a full beard but no mustache. He was altogether a distinguished figure, not portentous, for there was a modesty about him that was almost diffidence, and an evident sincerity. In the Legislature he addressed himself quite early to the re-establishment of South Carolina College, his Alma Mater,

---

23. *Ibid.*, pp. 117-18.
24. The minute book of this meeting is in the Watson collection.
25. *Darlington Press* (Darlington, S.C.), April 25, 1907.

being one of a few who followed this hard job through to completion. He served as one of seven elected trustees of the college (after 1888, University) from 1886 until 1890.[26]

He worked quietly in the several successive sessions that he served in the Legislature. The Senate Journal notes few speeches, nor was he much of a political trader. It was, rather, the quickness and breadth of his mind, and his personal independence, that moved him into a position of leadership. In 1880 he was named chairman of the Senate finance committee and remained in this job as long as he was in the Senate.[27] This was an important position, requiring strength, for every feather of public taxing and spending was a mountainous burden in a still prostrate state.

Things had, in the meantime, gone well with the Major in Charleston, though there was never any intention of remaining there permanently. In 1881 he left the partnership with George Norwood. A banking offer in Richmond attracted him, but his wife Sue demurred, on the grounds that Hartsville was a far better place to raise their children,[28] who by now were numerous, there being Margaret, James, David, Will, Jenny, Charles and Susie. So the Major came home to Hartsville. At the settling up of the partnership, the Major's share in cash, bonds and notes came to a little less than seventy-five thousand dollars.[29] He now had some of the money required to establish industry, if this was his ultimate intention. First, however, in the same year of 1881, he became the largest stockholder and first president of a bank that was established in the town of Darlington, this being the only bank in the area.

In 1883 the Major took the lead in establishing the Darlington Manufacturing Company, also in the town of Darlington, a cotton mill the likes of which he had spoken of in the darker days of 1869. Now perhaps some of the dreams were to come

26. R. E. Coker, "William Caleb Coker" (R. E. Coker), p. 65.
27. *Journal of the South Carolina Senate, Regular Session, 1880* (South Caroliniana Library), p. 33.
28. Conversation with Mrs. J. L. Coker, Jr.
29. Agreement dissolving the partnership (Watson collection).

true. As was the general custom in the early establishment of cotton mills in the South, there was a goodly number of local subscribers of stocks in small amounts, but the Major was the majority stockholder and, again, the president, though he was soon succeeded by Captain Coker.[30] The Major drove down from Hartsville twice a week.

Captain Coker continued in the Legislature, and by 1886 he was being prominently mentioned for governor, though he had made no personal effort in this direction. This year, ten years after Hampton's triumph, was the beginning of another decisive time in South Carolina. Political control during these ten years had, without any particular design, devolved into the hands of the so-called Bourbons, a loosely organized group of upper class people for whom Hampton was a good symbol. In a gentlemanly fashion they passed the offices among themselves. As a group they were neither corrupt nor incapable. They were merely themselves, and as poverty lingered on across the state, particularly among the small farmers, resentment grew against these leaders who apparently "forgot nothing and learned nothing." The South Carolina unrest was part of a general farmers' revolt that spread in these years across the South and West. In South Carolina this feeling of unrest found a harsh, effective voice in Benjamin Ryan Tillman, a man of monumental disrespect for tradition. By 1886, though at that time unwilling to run for office himself, Tillman had brought the farmers into effective political array. They loomed large in the state Democratic convention that met in Columbia to nominate candidates for Governor and other state offices.[31]

The Captain was one of a number of nominees for Governor. He was nominated largely on the basis of his evident fitness, for he had the backing of neither of the major contending groups. Nor had he sought such backing. He, and all

30. R. E. Coker, "William Caleb Coker" (R. E. Coker), p. 74.
31. Francis B. Simkins, *The Tillman Movement in South Carolina* (Durham: Duke University Press, 1926). See Chapter IV for account of the Convention of 1886.

the Cokers, loved Hampton—indeed, Hampton had been a house and hunting guest of the Captain's. At their best in holding public office as duty and responsibility, the Captain was congenial with the people loosely identified with Hampton. There has been in southern life—particularly in the eastern rural counties—a genuine strain of public service by better off, better educated, upper strata men. Whatever of paternalism and *noblesse oblige* has been present, the core of motivation has been relatively unselfish; the honor of office holding has been no more than co-equal with duty, and financial gain insignificant. This was the ideal, and the Captain approached it very closely. In Darlington County he was one of several men who were expected to give leadership in political affairs, not because of power but because of personal knowledge, probity, and station in life. In turn, of course, for his lifetime these demonstrated qualities gave him back political success insofar as he desired it.

Yet, for all of this, there were in him qualities of independence, a distaste for political arrangements and favors, and a personal need for withdrawal from the bustle of affairs, that stood between him and organized backing from the old guard. Their candidate was J. P. Richardson. For the same reasons, perhaps intensified, he did not have the backing of the Tillman group, though this was offered and refused. The details are a little mixed, but the substance is clear. Before the opening of the convention Tillman tried unsuccessfully to have his farmer delegates unite on J. C. Sheppard, a member of the old guard but still uncommitted as to the farmers' program. Sometime after this, perhaps during the balloting, Tillman wired the Captain the offer of his support. There were conditions. Just what they were is uncertain, but had they been absent the outcome would likely have been the same, for Captain Coker wired, in effect, that he would be governor for all the people and not for a special group.[32] He thus turned away from the nomination, for Tillman's support would have nominated him. On the first ballot Richardson received 112

---

32. *The Darlington Press*, (S.C.), April 25, 1907.

votes, Sheppard 68 and Captain Coker 48; on the second, as several minor candidates dropped out, Richardson got 137, Sheppard 80 and Coker 65. On the third ballot Richardson was nominated with 172 votes, but it is worth noting that on this ballot Captain Coker received 94 votes to Sheppard's 50. Actually, before the vote was announced there were changes to Richardson, apparently motivated by Coker's gathering strength for the next ballot.

Triumph of the old guard in 1886 confirmed the dissatisfaction of the farmers and made inevitable Tillman's candidacy for governor in 1890. The farmers' program was a good one by all present standards, and at this stage of his career Tillman was a much needed leader for equally needed improvements. But Tillman became a virtual dictator, a roiling, broiling figure causing tumult and unprecedented bitterness, and his program was increasingly obscured and diverted by personal, racial, and purely political issues. "Tillmanism," as cult and practice, was one major source of the later Bleasism and of other excesses in latter day South Carolina politics.[33] It is an insistent question, therefore, as to what might have been the course of events had the Captain accepted Tillman's support. He was, of all things, aware of the farmers' needs and equipped to seek solutions. Perhaps he could have bridged the gap and converted, as Aycock did in North Carolina, this emotional potential ever present in South Carolina into a more constructive outcome. The Captain withdrew from politics after 1886.

V

Both the Captain and the Major turned homeward for good in 1886. The two turnings had some connection. Major Coker had by that time determined to concentrate all of his interests in Hartsville. The store there had become increasingly successful since his return, serving a wide area of farmers, and Hartsville was beginning to be more than a cross-roads. The volume of goods to be hauled into the store, and of cotton out,

---

33. See Simkins, *The Tillman Movement in South Carolina.*

had become so large that a railroad into Hartsville was required. The Major's stated purpose to obtain a railroad into Hartsville raised some objections in Darlington, where the position as county seat and central trading place was much enjoyed. There was also some disagreement over taxes on the mill with Darlington officials, and the Major found the constant travel by buggy over the fourteen miles between Hartsville and Darlington burdensome. As decisive as these considerations was the bother of dealing with a large number of small stockholders, for the Major was of considerable independence of mind.[34] He therefore turned his main attention after 1886 to Hartsville, though he retained stock in both the bank and cotton mills.

Perhaps something more was involved than business arrangements and necessities. James was now 49, William 47. For both, the twenty-five years just passed had been strenuous, full of war and near poverty, of civil strife and personal uncertainty. Both had fought through with integrity, and had achieved a measure of success. At the beginning of middle age, then, their homing was not unnatural. Each had a large family; the oldest children were now coming to maturity, and the others not far behind.

The Captain, with his remarkable versatility, managed the mill quite well. Dividends were regular, though sometimes small, and during the hard times of the 1890's the mill was able to remain open. Other affairs did not go as well. After he had left the store at Society Hill, losses and indebtedness developed there. The Captain personally assumed all the debts. His oldest son, Allen, graduated from college, gave his time to the store, and under the new style of W. C. Coker and Son the store's affairs were set right. In the same way, the Captain assumed half the debts of a brick and iron works with which he was associated, though under no legal obligation to do so.[35]

Increasingly among southern cotton mills, substantial con-

---

34. Conversation with W. C. Wilson, Darlington, South Carolina.
35. R. E. Coker, "William Caleb Coker" (R. E. Coker), pp. 74-75.

trol was passing to individuals and concerns outside the region. This was largely a result of lack of capital and marketing facilities in the South. Few southern mills had the capital reserves with which to expand, or to weather serious financial difficulties, and there was relatively little capital to be had in the South. Capital was thus sought elsewhere, often in the brokerage houses through which the cotton goods were sold. This occurred at the Darlington Manufacturing Company in the 1890's, when money was secured for expansion. Differences developed between the Captain and the new stockholders relative to size of dividends, night work (which the Captain considered harmful to health), and other matters. Finally, in 1901, he decided to terminate his relations with the mill. Profits ceased soon after, and the Captain was urged to return to the presidency of the mill. He had decided to do so when final illness intervened.[36] The Captain died in 1907.

Of all the Cokers, the Captain was the most versatile and the most paradoxical. He was at once scholarly, philosophical, profound, and an excellent farmer and business man. His mind was exceptionally quick, and almost phenomenally accurate. The range of his interests, and his fundamental grasp of subject matter, were great. The children found no difficulty in getting him to aid them in translating Latin; ". . . the difficulty was to get the book back. It was fortunate that there were in the home library some old editions of the common Latin and Greek texts; for, once started on the reading of Virgil, for example, he would likely continue reading by himself until bedtime, turning the pages at short intervals and apparently reading the language almost as readily as if it had been English."[37]

His son Robert, later to become a distinguished zoologist, recalled that ". . . after taking 'conics' in college, I first learned from him, on returning home, what conic sections really were. On another occasion, I mentioned having had difficulty on an

36. *Ibid.*, p. 77.
37. *Ibid.*, pp. 76-77.

examination with the equation for the *catenary*. He said he believed that curve was not used in the text he had studied in college (forty years earlier) and asked what it was. I told him it was the curve taken by a telegraph wire hanging between two poles. He then asked how its equation was derived. I had started only the first line of the solution, when he immediately took the words from my mouth, saying 'I see,' and completing the derivation of the equation in perfect form."[38]

He did not possess mere facility, or a good memory. There was in him a rare combination of spirit and mind, lightened with a quiet sense of humor. His knowledge wore well in his thinking and became profound. His son Robert wrote many years later that "It is to him, also, rather than to any teacher of Biology, that I owe my first definite conception of one of the most fundamental qualities of life: Among other things he said with some dry wit, 'the primary object in life of an oyster is to convert the whole world into oyster' . . . a thought which goes to the very essence of the nature of organic life."[39]

There was in the man genuine modesty—and something that went, perhaps, just beyond modesty. It was not quite diffidence, for no man could speak more plainly or directly, or had surer confidence in his own thinking, or made less apology or explanation for what he thought or did. He simply was not constituted to push his abilities into the public eye, nor to compete for favor or wealth. Rather, once the matter at hand was dealt with he tended to withdraw, perhaps to hours of reading, or to his beloved flute playing, or to sitting quietly with his thoughts, smoking a long-stemmed pipe. His reserve increased with age, and he seldom contributed his opinion unless it was sought.

Yet his opinion was often sought in Darlington County. For he was a man pre-eminently of his people. The South has many moods, and one of its most constant is golden in hospitality and respect for the able man who does not display his abilities too prominently, and who is tolerant and easy going.

38. *Ibid.*, p. 10.
39. *Ibid.*, p. 19.

RESTORING LIFE 105

There has been loss here, since hard issues have often been decided on irrelevancies, and good men have often left action to lesser men. Yet there has been a gain, also, because this mood has been predicated on tolerance and respect, and on a timeless, resilient social maturity.

Occasion could rouse him to his full capacity. In 1894 there occurred in Darlington what in history books has come to be called the Darlington Riot. It was an outgrowth of the unmitigated bitterness engendered by Tillmanism. By 1892, when Tillman was elected for his second term as governor, there seemed to be a majority sentiment for prohibition in the State. The Legislature was proceeding to convert this sentiment into law, when, suddenly and with an amazing exhibition of personal power, Tillman caused to be enacted a state controlled dispensary system, not only demolishing prohibition but making the State part of the trade. This system is in rather common use today, but it was revolutionary for the times. To enforce the law's provisions against local manufacture and sale of liquor, the Governor had placed at his disposal a state constabulary; the constabulary's instrument was the search warrant. This now infringed upon sentiments of personal liberty, so carefully cherished in South Carolina, and around this issue gathered the Tillman opposition.

In late March of 1894 Tillman dispatched a large group of constables to investigate alleged violations in the town of Darlington, where Captain Coker was then living. Tension spread over this center of Tillman opposition. It seemed, however, that the constables, their work done, were about to depart in peace, when a fight between two local young men, in which one of the constables became involved, provided the spark. Before the shooting had stopped, one local man and two constables were dead, others wounded, and the citizens of the town were up in arms. Tillman called out several militia companies, only a part of which responded.[40]

Captain Coker had no part in the riot, except to develop an utter disgust for the total. Though he had not ridden for a

40. Simkins, *The Tillman Movement in South Carolina*, Chapter VII.

number of years, he saddled and mounted a horse in cold fury and rode to the courthouse square, expressing his sentiments to all involved in plain terms.[41] He continued to lead in restoring order. The *News and Courier* of Charleston for April 4, 1894, reported from Darlington under the dateline of April 3 that

On the afternoon train Messrs. W. C. Coker, E. Keith Dargan and George W. Dargan left for Columbia on the invitation of Governor Tillman to consult about the entire matter. Later in the day a letter replying to inquiries from Gen Richbourg was received at headquarters, which made everyone feel that the end was near. The inquiry was made by Gen Richbourg regarding the safety of the dispensary constables engaged in last week's affray if brought here as witnesses before the coroner's inquest. Twenty eight leading citizens of Darlington, headed by Mayor Dargan, Capt Coker and other prominent citizens, pledge themselves on their honor to use their influence in every possible way to see that these men are not interfered with.[42]

In 1905, two years before his death, the Captain had an opportunity to talk to his home people about the law. The occasion was the dedication of a new court house at Darlington. Though in poor health at that time, he spoke plainly and in the context of the history of the Pee Dee area: "Perhaps the lesson most needed today by our own people, under the conditions existing now, is that reverence for law and a cheerful and willing obedience to its requirements and acquiesence in its judgments."

It was his conception of the law that ". . . however inadequate may be the result which the wisdom of law-makers, and the learning of the interpreters of the law have attained in ascertaining and establishing absolute justice, yet it remains true that the ideal and purpose of the law, in all its complications, through all its intricacies, and through all its forms of administration, is simply this, to come at what is right, to defend the good and punish the evil."

---

41. Conversation with F. W. Coker.
42. The *News and Courier* (Charleston, S.C.), January 16, 1905.

He reminded his audience that lawful liberty had come at a dear cost in the Pee Dee area, and of the fact that they were "... the inheritors of a system of law and methods for its enforcement worked out by the long and trying experience of a race working its way through alternating anarchy and despotism to liberty and safety; and which, through its painfully acquired institutions, has attained to the highest degree of liberty and safety ever realized by any portion of the human race."[43]

At Hartsville, the Major was building his own railroad, and, though he was perhaps unaware of it, he was, with his sons now beginning to come of age, starting out on a course of remarkable achievement.

The Major had not intended to go into railroading. It was simply the last alternative. Earlier in the eighties, he had asked the Atlantic Coast Line to build a branch into Hartsville from their Cheraw and Darlington Railroad, about seven miles away at the nearest point. This failing, he had joined with men from other towns in an ambitious project to build a railroad from the Pee Dee River northwestward across the state, passing through Hartsville. This effort failed also, and in 1889 a final and unsuccessful request was made of the Atlantic Coast Line.[44]

The Major had had enough of refusals. And, besides, he now possessed a new resource. His eldest son James was newly home from Stevens Institute of Technology with an engineering degree. James could survey the road bed, and he understood the workings of a steam engine and railroad cars. So the Major decided to build the road himself. The Coast Line was at that time replacing its iron rails with steel rails. The Major secured the use of some of these iron rails, incorporated the Hartsville Railroad, and began to build. Joseph Lawton, who had married the Major's eldest child, Margaret, was in

43. *Ibid*.
44. J. L. Coker, *Hartsville, Its Early Settlers* (Pee Dee Historical Society, 1911). pp. 34-35.

general charge of the grading and filling, using for the most part labor, drag pans, mules, wagons and timbers from the Hartsville plantation. The Major watched over all. In the fall of 1889 James drove the first train into Hartsville, his bride from New York in the passenger car.[45]

The railroad would now serve the store and community. It could also serve a dream that young James had brought home with him from Stevens Institute, a dream to make at Hartsville paper from the pine that grew all across the countryside. James had laid the dream before the Major, and all the while the railroad was building it was under discussion.

45. Conversations with Mrs. J. L. Coker, Jr. and W. C. Coker.

6

Piney Woods and Paper: J. L. Coker, Jr. and Paper Making

I

JAMES LIDE COKER, JR., it will be recalled, was born at Society Hill in November of 1863,[1] while his father hovered between life and death in Tennessee, under the shadow of Lookout Mountain. James grew up through Reconstruction and the years following. His turn of mind was scientific, to chemistry and engineering, which turn he followed in 1884 to Stevens Institute of Technology at Hoboken, New Jersey. His aptitude with his hands and mind for engineering problems caused some comment at Stevens, including a question about his previous training. Having none, he told the truth: that what he knew he had learned in the blacksmith shop on the Hartsville plantation.[2]

It was a requirement at Stevens that seniors write a thesis. James and H. C. Ferris joined together to write on "The Sulphite Process of Manufacture of Cellulose for Paper Making,"[3] that is, how to make paper pulp by the sulphite process. In the way of all thesis writers, James and Ferris devoted the first third of their seventy-five page paper to the background and history of their problem. The remaining two-thirds were devoted to a detailed study of two operating mills, one in Michi-

[1] Hannah Lide Coker, *A Story of the Late War*, pp. 6, 21.
[2] Conversation with Mrs. J. L. Coker, Jr., Hartsville, S.C.
[3] Letter to author from Miss Frances Duck, Stevens Institute of Technology, Castle Point, Hoboken, N.J., March 7, 1949.

gan, the other in Wisconsin, in which they noted not only the details of operation but also the cost of pulp production per ton.

As he wrote, James began to think of the great abundance of pine trees that grew all across the South Carolina middle country. In the beginning there had been predominantly the great long leaf, destroyed by settlers clearing cotton lands, by lumbermen, by turpentiners, by farmers burning underbrush. In the old fields remaining as cotton wore the land out, and in the lumbered areas, there had succeeded in place of the long leaf the several varieties of short leaf pine—as plentiful as water and almost as free as sunshine.

Could not these pine be made into paper pulp chemically? James thought so, but neither he nor anyone else knew for certain. The existing pulp makers were not interested, for the northern forests were still bountiful, and the markets were nearer. So James came home with his proposal and made it to the Major—that they make the attempt at Hartsville to use the wasted pine. The Major, beyond doubt, thought back to his homecoming from Harvard in 1858, when the family at Society Hill suffered his enthusiasm for his fresh knowledge of chemistry, and when his father had agreed to some experiments on the Hartsville plantation. Certainly he was in no position to deny James a patient hearing.

But Major Coker had not been through the business rigors of war and reconstruction to accept easily a new and untried scheme that would involve perhaps the major part of his resources. He raised objections, as well he might. Hartsville was but a mere crossroads, a pinprick in the long, flat landscape of the middle country. All around was still the land of cotton. There was no power of any sort at Hartsville, no experienced mechanics or machine operators, and no railroad transportation. Young James was the only person involved who had even the slightest knowledge of pulp making. In the beginning there was no accurate way to estimate the cost or even all of the technical requirements. Most important, there was no knowledge anywhere of what southern pine would do when reduced to pulp.

So the Major demurred, gently perhaps, because he was anxious to see his son go forward. Most of the talking was done after supper on the piazza, in the early evening, when of all times the southern nature holds her own in an infinity of cricket sounds and gathering darkness. James persevered and finally Major Coker agreed to a limited effort: they would set up a pulp mill and make pulp for sale to northern paper manufacturers. If this turned out successfully, then perhaps a paper mill could also be built at Hartsville.[4]

After the railroad was completed, James went to New York in the early winter of 1889 to make arrangements for the construction of the pulp mill.[5] He had before him three jobs: first, to secure access to the sulphite process, parts of which were covered by patents; second, to secure advice and help in the use of the process; and, third, to draw up plans for the mill and to purchase machinery. This was a large order for a young man of limited experience; a hard education was before him.

The still new and developing sulphite process was substantially under the control of the American Sulphite Pulp Company.[6] James dealt with a director of this company, W. H. Parsons, Sr., who also had an interest in several paper mills. Parsons and his associates knew only enough of the plup and paper qualities of southern pine to be wary. They were not unwilling, however, for the Cokers to make the attempt to convert pine to pulp. After several conferences, James and Parsons reached and drew up an agreement, which James mailed to his father for approval on Christmas Eve of 1889. The terms were that the Cokers would construct a pulp mill at Hartsville and run it. Parsons would secure licenses from the American Sulphite Pulp Company for the use of the patented parts of the sulphite process at Hartsville. Parsons also would furnish advice and engineering help in the con-

---

4. Conversation with Dr. W. C. Coker, Chapel Hill, N.C. Also evidence in letters subsequently cited showing that paper making at Hartsville was considered before it became necessary.
5. James to Major Coker, December 24, 1889 (R. G. Coker).
6. W. H. Parsons, Sr., to J. L. Coker, Jr., November 22, 1889 (R. G. Coker).

struction and operation of the mill. The Cokers and their associates at Hartsville would retain seven-tenths of the stock and the remaining tenths would go to Parsons and his associates in consideration of the patent licenses and of their advice. These provisions were the backbone of the agreement, which was signed and dated December 30, 1889, and they seemed plain enough.[7]

James had reason to be encouraged. He had accomplished, or put in motion, all three of his jobs with one stroke, and had done so economically. The sulphite process had been made available, as had the requisite technical and engineering help. "Mr. Parsons thinks he can save us nearly all expenses for engineer's service...."[8] He remained in New York for some time during the winter of 1890 to learn, to draw up plans, and to place orders for machinery.

There were four main steps in the sulphite process for James to master. First there was the preparation of the wood, which involved cutting, barking and reduction to small pieces. This latter process was called chipping. Quite likely he learned not to attempt to reduce the heartwood of pine to pulp because the high content of resin in this part of the tree prevented good pulping. Parsons and his associates probably had learned this from earlier experience with northern jack pine. The second step was the making of the sulphite solution, or liquor as it was commonly called, in which the chipped wood was cooked. A first cousin, Howard Edwards of Darlington, was sent in April of 1890 to a pulp mill at Saugerties, New York, to learn in detail about making this sulphite liquor. The third step brought the chipped wood and the sulphite liquor together in huge, steel, kettle-like containers, called digesters. The Cokers installed two at Hartsville, each of a rated capacity of two and a half tons of pulp. The introduction of steam under pressure into these digesters released sulphurous acid from the sulphite solution. The acid in turn freed the wood fibers from lignin and other materials. In the fourth step the

7. Copy of agreement (R. G. Coker).
8. James to Major Coker, December 24, 1889 (R. G. Coker).

pulp was drained from the digesters—called "blowing" the digesters—and washed and screened to remove all material except wood fibres.[9]

James consulted in some detail with Parsons and Parsons' engineers in regard to machinery and mill buildings. He had been at a disadvantage in drawing up the original agreement with Parsons, for he was not primarily a business man and in any event Parsons held the top cards. On the technical matters, however, and in spite of his inexperience, he held his own, both as to what he wanted and as to what the Cokers could afford to finance. When the details of machinery and arrangements had been worked out, the over-all design of the mill was made by the Boston engineering firm of Lockwood and Greene.[10]

II

The mill site was on the bank of Black Creek, about a quarter of a mile behind Major Coker's house. The ground was cleared in the spring of 1890. Around July 1st construction of the mill buildings was begun. Howard Edwards, returned from New York, supervised the day-by-day details of the building. The master builder was Henry Gandy, from the nearby community of Doversville. With a crew of Negro men as helpers, he cut the great longleaf pine that grew along the creek bank, laid the foundations and erected the buildings in the strength of hewn pine timbers.[11]

As construction proceeded it became apparent that a rural countryside empty of mill buildings and running machinery was not the only void that confronted the Cokers. Both James and his father began the venture with a minimum knowledge of pulp making that only hard experience was to increase—this requisite experience appearing promptly. Some of their personal inexperience may well have been offset by more study.

9. Robert H. Clapperton and William Henderson, *Modern Paper Making* (Oxford: Basil Blackwell, 1941), pp. 56-58.
10. Major Coker to Lord and Burke, Attorneys, Charleston, S.C., May 18, 1892 (R. G. Coker).
11. Conversation with Mr. Howard Edwards who was on the scene.

James conceivably would have benefited from practical experience in an operating pulp mill. Major Coker obtained the answer to several obvious business questions later than seems necessary.[12]

Fundamentally, however, their difficulty was cultural, reflecting the great deficiency that then existed throughout the South in what is commonly considered the ordinary facilities of industry: technical advice, financial help, and a knowledge of men and companies in any particular industry.[13] These deficiencies of the South in industrial facilities were multiplied in making pulp at Hartsville. The middle country had not come as far as the Piedmont in industry; Hartsville itself was almost open country; and not nearer than New York were there any facilities for making or selling paper pulp. These deficiencies unfolded as construction proceeded, when almost all of the many questions that appeared had to be referred to New York. The reliability of a machinery manufacturer depended on Parsons' advice, about which advice the Cokers had little real knowledge.[14] Similarly, the hiring of expert help was accomplished by long range letters, on Parsons' guarantee and at a salary out of line with the Cokers' resources and the going rates in the South.[15] The purchase of supplies was made with almost no opportunity to check on prices and quality.[16] As to insurance, James wrote Parsons: "Could you not place the insurance on our plant for us, we are at rather long range to do anything with the insurance men and no doubt you could do more with them—get better rates than we could."[17]

Perhaps the greatest deficiency was lack of capital. Major Coker was wealthy by local standards. It is unlikely, however,

---

12. Such as freight rates, costs of production, how to ship pulp.

13. Francis B. Simkins, *A History of the South* (New York: Alfred A. Knopf, 1953), pp. 329-30.

14. W. H. Parsons, Sr., to J. L. Coker, Jr., August 14, 1890 (R. G. Coker).

15. Major Coker to W. H. Parsons, Sr., December 12, 1891 and December 17, 1891 (R. G. Coker).

16. See numerous letters from J. L. Coker, Jr., to W. H. Parsons, Sr., and W. H. Parsons, Jr. (R. G. Coker).

17. J. L. Coker, Jr., to W. H. Parsons, Sr., October 6, 1891 (R. G. Coker).

that his available surplus exceeded $75,000,[18] and all along he was heavily involved in giving credit at the Hartsville store and in buying cotton. It was necessary to keep the mill expenditures under short rein; the cost of building came close to $50,000 and only a few months of losing operations would be required to exhaust his funds. There had been relatively small stock subscriptions from members of the family and the Major's close friend George Norwood in the beginning. After that the entire burden was on Major Coker. As Parsons wrote him, "We do not, at the moment, know any one who would care to subscribe for the five shares of stock. It is so far away from New York, that parties here do not, as a rule, seek investments of this sort."[19] In practice the store paid the bills, acting in effect as banker to the mill. When convenient, these charges against the mill on the store books were converted to stock issued to Major Coker.[20] In such a situation the Cokers were anxious to practice economy. Considering their inexperience, it is not surprising that on occasion they practiced bad economy.

The installation of machinery, therefore, was slow and halting. Two digesters were ordered for delivery in late February of 1891; but the first one was not shipped until the middle of May.[21] Trial production was finally begun in September of 1891,[22] and revealed many problems. W. H. Parsons, Jr., wrote on September 9, "I am extremely disappointed at the failure of your lining [of the digesters]. . . ."[23] Two months later Parsons, Senior, wrote that the burning of the fiber stock was ". . . due to the fact that you have not sufficient acid in the digester."[24] In late November there had been some progress, though nothing conclusive, when Major Coker wrote that "I think we are doing very well with the 'acid making' and the

18. This is an estimate, there being no accounting of his financial position for these years. He had not made sensational profits from the cotton mill in Darlington.
19. W. H. Parsons, Sr., to Major Coker, June 9, 1890 (R. G. Coker).
20. Minute book of Stockholders' and Directors' meetings of the Carolina Fiber Company (R. G. Coker).
21. W. R. Parsons, Sr., to Carolina Fiber Co., October 6, 1890, and J. L. Coker, Jr., to W. H. Parsons & Co., May 12, 1891 (R. G. Coker).
22. W. H. Parsons, Jr., to J. L. Coker, Jr., September 9, 1891 (R. G. Coker).
23. *Ibid.*
24. W. H. Parsons, Sr., to J. L. Coker, Jr., November 9, 1891 (R. G. Coker).

'cooking' in our fibre works, but we are not doing well yet in the 'washing' and in working the screens etc., in wet room." He went on to reveal further their inexperience: "I notice that it [the pulp fibre] is very fluffy and easily assumes a wooly condition . . . is that an advantage or disadvantage? The fibre is very long, I think."[25]

In early December of 1891 Major Coker wrote the Atlantic Coast Line for freight rates on pulp from Hartsville to West Newton, Pennsylvania, where one of the Parsons' paper mills was located. The reply spread a cloud over the whole venture: shipping charges would be so high as to make impossible the sale of pulp, at least to any paper mill then in existence.[26] All along the assumption had been that the pulp, if successfully made, could be sold. This development made immediate the question of installing a paper mill at Hartsville, so that the pulp could be converted into paper there. James' original conception had included a paper mill. It had never been abandoned but held in abeyance, cautiously, until the financial and technical measure of pulp making could be taken.[27] Undoubtedly it was hoped that pulp making could be put on a profitable basis before the larger outlay for a paper mill was assumed.

However, with a decision thus prematurely necessary in December of 1891, Major Coker reacted characteristically. He wrote Parsons for a rough estimate of the cost of a paper mill. Parsons' figure was between thirty and fifty thousand dollars, which at least was not so large as to put an end to a hope.[28]

But nothing was possible, of course, until satisfactory production of pulp could be reached. That remained their first

25. Major Coker to W. H. Parsons, Sr., letter undated but evidence indicates that it was written in November, 1891 (R. G. Coker).
26. Major Coker to W. H. Parsons, Sr., December 16, 1891, and W. H. Parsons, Sr., to Major Coker, December 19, 1891 (R. G. Coker).
27. In a letter to W. H. Parsons, Sr., dated December 12, 1891, Major Coker mentioned the possibility of putting in a paper mill. This was a day or two, at least, prior to the time that rates were received from the Atlantic Coast Line. Also on December 1, 1891, W. H. Parsons, Sr., wrote Major Coker: ". . . if you should decide to put in a paper machine . . ." (R. G. Coker).
28. W. H. Parsons, Sr., to Major Coker, December 17, 1891 (R. G. Coker).

job. In December James became too ill to work.[29] An expert pulp maker from the North was hired on Parsons' recommendation to take over temporarily James' work at the mill. His stay was short. On February 13 Major Coker wrote Parsons:

> Mr. Brown returns to Angeliea tomorrow or next day. He has shown a disposition to do all that could be expected, but he does not understand this wood and I saw it would not pay us to keep him longer, so compromised with him on his salary and let him go. He is a faithful and good man and I think could work spruce wood well. . . .[30]

Troubles dogged them. The digester linings, especially, continued to be damaged by the strong action of the sulphurous acid. A machine for chipping the wood had to be installed. The proper regulation of heat, pressure and acid in the digesters was learned only through trial and much error. On February 13, 1892, Major Coker wrote Parsons, "As for our mill it looks very dark and uncertain,"[31] though he continued to hope realistically: "Those results may be turned to advantage if we can cooperate in furtherance of our enterprise."[32] By early March of 1892 conditions had improved somewhat: "We have been very successful with our cookings during the past week. . . ."[33] "We have just made a good cook of pine (about 5½ cords of unbarked wood) which will turn out at least 2½ tons of fiber, the cook was on just eleven hours."[34] This now, more than two years after the beginning, was the first indication that the threshold of commercial production of pulp had been reached.

Yet, actually, the Cokers were deeper in the woods than ever before. Early in March of 1892 trouble of a different but entirely serious nature appeared. Some time previously the

29. Major Coker to W. H. Parsons, Sr., December 12, 1891 (R. G. Coker).
30. Major Coker to W. H. Parsons, Sr., February 13, 1892 (R. G. Coker).
31. *Ibid.*
32. Major Coker to W. H. Parsons, Sr., March 7, 1892 (R. G. Coker).
33. Major Coker to W. H. Parsons, Sr., March 12, 1892 (R. G. Coker).
34. Major Coker to W. H. Parsons, Sr., March 16, 1892 (R. G. Coker).

Cokers had asked Parsons to deliver the patent licenses, as stipulated in the original agreement. Parsons refused. There was in the agreement a general passage that the Cokers construct "first class Sulphite Pulp mills." This passage stood without definition except that the operation at Hartsville was to be "of the capacity of at least five tons per day." Parsons denied that the mill was first class, and now proposed that the Cokers buy the licenses outright, for cash, rather than issue him stock.

So far as his stated reasons are concerned, Parsons was standing on a technicality. At that stage, whether the mill was first class could be determined only by continuous operation, which the Cokers could not undertake without having the legal right to use the process under patent, and which they were financially unable to undertake until there was a market for their pulp. The Major asked Parsons to stipulate those matters which were not first class, but Pasrons would not do so. In actual fact, Parsons had been made aware of the details of the mill construction from the beginning; he and his engineers had been responsible for most of the plans and had been consulted closely all along. In almost every instance, Parsons approved the installations; all of his objections were mild ones, and nowhere had he indicated that any part was not first class. The pulp produced by the trial runs met his approval.

With respect to the matter of a five ton daily capacity, Parsons' grounds were a little more substantial. The mill was rated at five tons, but no more. Experienced in these matters, Parsons knew that in actual operation a rated capacity somewhat in excess of five tons was normally required to produce five tons of pulp day in and day out. He had so advised the Cokers in 1890.[35] Perhaps they did not take him as seriously as they might have, but in any event they barely had funds for the minimum. This was in the beginning, and Parsons had been cooperating since this original objection.

The truth seems to be that Parsons did not think that the

---

35. W. H. Parsons, Sr., to J. L. Coker, Jr., January 18, 1890, and August 14, 1890 (R. G. Coker).

Cokers were capable of running a pulp mill, or a pulp and paper mill, profitably and efficiently, if ever they did get into commercial production. From his point of view it was not an illogical conclusion. Things had gone slowly and haltingly in that far-off unknown place, amateurishly even, and obviously on a shoestring. He had been skeptical from the first that a man as young and inexperienced in pulp making as James could swing the operation at Hartsville. He had urged that the Cokers engage an experienced pulp maker, and though James "... always met my suggestions kindly and respectfully yet he seemed to think that he had all the requisite knowledge and experience."[36] When such a man was hired because of James' illness in December of 1891, it probably did not increase Parsons' sympathy for the Hartsville enterprise that the Cokers quickly found the expert wanting. On at least one occasion James and Major Coker disregarded Parsons' advice only to have to return to it later.[37] A quality of independent mind has been characteristic of the Cokers as an advantageous trait. Under the circumstances, however, it did not impress Parsons favorably.

As the difficulties of production continued through the winter and spring of 1892, with James ill and the necessity for the construction of a paper mill at Hartsville confirmed, Parsons' doubts grew. In early March of 1892 he came to Hartsville for a few days. Getting there was unpleasant over the rough southern roadbeds. There was a change of trains at Florence, another at Darlington, another at Floyd's Station, and the final seven miles over the rough single track the Cokers had built into Hartsville. If Parsons thought that he was at the end of the line, then he was not mistaken. Hartsville was a crossroads, and very little else, in the flat landscape. There were no electric lights, no plumbing, no paved streets, no entertainment. A cotton field stretched a mile away to the south from Major Coker's front yard. The flat landscape, to be so lovely within a few weeks, was rather drab in early

36. W. H. Parsons, Sr., to Major Coker, December 14, 1891 (R. G. Coker).
37. Major Coker to W. H. Parsons, Sr., April 13, 1892 (R. G. Coker).

March. The mill on the creek bank was sound but not elaborate, and the machinery was not humming. Doubts were confirmed by all this, and perhaps outraged when Major Coker suggested that Parsons join financially in the construction of a paper mill. Almost literally, Parsons ran; certainly he left hurriedly without giving the plant and the books more than a casual inspection.[38] He wanted out, but with a profit. So he threatened to withhold the licenses unless they were purchased with cash instead of stock as the agreement stipulated.

Parsons' action was not admirable, but to his credit it must be said that he really had no way of knowing how much he was underestimating the Major, James, and the whole situation at Hartsville. He mistook Major Coker's inexperience in the field of pulp and paper making for inability, and it is obvious that he felt confident of bluffing the Major into buying the licenses. He had chosen the wrong man. Since 1861 the Major had had adversity for constant company, and on many occasions catastrophe had not been far off. He could not be bluffed or intimidated by the threat of trouble; though he was rigorously fair, he was a consummate businessman; and with his remarkable facility for growth he could learn whatever was necessary about the pulp and paper business. The Major, once he had discovered Parsons' purpose, was equally anxious to sever the connection by buying the licenses outright, but not until "we can properly proceed"[39]—that is, until Parsons' threat of court action had been removed from over his head. He would not be coerced. He wrote Parsons: "I was anxious to see if it could not be settled between ourselves. Therefore, irrespective of our strict right, I desired to have a detailed statement of your objections, as apart from any legal obligations, if they appeared just and reasonable I was desirous of meeting you in the spirit of harmony and conciliation. You have however declined to meet me in this way."[40] When Parsons ended the negotiations by threatening suit Major Coker put the matter

38. *Ibid.*
39. Major Coker to Lord and Burke, May 10, 1892 (R. G. Coker).
40. Major Coker to W. H. Parsons, Sr., June 6, 1892 (R. G. Coker).

in the hands of a Charleston law firm and adhered closely to their advice.[41]

If Parsons had made a mistake in his estimate of Major Coker, he had made an even greater mistake in his estimate of James. James was essentially a creative and improvising engineer; here lay his great skill and in the new world of science, machines, and industry that skill fell on fertile ground. The creative process absorbed all of his attention and all of his energy. The technical job called forth an integrity of application that allowed him to hold nothing back. His illness in the winter and spring of 1892 was caused by overwork and worry; many times in later years he was to be forced to leave work for the same reasons.

James, enthralled with creation, was not a good business man, nor an especially good administrator. Such matters, in fact, for him were something to be gotten out of the way so that the technical job of building and making could be taken in hand. More than this, James was inflexible to the give and take of everyday business transactions; he could not shrug off imperfections and superficiality in people with whom he was dealing. Being completely without deviousness himself, he was fundamentally incapable of foreseeing it in other people; and after the act, his condemnation was complete, final and severely taxing on his own energy. His general approach to men and affairs was revealed in his description of one of Parsons' engineers: "I like the man and the way he talks. He seems to be a practical straight forward fellow with a mechanical head."[42] He was inclined to attribute a like evaluation to people who did not deserve it. These qualities of James, while admirable, did not, when combined with his inexperience, commend him to Parsons as a business administrator who could put over the Hartsville venture.

But James did not stand alone. The Major was there, and it was on the relationship between father and son that the pulp and paper making would stand or fall. Major Coker had

41. See correspondence between Major Coker and law firm of Lord and Burke, Charleston (R. G. Coker).
42. James to Major Coker, January 6, 1890 (R. G. Coker).

a fine feeling for growth and development in his sons. That he was somewhat austere in appearance and exacting in performance ought not to conceal the fact that he neither stifled their originality nor condemned their mistakes. Thus he had not pursued his original objections to the pulp mill in the face of James' insistence. Except as he set the limits for spending, the Major gave James free rein in the organization of the project. That he was reluctant to modify James' program is revealed by the fact that he signed the badly drawn agreement with Parsons, which, it will be remembered, had been made in New York in conferences between James and Parsons. Nothing else will explain the fact that Major Coker signed such an agreement, for he understood contracts well, having drawn up a good many in his own hand.[43] He accepted Parsons' good faith on the basis of James' opinion of the man: "When my son . . . assured me of Parsons' good faith to us . . . I agreed."[44]

If from Parsons' viewpoint the operations at Hartsville up to the spring of 1892 were unsatisfactory, Major Coker, on the other hand, was in a position to realize the tremendous achievement that James, as young and inexperienced as he was, had made in the face of many difficulties to bring the pulp mill to the point of practicable operation. He could also see James' growth and increasing ability as experience accrued. His confidence in his son was unabated.

This confidence found expression almost immediately. By June of 1892, when operations were shut down completely to await the outcome of the Parsons matter, James had in mind two technical developments that would remove the necessity of having access to the patents under Parsons' control. One of these developments concerned the apparatus used to make the sulphite liquor, and differed radically in certain respects from the installation controlled by Parsons. He provided a better means of cooking the sulphur and a construction where-

---

43. See agreements between Major Coker and G. A. Norwood establishing their partnership and dissolving it. These two documents were drawn by Major Coker (R. G. Coker).

44. Major Coker to Lord and Burke, May 17, 1892 (R. G. Coker).

by it was not necessary to halt production in order to make the frequent cleanings of the apparatus. He was well along with this development in the summer of 1892, though a working model had not then been constructed.[45]

Much less, if any, work had been done on a scheme to install a radically different lining in the digesters, which was also under one of the patents Parsons was to make available. The digester lining was perhaps the most important part of the installation controlled by Parsons, though the linings installed under Parsons' direction had never been completely satisfactory, tending to develop leaks under the influence of the acid. James' arrangements, when eventually worked out, rendered the lining self-sealing. Whereas the original installation had been merely a special mixture of cement laid on the inner side of the steel shell of the digester, he designed the following arrangement: inside the shell he built a lining of brick or tile blocks and left between this lining and the shell a small space. This space he filled with sand. Through the outer steel shell and into this layer of sand there was introduced a salt solution under pressure. This salt solution permeated the sand and reached the inner lining of brick. Where the sulphurous acid broke through the brick lining it met the salt solution and formed there an impervious precipitate.[46]

Neither of these developments, as James and Major Coker paused in the summer of 1892 to await Parsons' next move, were far enough along to be tested. Nevertheless, James and his father had reached the point where a definite decision as to installing a paper machine had to be made. The affirmative decision was reached, and basic to that decision was Major Coker's confidence that one or both of James' inventions would be successful, and that James could handle the pulp-paper combination satisfactorily.

---

45. For description of this apparatus see letter of patent (R. G. Coker). Also, a letter from Major Coker to James, August 13, 1892, indicates that by that date the liquor apparatus had not been installed at Hartsville.

46. See letters of patent (R. G. Coker), U. S. Patent No. 609,733, August 23, 1898.

III

James went North in August to make arrangements for purchasing and installing a paper machine. Experience had been a hard teacher. He proceeded with care, in close consultation with his father by letter, though with increased poise and confidence. Excerpts from Major Coker's letters show their caution. August 4: "Be careful not to pledge us to purchase." August 8: "As to the Horne beating engines, could you not get a price from them writing from Pusey & Jones office? This might give them an idea that we are pretty well informed about prices." August 11: "There is one cost, (machine shop tools), which has been omitted in all estimates, which will likely add $2000 to the present estimate. Then to begin to move will take at least $5000 more—So we must have 45 or 50,000 dollars cash & credit to proceed." August 18: "I think you had best interview Mr. Savery, make out specifications, get *his* best *offer* of terms and then leave the matter open for a few days." August 18: "When you finish up there, perhaps you had best come home after doing what you think best in Washington & we will at once decide and either go forward or postpone the matter."[47]

The decision was to go forward. On September 19 James signed a contract with Pusey and Jones of New York City for the purchase of a Fourdrinier paper machine, the machine to cost $19,050.[48] Construction of the mill began in late September, Major Coker writing James on September 29, "I will be glad to see you back as soon as you can get away, as I do not feel competent to carry on the building (even the foundation)."[49]

Building and installation proceeded during the winter of 1892-93 and was substantially completed in March of 1893 when Major Coker, reporting to the stockholders, summed up the situation:

Since our last meeting, after taking time to consider what should

---

47. Letters (R. G. Coker).
48. Contract for purchase of machine (R. G. Coker).
49. Letter (R. G. Coker).

PINEY WOODS AND PAPER

be done in the face of W. H. Parsons' refusal to carry out his contract ... it was at last determined with the knowledge and consent of all concerned to add to our plant all that was necessary to manufacture paper and these additions are well on toward completion. For linings for our Digesters we are using a device of J. L. Coker, Jr. which will soon be ready to be tested and which we hope will prove successful. ... Our great problem is, can we use our wood in making a sulphite stock which can be economically made into good and saleable paper. If we can we can go forward hopefully; if we cannot it will be for you to consider what next to do. ... I will not discuss these questions, we will soon be in position to make such trials as will show whether or not our pine sulphite can be adapted to the processes of paper making.

We have thought best to get a first-class paper machine, one of Pusey & Jones Co's. build which can turn out 5 to 8 tons of paper per day of 24 hours, and we hope this may be started experimentally about April 1st. Below is statement showing the condition of our company on March 1st 1893 which I beg to submit for your careful examination and verification.[50]

Major Coker's word "experimental" was apt. Small trial runs were made during the summer with indifferent success.[51] One bright spot was the fact that James' digester linings and liquor-making apparatus operated satisfactorily. Apparently it was thought that some of the difficulties that they were encountering lay in the pine wood itself, for samples of wood were sent to the paper engineering firm of Griffin & Little in Boston where the wood was converted to pulp. The report of this firm, submitted on September 13, 1893, was encouraging both as to quality and cost.[52] Operations proceeded on a larger scale as difficulties were overcome.

Yet there was one further hard lesson to be learned in industrial production: that in the shift from experimental to full scale operation unforeseen problems almost always develop. For James and the Major the new problem was resin. Resin was no stranger; it is one of the most familiar of things in the South. When the clean juicy wood of a pine tree is cut, resin covers

50. Minute book (R. G. Coker).
51. See correspondence between the Cokers and Griffin and Little (R. G. Coker).
52. Copies of this report (R. G. Coker).

over the wound, sticky and amber colored as it oozes out of the tree. Later, through exposure to air, it turns dark brown and becomes hard and impervious.

The Cokers knew that resin would give their paper a light brown coloring and would appear as occasional dark blemishes in the paper. This was of relatively little importance since their intention was to make rough wrapping paper. They had known from the beginning that the sulphurous acid did not dissolve the resin; that it merely separated most of the resin from the wood fibers. For that reason the heartwood, which has a high resin content, had not been used. Presumably, the problem of the remaining resin found in the sapwood was solved in the washing of the pulp, where most of the resin detached by the acid from the wood fibers was washed and screened out of the pulp along with other extraneous materials. Indeed, not enough resin remained in any one cook of pulp to affect the quality of the paper made from that amount of pulp.

In the continuous process of converting pulp into paper on the great new paper machine, however, the remaining particles of resin would collect on the meshed wire screen onto which the pulp was poured. After even a short period of operation, these blobs of resin became quite large, and the result was paper containing many weak watermarked spots—paper that was commercially useless. The resin stuck hard to the wire screen; removing it was difficult and time consuming. What was supposed to be a fast and continuing process proceeded in a halting and broken way.

Local efforts failing, experienced paper makers were brought in from the North during 1894 and 1895. The sum total of progress was the discovery that kerosene would remove the resin from the wire screen with least effort, but this did not solve the problem satisfactorily. A poor, non-commercial grade of paper was the product. After almost six years of effort, at a cost of around $120,000, operations were unprofitable and prospects gloomy.[53]

53. Conversation with Mr. Howard Edwards, Cedartown, Georgia, who was working then at the Carolina Fiber Company as Superintendent. Later he held the offices of Secretary and of Treasurer.

PINEY WOODS AND PAPER

These years had been hard on James. Several times the strain had made him too ill to work. Still he kept on at the resin problem. Some time, probably in 1896, his attention turned from the manufacturing process to the wood itself and the pieces of a solution began to fall into place. Always a close student of nature, he noticed that old, weathered wood did not have the high resin content of fresh-cut green wood. Going to the pine fields, he discovered that wood cut in the late spring or early summer when the sap was rising and left to lie where cut for several months, with the bark and limbs on, contained less resin than did wood handled otherwise.[54]

This discovery was the key. Some resin remained in wood treated in this fashion, but not enough to impede operations. The last important manufacturing hurdle was over. For the first time, anywhere, and in quantity, southern pine was converted chemically into paper in the little village. A new era was made specific to Hartsville, and a town born. On March 9, 1898, at a meeting of the stockholders, Major Coker ". . . made some remarks on the business outlook for the year, which he thought were rather brighter than heretofore."[55]

IV

The outlook was indeed brighter, and the whole family knew it. On February 14, 1899, the Major's second son, David, wrote the third son, Will, that the mill ". . . is worth 100,000 more than it was 2 years ago."[56] This was a main turning point, whose effects were far reaching in the years to come. A bold new step had been taken, with success, and it was example and encouragement for other steps to be taken later. James had brought his learning home; he and the Major had put it to use. Industry was now in Hartsville, and there was another string to the bow.

All through the nineties the total resources of the farms and

54. Conversation with W. C. Coker, Chapel Hill, N.C., and with Mr. Howard Edwards.
55. Minute book of Stockholders' and Directors' meetings of the Carolina Fiber Company (R. G. Coker).
56. D. R. Coker to W. C. Coker, February 14, 1899 (W. C. Coker).

the store had been required to support the costly work at the paper mill. These were now released, and to these were added the annual increments from the paper mill. There were others in the family at Hartsville who wanted to kick up their heels. The Major did not stop them.

The new developments grew out of what was going on at Hartsville. The first new activity began in 1899.[57] The Cokers were making rough paper; the Major, from his Darlington experience, knew a good deal about cotton manufacture. There was a considerable relation between the two, for the great amount of cotton yarn that does not go directly to the loom after it is spun, but is stored and transported, is wound on paper cones. The paper cones are about six inches high and about two inches at their largest, or bottom diameter, from which they taper almost to a point at the top. Many millions are used each year, and they are expendable.

At that time, in 1899, making cones was a simple and largely hand operation. A single operator ran a small, foot powered machine, the operation being very similar to that of a foot powered sewing machine. The shaped paper was fed into the machine, where it was wet with glue and wrapped around a steel cone. The paper cone thus formed was hung to dry in a loft.

The Cokers, having paper and knowing something of the cotton mill business, decided to go into cone making. They would also make paper tubes, this usually being a correlative job with cone making, since the principle was virtually the same. They brought W. F. Smith, an experienced cone maker, to Hartsville from New Bedford, Massachusetts, and went to work. The main facts are clear, but there is some confusion as to how Mr. Smith was contacted. One version has it that Mr. Smith, wanting to go out on his own from the Pairpont Company, where he worked in New Bedford, advertised in a trade journal for partners with capital. Major Coker responded and the connection was made. Another version has it that James and Mr. Smith, total strangers, struck up a casual conversation

---

57. J. L. Coker, *Hartsville, Its Early Settlers*, p. 36.

on a train; that each talked about his work, and from this came the interest that resulted in cone making in Hartsville. Perhaps both versions are essentially true.

Whatever the case, it is certain that James did the early talking and that he was highly stimulated in regard to the technical details, and that Major Coker guided the business arrangements. All of this appears from the following letter from the Major to Mr. Smith that certified the undertaking:

Mr. Walter P. Smith 3/20 9
    New Bedford, Mass.
Dear Sir:

Yours of 17th recd. I supposed after your conversation with my son everything was understood—But am quite willing to put everything in writing.

Here is what I think to be the scheme.

1st Form a company   capital about $3000.
    for machines and working capital
    For lot and building say   2000.
Incorporate this company if you wish.

2. We subscribe for and pay in sixty per cent of this capital. 60% of 5000—is $3000.

3. You to give your time to the mechanical work, building the machines at our shops, and superintending the mill when built. We to attend to the finances, selling, keeping & collecting accounts.

If you would prefer to keep the capital only $3000 & rent building that will be all right but I think the purchasing of house & lot would be better for the company, but that may be as you prefer.

This company would of course furnish paper as low as it could be bought elsewhere or else the new company would be expected to buy where it could buy cheapest.

I just now have a letter from McColl Manufacturing Company in adjoining county saying, they use cones like your no 1—6000 per day and pay for them 2.25 per thousand.

Answer this at once and oblige.

                       Yours truly,
                       J. L. Coker[58]

[58]. This letter copied from Major Coker's letter book, pp. 295-96 (R. G. Coker).

Now Mr. Smith had not been to Hartsville when he agreed to the above arrangements. When he did come he arrived at night. He was put off the train in the dark, in a cotton field in front of the Major's and James' houses. James guided him to his home by lantern light, and before he crossed the threshold, Mr. Smith had made, and expressed to James, his decision to depart by first conveyance and never return. A good dinner did not improve his humor. Somewhat desperately, James took him forthwith to the paper mill on Black Creek. They did not return until the small hours of the morning, and they were absorbed in their talk and plans. The paper mill, in good operation, had convinced Mr. Smith that perhaps something, after all, could be made in Hartsville.[59] Operations were soon set up in an old tobacco warehouse.[60]

The company, that was begun in this way, and on a subscribed stock of $3,000, is today the pre-eminent producer of cones in the world. It is complex and mechanized, a service industry basic to all textile operations, and is the largest activity of the Cokers. All of this was to come slowly and is a story to be told fully in later pages, where it takes shape around new mechanical developments in cone making, and around the guidance of the Major's youngest son, Charles.

One of the Major's main helpers on the farms, in the store and in school activity at Hartsville during these years of the nineties had been his son-in-law, J. J. Lawton, who had married the Major's oldest child, Margaret. Joe Lawton was born in Allendale, in Barnwell County, South Carolina, on April 18, 1861, the son of a country doctor. He attended Furman University, and in 1883 came to Hartsville as farm manager for the Major. In 1884 he became a partner in the store.[61]

Joe Lawton was eternally vigorous and energetic, and the Major had a way of saying that if he wanted something done

---

59. This account given by Mrs. J. L. Coker, Jr.
60. J. L. Coker, *Hartsville, Its Early Settlers*, p. 57.
61. Ruth Lawton Wilds, "Biography of J. J. Lawton," typed MS, March 23, 1934 (E. H. Lawton).

at a certain time and place, he would tell Joe Lawton and it would be done as specified.[62]

In 1900 J. L. Coker and Company—being by this time a three-way partnership between the Major, his second son, David, and Joe Lawton—built a cotton oil mill in Hartsville.[63] While this, like the store, was a partnership, Joe Lawton became president, and the oil mill was his special concern. Under his management it was immediately successful.

Also in 1900, rounding out the use of local resources, there was established a cotton mill.[64] This was not a Coker project in origination, but the Major and the others encouraged it, and the Major was a very large stockholder.

By 1900, also, the beginnings of the great venture into seed breeding had been made, though without conscious design at the time, and without awareness of where these beginnings would lead.

62. Conversation with Mrs. D. R. Coker.
63. J. L. Coker, *Hartsville, Its Early Settlers*, pp. 37-38.
64. *Ibid.*, pp. 38-39.

7

David Coker and Pedigreed Seed

I

DAVID, THE MAJOR's second son, graduated from South Carolina College in 1891, with a degree in liberal arts. Coming home, he went to work in the store where, as Caleb and the Major before him, he faced in all directions toward the southern cotton economy. In 1897 bad health caused him to leave daily work at the store temporarily.[1] During this interval he turned to growing things, letting his mind and curiosity run freely, for there was no urgency about what he was doing, and the point was as he chose to make it.

I recall particularly how he surprised me and others by inventing (so far as I know) a method of filling out gaps in his sweet corn rows by transplanting extra shoots from the other hills. He would twist off about half the length of all the leaves and add a small amount of water, losing very few of the transplanted plants.[2]

In the spring of 1898 David carefully measured off four plots of ground near his home. Three he fertilized variously, one not at all. In each of the four plots he planted, in equal amounts, four varieties of cotton. The growing of the cotton was carefully observed during the summer, and that fall the harvest was carefully measured. The results were published by the Clemson College Experiment Station,[3] but before that they

---

1. *Coker's Pedigreed Seed Catalogue,* Spring, 1927, p. 1.
2. Letter to author from W. C. Coker, August 16, 1949.
3. "Varieties of Cotton," *South Carolina Agricultural Experiment Station Bulletin,* 42 (March, 1899), p. 7.

had been discussed with the Major, who, on almost exactly the same spot, had conducted altogether similar experiments in that now long ago time before the Civil War.

For that matter, all others in the family were interested also, not in an intense, dedicated way over the specific results, but in the way of a family that enfolded Nature as a topic of conversation, a delight, a spiritual resource, an intellectual avocation. The children's growing years at Hartsville had been outdoor years, where their waking interests were almost synonymous with the great variety and color of growing things. It was a great day when a new story could be told—of, say, a frog meticulously shedding his skin, rolling it into a round ball and popping it into his mouth. The Major talked of Nature to the children, sitting together on the piazza or walking through the woods on Sunday afternoons. All the children were keen students, with respect for Nature's inexorable processes, and there was in the family the feeling that to work with Nature was worthy of a person's time and energy and best efforts.[4]

In fact, at this very time when David was experimenting, his next younger brother, Will, was at Johns Hopkins University working toward his doctorate in Botany. In 1900, probably, Will made a talk to the Botanical Club of the Department of Agriculture in Washington. On that occasion he met Dr. H. J. Webber, just recently placed in charge of the Department's cotton breeding program. Webber introduced Will to the exciting possibility of breeding plants, especially cotton, as one did animals, so as to fix desirable characteristics in field plantings, and to eliminate undesirable characteristics. Will, of course, brought this information home to Hartsville, and the Major and David became interested.[5] In July of 1901, the Major with his usual care to see that the boys' enthusiasm did not exceed reality, invited Dr. Webber to come to Hartsville. Webber was glad "... to call on you and look over the agricultural features of your locality to some extent."[6] There

4. Conversation with W. C. Coker.
5. *Ibid.*
6. Dr. H. J. Webber to Major Coker, August 9, 1901 (Watson collection).

was a meeting of minds. And of resources, for Webber's funds were limited and the Cokers could help in some of his work. During the following winter and spring, Major Coker sent Dr. Webber three quarts of Jones Big Boll cotton seed for use in his experiments, and at Hartsville Dr. Webber asked the Cokers to plant two varieties of Egyptian long staple cotton seed and a single variety of peas.[7]

The central interest, however, was to improve, through breeding, one of the domestic upland cottons—to develop a productive, long staple cotton that could be grown at Hartsville and throughout the South. As to ways and means, David was quite interested, but he had in the meantime returned to the store as manager of the buying and selling, and therefore could not give full time to the work. Will's roommate at Johns Hopkins was Daniel N. Shoemaker, "a big-boned, red haired farmer in appearance,"[8] who expected to finish his doctoral work in 1902 and was also interested in plant breeding. Arrangements were made for Shoemaker to come in 1902 to teach at the Welsh Neck High School at Hartsville and, in conjunction with David, to carry on the breeding work.

In the fall of 1901 Will and Shoemaker came to Hartsville from Baltimore and from a field on the plantation selected thirty outstanding plants, taking the seed from these plants to be used as the basis of breeding. During the next crop year of 1902 the seed from each of the plants was planted in a separate row, the thirty rows being side by side so that the yield of the progeny from each stalk could be compared. That fall Shoemaker selected a number of the most outstanding plants from these rows, and in 1903 these were planted as before—the seed from each plant in a separate row. In 1903 Shoemaker departed to take full time work with the U. S. Department of Agriculture, leaving the breeding entirely to David, and from this time onward it was to be the center of his work.[9]

David's object was to breed ". . . a productive, large boll,

7. Major Coker to Dr. H. J. Webber, February 11, 1902, and C. W. Coker to Dr. H. J. Webber, May 12, 1902 (Watson collection).
8. Letter to author from W. C. Coker, August 16, 1949.
9. *Coker's Pedigreed Seed Catalogue*, Spring, 1927, p. 1.

high percent variety that will run 1¼ in the field."[10] Increased staple length was the main object, but it had to be associated with high yield and other desirable characteristics, else it would have no commercial value. These desired characteristics were present in isolated plants; by planting a row from the seed of a single plant, David was seeking to find the plant that would reproduce itself uniformly, rather than reproducing some good and some bad plants. He was looking for a climax row, from a plant prepotent to reproduce itself. There was no such row in 1904, nor in 1905.

In 1906 the good row appeared. It "was the most beautiful and uniform row of cotton up to that time that I had ever seen. It had large round bolls, was very fruitful and open-growing, with a strong wiry 1-3/16 staple."[11] Perhaps this was the climax row, and only further testing would provide the answer. The seed from this entire row—identified as row 16-1-2-4-1—were saved, along with those of several other outstanding rows so that comparison could be made. These seed were put both to plant-to-row tests and increased in larger plots during 1907. The 16-1-2-4-1 maintained its leadership.[12] In the plant-to-row tests based on the best individual plants it had a very high production "the lint of which will average I think, 1-3/16 to 1¼. If it should run 1¼ I will have attained the mark for which I have been so long working for. I know that its productiveness is far beyond that of ordinary short staple cotton and has all the other desirable features including the very large boll."[13]

The 16-1-2-4-1 row again proved superior to other progeny in the 1908 tests. This particular strain had now been bred since the first selected planting in 1902. It had steadily increased in uniformity of staple length, so that under normal growing conditions it would produce a uniform 1-3/16 inch staple. Under excellent conditions it would produce an inch and a quarter

---

10. D. R. Coker to Messrs. D. M. Jones & Co., Gastonia, N. C., November 16, 1907, in store books of J. L. Coker and Company (Mrs. D. R. Coker).
11. *Coker's Pedigreed Seed Catalogue*, Spring, 1927, p. 1.
12. *Ibid.*
13. D. R. Coker to Robert Chapman, January (date illegible), 1908, in store books of J. L. Coker & Company (Mrs. D. R. Coker).

staple, and only in crop failure conditions would the staple run less than one and an eighth inches. This cotton had the desirable large bolls, fifty-five of which would add up to a pound of cotton, and almost every stalk would produce a pound of seed cotton. The percentage of lint in every pound of seed cotton was commercially adequate. Uniformity and prepotency had been established. An upland staple cotton, practicable to plant and cultivate, yielding well in comparison to short staple cottons and, above all, eligible for a premium on its extra staple, had been established. David had come close to "the mark for which I have been so long working for." Having reached this climax where these characteristics seemed definitely fixed he named the new variety Hartsville, increased it as much as possible in 1909, and that fall and winter sold the seed to many farmers in the Hartsville area for planting in the spring of 1910.[14]

II

As something to occupy a young man's curiosity breeding cotton was altogether satisfactory; as an accomplished fact, with the result plainly set forth, it represented at least a commendable achievement. But whatever affected cotton was a vital and practical matter in the lives of every person in the Hartsville area. The Cokers' position in the community virtually guaranteed a trial for the new cotton; this position also required that they not lead the farmers up a blind alley, and there had been considerable general skepticism about the breeding being worthwhile. The new cotton had to stand or fall in the market place. Nor was David irresponsible; he would not sell seed that would produce unmarketable cotton: "We want to sell the seed . . . to farmers in this neighborhood, but first wish good assurances that we can get a premium for this cotton . . ."[15]

There were certain historical difficulties that made the mills wary of upland staples:

14. *Coker's Pedigreed Seed Catalogue,* Spring, 1927, p. 1.
15. D. R. Coker to Messrs. D. M. Jones & Co., November 16, 1907, in store books of J. L. Coker & Company (Mrs. D. R. Coker).

DAVID COKER AND PEDIGREED SEED

Previous to 1907, small amounts of "Allen," "Floradora," "Sunflower" and other varieties of staple cotton were planted in this territory. Whenever staple premiums were high the acreage expanded considerably, only to decrease to practically nothing when premiums went under 3 cents per lb. These cottons, being much less productive than short staple sorts, could not be planted profitably where they command a premium of less than 3 to 5 cents per lb. This in and out movement of these varieties prevented the establishment of the staple industry on a firm basis. The seed rapidly became mixed, and the product was very unsatisfactory to the mills using it. So much so that I have never talked with a mill man who had ever spun a bale of these older staple varieties from this section who would buy any more of it at any price.[16]

Nevertheless, David had begun as early as 1904 to test out the possibilities of the market. While saving the most outstanding plants for breeding purposes, he had from the beginning used many of the other plants of slightly less excellent character for field plantings on the Hartsville plantation. These produced good cotton of extra length, and in 1904 he shipped to a Boston cotton broker ". . . nine B/c Marked J. L. S. strict to G. M. with about 1¼ in. staple . . . would be glad to have your opinion as to whether this cotton is worth more than our ordinary short staple uplands."[17]

The mixed reception accorded the upland staple is revealed in a later letter to the same brokerage firm. "Yours of Jan. 11 to hand. We are a little surprised at what you say of our J. L. S. cotton. We shipped a part of this same lot to Philadelphia and our broker reports it as about 1-3/16 inch which is about what we expected. He also reports that it will bring some premium over ordinary uplands on that market."[18] While the cotton brokers did not fall over themselves in enthusiasm, there was sufficient encouragement to keep on. In 1907 twenty-three bales "sold for 2c premium and the second

16. Address by D. R. Coker before Darlington County Agricultural Society, Mineral Springs, August 13, 1912, published in the *Hartsville Messenger*, August 22, 1912.
17. D. R. Coker to Messrs. Barry Thayer & Co., December 30, 1904, in store books of J. L. Coker & Company (Mrs. D. R. Coker).
18. *Ibid.*, January 13, 1905.

picking is just being ginned and we will not offer it for less than 12½c."[19]

In November of 1907 he made what seems to have been a major and considered move. To D. M. Jones and Co. of Gastonia, N.C., he sent

samples representing a lot of 49 bales of cotton which we have on hand.... This cotton is the second picking from 110 acres on our farm and is descended from a stalk selected by the writer in 1902, from one stalk in 1903 and from two stalks in 1904. By this breeding the writer had substantially lengthened the lint and increased the productiveness of this cotton and found no difficulty in selling the first picking of 23 bales at 2c premium over ordinary short cotton.

We class this cotton as full 1⅛ staple and have submitted it to several experts, none of which have classed it below this. Please submit these samples to some of your mills and let us know the best offers you can get and what your commission charge for selling will be.[20]

The forty-nine bales were eventually sold in New England through a Norfolk broker, but David clung to the necessity of proving the case to the mills: "I wish you would before next fall ascertain from the manufacturers who spin the 23 bales #16 sold you early in the season and the 49 bales which are now going forward, how they regard the spinning qualities of the cotton. Possibly they may be willing to give us an order through you for a round lot from this seed next fall."[21] Again and again there appeared the conviction that a successful market could be established, ". . . if the mills will cooperate with me and contract with me and other responsible parties for the product of my extra staple seed."[22]

A clean shot at the South Carolina mill owners, who were

19. D. R. Coker to R. W. Merritt, October 24, 1907, in store books of J. L. Coker & Company (Mrs. D. R. Coker).
20. D. R. Coker to Messrs. D. M. Jones & Co., November 16, 1907, in store books of J. L. Coker & Company (Mrs. D. R. Coker).
21. D. R. Coker to John H. Rogers, February 5, 1908, in store books of J. L. Coker & Company (Mrs. D. R. Coker).
22. D. R. Coker to Robert Chapman, January (date illegible), 1908, in store books of J. L. Coker & Company (Mrs. D. R. Coker).

DAVID COKER AND PEDIGREED SEED 139

by this time a considerable number, came along in 1908. He was invited to speak before the South Carolina Association of Cotton Manufacturers in June of 1908 on the subject of his plant breeding. He went straight to the point:

... The State of South Carolina now produces an average cotton crop of about one million bales per annum. The mills of the State consume over three-quarters of a million bales, but purchase a large percentage of their requirements in Mississippi and Alabama. This shows that much of the cotton produced here is not suited to the needs of our spinners. In fact it is well known that the average staple of the North and South Carolina crops is shorter than any produced elsewhere in the United States. The mills of these States requiring cotton longer than one inch are, therefore, losing a part of the advantage to which their position in the cotton belt entitles them.

... The real value of a pound of cotton is the sum of its spinning qualities, and when the spinning value, and that alone, everywhere determines the price, inferior and undesirable varieties will quickly disappear and improved types will take their places.

... The plant breeder has already added millions to the value of the grain crops of the North and West, and has revolutionized the tobacco and fruit and truck industries of several States. But though he is now doing some work on the cotton plant, some measure of co-operation from the mills will be necessary if his efforts are to have in this section the prompt and important results that they have had over wide areas in other parts of this country.[23]

The Association appropriated a thousand dollars to help the extension service promote good cotton seed; August Kohn sent the speech to the newspapers, saying, "It may be a fad, but it is a good one, and one that will mean much to the cotton planters of South Carolina."[24] But the case was not made. In general, the mill owners were little better organized, or more progressive minded, than the farmers. In fact relatively few of the South Carolina mills used staple cotton.

It remained for David, in most cases, to go to the individual

23. D. R. Coker's speech to the South Carolina Association of Cotton Manufacturers, June 11, 1908, reprinted in the *Hartsville Messenger*, June 18, 1908.

24. In Mr. Kohn's preface to David's speech, the *Hartsville Messenger*, June 18, 1908.

mill treasurer. Taking with him samples of cotton, he urged, pleaded and even begged the mills to give the new cotton a trial. He went also to North Carolina, where there were more mills using staple cotton than in South Carolina. In this way he made as many as possible of the North and South Carolina mill men aware of the possibilities of upland staple, and a few seemed willing to use it in quantity, notably Lewis W. Parker of Greenville, South Carolina, and Andrew E. Moore of Gastonia, North Carolina.[25]

He was like a man building a house who was forced to stand one wall up and leave it without support, hoping that it would remain standing until he had raised an adjoining wall. He could not interest the mills substantially in the upland staple on the Hartsville market until the farmers grew this cotton successfully in quantity over a period of several years; he could not in conscience sell the seed and urge the production of staple cotton without there being a reasonably sure market. In this latter he had gone as far as possible.

Thus the situation stood when the first crop of Hartsville cotton came on the market in the fall of 1910. Fortunately, the amount of seed available had been small and consequently only about 700 bales were produced this first year. David bought all or nearly all of this cotton at a good premium and placed it with mills where its spinning performance was satisfactory.[26]

With this good start, and the great amount of proved long staple seed now available in the Hartsville area, 20 per cent of the cotton acreage around Hartsville was planted in long staple cotton in 1911, producing about 2,000 bales. This acreage was successfully grown but difficulties involved in its sale showed David that he had a monster of his own creation on his hands.

The local market simply was not ready to handle this large amount of staple cotton. Aside from David, few of the local

[25] D. R. Coker, "Breeding Work and Status of Coker's Pedigreed Seed Company," in addresses and speeches file, 1929 (Mrs. D. R. Coker).

[26] D. R. Coker, "Long Staple Cotton at Hartsville," in unmarked brown folder, 1917 (Mrs. D. R. Coker).

buyers were prepared to buy and dispose of staple cotton at any considerable premium. Some farmers were disappointed, and David hastened to publish in January of 1912 an explanation of the marketing problem that was peculiar to staple cotton but did not exist in regard to short cotton.

... There is really no standard market for all lengths of long staple cotton in the same sense as for short staple cotton. One week a buyer may have an order for 100 bales of a certain length and grade at a price, and the next week he may be unable to get a bid for the same length and grade from any source. One buyer may have orders for certain lengths and grades, while another buyer is entirely without orders for the same class of cotton, though the second buyer may at the same time have orders for different lengths and grades.

... The suggestion that the owners of long staple cotton should not dispose of it without submitting samples to several buyers is a most excellent one, and one which I have recommended to many of my customers and in several instances I know that, by my advice, they took their cotton to other markets and received better prices for cotton lengths and grade than I could give.

The implication that a buyer is dishonest or ignorant when he offers less for this cotton than another buyer is not warranted.

It is simply a matter of having good orders or not having orders for that particular grade and length.[27]

While adequate local marketing facilities were necessary to maintain the morale for growing staple cotton in quantity in the Hartsville area, it could safely be presumed that a continued mill demand would provide the local buyers. Mill demand for staple cotton depended upon the quality of the cotton, as well as quantity. Since staple cotton was used primarily in fine goods, or where great strength was required, it was necessary that the cotton, in addition to having a long staple, be also of good grade—that is, be clean, dry, strong, and of uniform fiber. As the quantity of staple cotton increased it became evident that much of it was poorly prepared for mar-

27. D. R. Coker, "Market for Long Staple," published in the *Hartsville Messenger*, January 11, 1912.

ket. David undertook energetically to stress the importance of grade in staple cotton.

> ... If possible, the picking should be kept up with closely, as there is a tremendous difference in value between low grades and high grades. In fact, low grades are at times almost unsalable.
>
> ... It is necessary for the farmer to understand all the problems of cultivating and marketing staple cotton in order to handle this business intelligently; and those who go into it in the haphazard, slip-shod way will be much disappointed in results.[28]

Despite these difficulties, in 1912 over 85 per cent of the cotton acreage around Hartsville was planted in staple cotton. The premiums paid for this crop on the average at Hartsville were rewarding. While short cotton sold for 12 cents, the staple cottons were selling on an average between 17 and 18½ cents,[29] and in many instances several cents higher.

In August of 1912 David had reported through the newspaper that "I have, during the summer, visited most of the southern mills to whom I have sold staple cotton during the past few years, and find that all of them are pleased with our cotton and expect to use it largely in the future. I have also visited many New England mills and find their Treasurers willing to give our cotton a fair test this season."[30]

With this success and these prospects practically all of the acreage in the Hartsville area was planted to staple cotton in 1913,[31] and of course by now this planting had begun to spread considerably over a wide area in South Carolina.

The year 1913 turned out to be a poor one.

A cold wet spring made it extremely difficult to secure stands, and there was much replanting. The crop got a late poor start and the growing season, owing to the extremely early frost, was the shortest on record in this section. Under these conditions our staple varie-

---

28. D. R. Coker, "The New Upland Staple Varieties—Shall We Plant Them?" January 1, 1912 (W. C. Coker).

29. *Coker's Pedigreed Seed Catalogue*, Spring, 1923, p. 13.

30. Advertisement of J. L. Coker & Company in the *Hartsville Messenger*, August 22, 1912, signed by D. R. Coker.

31. To Hon. E. J. Watson, January 19, 1941, published in the *Hartsville Messenger*, February 19, 1914.

ties showed up very poorly as compared with that of extra early varieties of cotton, though all farmers who succeeded in getting a stand of staple cotton in April made full crops and were quite satisfied with the results. The extreme depression in the staple spinning industry operated to curtail premiums very materially, and the average price secured for good grade 1-3/16" cotton was only about three cents over the corresponding grade of short staple.[32]

In this situation David continued to feel his responsibility toward the success of what he consistently called the staple cotton industry, although in January of 1912, before the large crop of that year had been planted, he had by circular and paid advertisement in the *Hartsville Messenger* said that "I do not wish the impression to get out that I or my firm are undertaking to guarantee a market for this cotton, here or elsewhere." Despite this, he bought a good deal of cotton in 1913 for which he had no mill orders, and at one time had "about one half million dollars worth of staple cotton, much of which we would not have bought if it had not been for our interest in the Hartsville cotton market."[33] His carry-over that year was eight hundred bales, which were eventually sold as the spinning industry revived.

Such adversity, inevitable in cotton farming, was perhaps timely in 1913, for the uncertain war years were ahead, and it was encouraging to see that the industry had developed a hard core. While some farmers were inclined to abandon the long staple, "I hear no talk among those of our farmers who have been planting staples for three or four years about such abandonment."[34] David's work with staple cotton was to be as unceasing, and as perennial with problems, as agriculture itself, but the passage of this crisis of 1913 was a milestone marking at least the establishment of the industry in the Hartsville area. In 1914, when cotton prices dropped because of the war in Europe, staple cotton fell too; but even so the premium for inch and three-sixteenths cotton was 55.55 per cent at Hartsville, and 75.00 per cent for inch and five-sixteenths.[35]

32. *Ibid.*   33. *Ibid.*
34. *Ibid.*
35. *Coker's Pedigreed Seed Catalogue*, Spring, 1923, p. 13.

Reflecting a condition of several years' standing, the *Columbia State* could write editorially in September of 1917 that "Hartsville, S.C. is one of the principal long staple cotton markets in the State and it is a market in which the producer gets the value of his product, the cotton being carefully graded and the right price paid regardless of local competition or the lack of it in buying." The paper went on to say that it could "give farmers no better advice than that they keep themselves informed in respect of Hartsville."[36]

III

The seed breeding had begun as a personal and limited excursion by a young man with other important jobs. But it did not end so, nor solely with breeding pedigreed seed.

The prospect of agricultural improvement quickened David to growth. It touched all his capacities of mind, spirit and energy, and of ambition; it pulled him outward in expanding circles of awareness and comprehension of the monumental dimensions of that vast, tangled preserve of southern agriculture where little had changed in seventy-five years. It was dangerous to venture forth, for even whole social movements had been swallowed up in the matted growth. Southern agriculture was people and the way they thought and worked, an indestructible heritage; it was lack of education, of doctors, of roads, of market facilities; it was leaching soil and a still colonial economy; and a still unprofitable dedication to cotton.

Yet David really had no choice; he had found his job, and though it gave him no little heartbreak, it called forth all that was in him, and he grew as he worked. In hard times there was renewal from something better growing in the ground; in other times, especially in the young years, there was a joyousness and an insatiable appetite. In 1907 he wrote the South Carolina Experiment Station that

My firm are large handlers of fertilizers and fertilizer ingredients, and the farmers are constantly calling on me to advise as to the best mixtures to apply to the different crops. Recently several of our customers asked me to make them up a formula for their tobacco

36. *Ibid.*, Spring, 1918, p. 12.

crops, they have been using heretofore the 8.3.3 to add from 50 to 100 pounds Sulphate of Potash, with good results. It appears to me now from the analysis of Leaf Tobacco that the large amount of Phosphoric Acid contained in this commercial fertilizer, is not required in this crop, and I have, therefore, worked out three formulae, which I will submit to you and ask for your criticism and suggestion.

The first two have as their phosphatic basis Peruvian Guano. The third, commercial dissolved bone. The cost of the first to the farmer is $13.84, the second is $12.55 and the third is $12.14 put out. The Phosphoric Acid calculated in No. 1 and No. 2 is the total available and unavailable in the Peruvian, but experiments here and elsewhere seem to prove that the total content of this element in Peruvian is readily available.

... I would be glad if you would give me careful opinion on the above and advice that would help me to help the farmers of this section. Please especially advise as to the best forms of Ammonia and Phosphoric Acids for Tobacco and what amount of Phosphoric you consider necessary. I would be pleased to have any bulletins that you may have that will help me. Am particularly anxious to get some tables, showing the plant food removed from the soil by different Southern crops.

He could not stop there. Going on:

I am particularly anxious to get some analyses of Southern corn as compared with Northern corn as I have been informed that the protein and fat of the Southern product is much greater and, if this is true, it should be generally known. If you have no data with reference to corn analyses, would you make some analyses for me if I send you sample of corn raised in this section and of Western corn sold in this market.

In writing me, please give me the analyses of hard wood ashes. Some of our farmers in the sand hill section burn black-jack, red oak and hickory, and use the ashes as fertilizer, and one of them has asked me about its value as a fertilizer. I would also like to have the analysis of pine ashes.

Hoping that the above requests will not be too great a tax on you and assuring you that the information requested is intended for general distribution in this section, I am,[37]

37. To S.C. Experiment Station, Clemson College, January 10, 1906, in store books of J. L. Coker & Company (Mrs. D. R. Coker).

All that he asked was, indeed, "intended for general distribution in this section." To know a thing was, for him, to tell it to the farmers—at the store, on the seed farm, in the streets of Hartsville. In print he had the facility for making matters clear, and with an economy of words. He did not talk down; rather, as have all the Cokers, he thought his advice worth a plain statement. Thus, in the *Hartsville Messenger,* on November 3, 1908:

Time to sow oats, right now. Be sure to prepare your land thoroughly. Use two horses or disc plow if you have one, and harrow thoroughly, making a fine, smooth seed bed. Sow good seed of the best rust proof variety. Two bushels per acre are enough on good land.

200 pounds acid phosphate, 200 pounds kainit and 100 pounds meal now, with 50 to 100 pounds nitrate in the spring should insure you a good yield, if you have properly prepared the land.

Better to sow only one acre on thoroughly prepared land than five acres on clods and turfs.

If your scuppernong vines need trimming and your arbors need fixing up, now is the time to do it. If you wait as late as December to do this work your vines may bleed where they have been cut or broken and your next crop will be small.

Don't wait too long to clean up and plow your garden for next spring. If you plow in a heavy coat of manure in November it will have rotted by spring, and culture will be easier and crops finer than where the manure has been put in late.

You ought to be eating plenty of fall vegetables now. We know of people who have tomatoes, snap beans, butter beans, onions, spinach, lettuce, turnips, Irish potatoes and collards now.

Cut your sugar cane and dig your sweet potatoes right away. If you wait longer, we may have a heavy freeze and ruin these crops.

Don't fail to select your seed corn from the field. Select firm, good, strong, upright stalks that are growing where the stand is perfect.

Select ears that are large and well formed, and that do not grow too high on the stalk.

Save your 25 best ears for "an ear to row" test next year.

Damaged cotton is beginning to come into market.

Cotton is our most valuable crop. It is folly to allow it to rot after it is made.[38]

He recurred time and time again to the dictum that "the scale is the only reliable test."[39] In a culture that often placed high value on tall tales and easy generalizations he was rigorously scientific. "Great harm is constantly being done to the cause of agriculture by men who make positive statements with small basis of fact or experience behind them."[40] Such methods were not entirely foreign to southern agriculture. There had always been a strain of scientific agricultural interest in southern culture, carried especially by such local groups as the Darlington County Agricultural Society. There were by now experiment stations and other agencies who were doing and spreading this type of work. Yet the new methods were virtually unknown to most of the farmers, alien to their folkways, and David was, in his area, breaking the ground as he put them in everyday terms.

IV

David bought cotton in a vacant lot beside J. L. Coker and Co. He saw the cotton farmer as a lonely figure, hauling his cotton to market in a rattling, high sided wagon pulled by a pair of indifferent mules, and outlined against an autumn sky. Hamstrung by debt, bad transportation, and often by ignorance, the farmer sold tight-lipped into a market of which he had little knowledge and less control. So far as he was concerned, the market was the local buyers in Hartsville. The upper limits of the prices these buyers could offer were controlled by the national and world markets. Downward they had considerable leeway.

These buyers bought "hog round"—one price for good cotton and for bad cotton. Exclusive of staple, cotton is bought by grade, and grading cotton is a skill, almost an art,

38. D. R. Coker, "A Few Farm and Garden Notes," published in the *Hartsville Messenger*, November 5, 1908.
39. Speech by D. R. Coker before the Darlington County Agricultural Society, published in the *Hartsville Messenger*, August 18, 1910.
40. *Ibid.*

in which a buyer unceasingly pulls the cotton in his two hands, exposing the basic fiber, feeling its fineness and strength, looking at its evenness, its color and freedom from trash. All these qualities merge together and come out in the resonant sounding grades that begin with "good ordinary" and run through the middling grades (strict, good, strict good) on up to "middling fair." The local buyers as a rule disposed of the cotton to brokers and mills by grade, receiving a premium for the better grades. In buying from the farmers, the "hog round" practice was to pay a single price for all grades,[41] and this price was a lowest common denominator.

A man's good farming had no identity and little reward in such a system. There was no reason to grow good cotton, prepare it well, and take an intelligent interest in the market for no gain at all. This local situation reflected the fact that the world's cotton markets were bulk markets where the great mass of poor grade cotton was a sodden weight on the whole structure.

When in 1897 David began buying cotton, the "hog round" method was in operation at Hartsville, with one other large buyer and several smaller buyers in the market. David began to buy cotton by grade. After he had determined the grade of each bale of a farmer's cotton as it was hauled up on the wagon and sampled, he would write down on a piece of paper the grade, and the price he was willing to offer that day for that grade.[42] The farmer could then accept the offer, or he could take his piece of paper, and his cotton, to the other buyers, seeking their best price with a firm offer in hand. Whatever his choice, the farmer knew just what grade he had for sale, what its current market value was, and he had it all in writing. There was of course some opposition from other local buyers, but in a short while they were forced to adopt his practice of writing down the grade and price, and of buying each bale at something like its true market value.

41. From personal recollection of W. H. Sory, Coker Cotton Company, Hartsville. See also letter from D. R. Coker to H. P. Ferris, September 17, 1936 (Mrs. D. R. Coker).

42. *Ibid.*

So light began to filter through and illuminate the business of cotton. A farmer would take or leave a price on his cotton; there was little arguing with the market. Grade was a matter of determination by the individual, on the basis of what the eye could see and the hand could feel. It was low grade because it was blue tinged, or dirty, or full of trash, or had been badly cut up at the gin, or had been ginned when wet, or picked too early or too late, or a combination of several or all of these factors.

Naturally, a farmer would say something, in pleasure or disappointment, about the grading of his cotton. This was what David was looking for. Thousands of times, on almost every possible occasion, he would point out to the farmer just why the cotton was graded as it was, what was right and what was wrong with it. If it was mixed as to texture, fiber strength, staple length and other qualities, then obviously the seed had been badly mixed and he told the farmer so. David struck particularly at the senseless loss of good cotton through poor preparation.

Through these efforts that continued all his life, David sought to make the farmer a full, responsible participant in the transaction of selling his cotton, rather than a mute grower and hauler whose work-scarred hands were merely folded in patience at the market place. So far as the Hartsville area was concerned, he was largely successful; but the price limits, after grade and staple had been ascertained, were set by the national and world markets, and these were often crazy dervishes.

V

At best, the cotton farmer could do but poorly. Growing little else but unprofitable cotton, he was only half at work. So was his land, where little of food for man and feed for animals was grown. Cotton robbed the soil in summer, and left open fields to leach in winter. David knew this; so also did many others. David Rogerson Williams had known it; the Major had known; Captain Coker had demonstrated it in the 1860's. There was no secret; any weekly newspaper of the times was full of it.

There were many reasons why it was difficult to make a change. The most stubborn, the first and last, was the simple fact that cotton brought in considerably more cash money per acre than any other crop that could at that time be grown generally over the South. If the labor of women and children be discounted; if the rent of the land, and above this the excessive erosion, not be counted in; and if the absence of adequate schools, roads and community and health facilities be otherwise culturally compensated for, then the cash money that cotton always brought in was not inconsiderable. It was in fact the people's life, for today and for tomorrow. As a Hartsville editor wrote in torment: "What can he do? He must pay his debts to the merchant, the merchant must pay what he owes to the wholesale dealer and said dealer must account to the manufacturer or jobber."[43]

By the turn of the century the South had virtually forgotten how to grow corn, and the yields of oats and wheat were pitiful. These crops had not been brought to any kind of economic adequacy under specific southern conditions of soil, climate, growing season and hazards of disease. Midwestern corn and small grains could not be grown in the South. If it was illiberal to ignore the South's position of advantage in regard to the world's supply of cotton, it was also foolish to talk of raising food and feed and of growing cover crops until an obvious economic reason for growing these crops could be demonstrated.

For the latter, David, though heavily involved in store work and in the early breeding of the Hartsville cotton, did not miss the first promising development that came along.

... In the winter of 1904-5 I heard much talk of a remarkable yield of corn made by Mr. McIver Williamson on about ten acres of his farm. This land was said to be poor and light and the yield was reported as 84 bushels average—the best two acres producing 125

---

43. Editorial in the *Hartsville Messenger*, October 26, 1911.

bushels per acre. These figures were later confirmed by Mr. Williamson.

I was not long in finding out that Mr. Williamson was using a method of culture very different from that in common use, and a few questions as to his previous experience convinced me that he had made a discovery of incalculable benefit to the South and had demonstrated its value in a way so conclusive that none could doubt who took the pains to investigate.[44]

He joined Mr. Williamson in testing carefully and publicizing the new method, in the usual practical way. He concluded bluntly: "The Williamson method has knocked out the last prop of the all-cotton-raising, corn-buying Southern farmer, and those who are still buying the sorry, damp stuff that brokers sell for Western corn deserve very little sympathy."[45]

He had already begun to test out winter cover crops and found that a variety of Italian rye known as Abruzzi contributed more humus to the soil than any of the other cover crops then adapted to the eastern South. He began to breed oats in 1908, the year young George Wilds came to help with the work. There was some progress in these early years, but this is a story to be told later, for climax results were a long, patient time coming. What is important is to note that this direction of breeding reflected his increasing awareness of the dimensions of the southern agricultural problem, and his tendency to couple advocacy with field work.

It seems clear that in David's mind the framework of the "new agriculture of the South" was to be described in two terms: diversification and specialization. "At first these terms may seem contradictory but they are not.... The first would prevent the tremendous outgo of money for products that can be more profitably raised at home, the second would give us money crops of the highest possible quality and the greatest

44. D. R. Coker, "Factors Limiting Corn Production in the Cotton Belt—How Some of Them Can Be Removed," speech before County Agents of the Farm Demonstration Bureau, Clemson College, February 13, 1914, published in the *Hartsville Messenger*, March 5, 1914.

45. D. R. Coker's preface to Mr. Williamson's article in the *Hartsville Messenger*, April 16, 1908.

value in dollars and cents. All over the South we see instances of communities taking up a special crop and becoming prosperous by learning how to grow and market it successfully. The cabbage and cabbage plant industry of Young Island, S.C., the strawberry industry of Chadbourn, N.C., the tobacco industries of Mullins, S.C. and of Quincy, Fla. (both entirely different from each other) and the celery industry of Sanford, Fla., are all illustrations in point."[46] The staple cotton industry at Hartsville was also an illustration in point.

The South has wonderful agricultural possibilities but no country can develop fully as long as it scatters its energies too much. Each section should have one or more specialties, every feature of which should be thoroughly learned by the farmer. The marketing also must be thoroughly studied.[47]

"Staple cotton is a specialty" and of course had a limited market. It could not be grown to supply the bulk markets of the world. Nevertheless, it was becoming increasingly obvious that the general cotton farmer must of necessity become a skilled producer. Neither the land nor the people could exist indefinitely under the system of extensive planting on any and all kinds of land that produced small yields per acre. A minimum goal had to be ". . . a severe reduction of the cotton acreage, but not a reduction of the crop."[48] This would free the land for growing food and feed, for cover crops and for developing other money crops. This required an increasing skill and competence on the part of the cotton farmer, new and better ways of cultivation, attention to preparation, and an appreciation of the value of pedigreed seed. The attainable objective, as David saw it in these prewar years, when there existed a great world market for American cotton, was the planting by the average cotton farmers of not more than 50 per cent of

---

46. D. R. Coker, untitled manuscript dated March 9, 1915 (Mrs. D. R. Coker).
47. *Ibid.*
48. D. R. Coker, "The New Agriculture in the South and Its Relation to the Cotton Spinning Industry," speech delivered before the National Association of Cotton Manufacturers at their Annual Meeting, April 23-24, 1913, in Boston, Massachusetts.

his cultivated land in cotton, the remainder being devoted to corn, oats, and to food for home consumption.

VI

During these early years, David's office was at the back part of J. L. Coker and Co. Storekeeping, seed breeding, cotton buying, and general agricultural advice were all mingled together. His office adjoined the bookkeeping and credit departments, those timeless crossroads of southern agriculture, where farmers came to establish their credit and pay their bills. His door was always open, and there were few who passed who did not stop to talk. Later when the seed breeding and the cotton buying required a separate building, his office there was at the entrance, and his window opened on the sidewalk. Again the door was always open, and so was the window in good weather. Perhaps through no other window has so much agricultural advice passed.

He was thus reminded daily who it was that worked the land, raised families on it, who, indeed, put the seed in the ground. These people were the intermediaries between advice and practice. They were people for whom he had abiding respect, the yeomanry of the South—like the Cokers at New Providence, or, by and large, like the men in the Major's company. They were the personalized objectives of his work, always present, both means and end. It was part of his idealism to visualize them as independent, educated, they and their families living fully in the main stream of American life.

This objective was the common, unifying element of his work. As it became clearer it emerged powerfully simple—somehow Jeffersonian and yet having a recurring pertinence to the efforts of a modern America. He began to talk more and more of a sound "rural civilization" as a necessary and fundamental part of an industrial America.

Yet in David's lifetime the independent farmer was passing out of southern agriculture, day by day, gradually but surely. "Recent statistics show that in most of the Southern states including South Carolina our lands are getting into the hands of fewer owners and that the tenant farmers are growing in number year by year."[49] The tenant alone was not concerned, for:

No agricultural country has ever become permanently prosperous where the lands were owned in large bodies by a few people. Some means must be devised to enable the industrious tenant farmer to purchase land. Under the present condition of affairs he has small incentive to industry and economy and no hope of ever owning a home. If he is improving the place he is living on, the chances are that the rent will be raised or that he will be forced to move. 93 per cent of the tenant farmers of the South remain on one place not more than three years and about 50 per cent of them move every year.[50]

He returned always to the central theme: "How can men become happy and prosperous citizens and raise their families in reasonable comfort under such blighting conditions?"[51] And then to specific action: "We must have legislation by which the state and National government will assist these farmers to own their homes and the bankers are well equipped to lead in the agitation for proper legislation along this line of rural credits."[52]

In certain respects tenancy and related human problems constituted the southern agricultural problem. Certainly it was possible to begin with the tenant, expand the analysis to include the factors that produced him and influenced him, and thereby have both an understanding and the basis of a program for the improvement of southern agriculture. David's increasing awareness of the human and cultural factors pertinent to the South led him to just such an analysis. He delivered it before the Darlington County Agriculture Society in 1915, under the title of "How Our Agriculture Can Be Improved." The emphasis upon tenancy and related matters was sufficiently new for him to be careful to say beforehand that he knew many of

---

49. D. R. Coker, "The Relation of the Banker to the Farmer," undated manuscript, apparently written in 1915 (Mrs. D. R. Coker).
50. *Ibid.*
51. *Ibid.*
52. *Ibid.*

DAVID COKER AND PEDIGREED SEED

his listeners would be surprised at both the points included and the priority of their listing.

I. I believe that our industrious white tenants must be more permanently attached to the soil, either by long term leases, or by actual ownership of the land, the second vastly to be preferred. Year by year our lands are coming into fewer hands, and the proportion of farm tenants is increasing. I am told that 50 per cent of Southern farm tenants move every year, and that 93 per cent move at least once every three years. Such a condition is fatal to general prosperity and advancing citizenship. It retards the development of schools, good roads, and good government, for few can be induced to take much interest in these questions who do not expect to permanently identify themselves with any community. Nor can we have a rational system of crop rotation and soil improvement under a shifting tenant system.

II. I will mention as next in importance rural sanitation. Families that are permanently settled and disposed to industry cannot make progress of any kind without good health. Sections of our country are almost annually visited by malaria and typhoid fever. Almost the whole country was ravaged this spring by dysentery, and thousands of children were carried off by it. A man of the finest and truest Darlington County type, an intimate friend of mine, recently died in an adjoining county with a complication of typhoid and dysentery. Hookworm is still prevalent in large sections of the State, including our own county, and tuberculosis is common. All of these are preventable diseases, and our people must be instructed as to the importance of preventing them. The appointment of a county health officer I believe to be the first and most important step in this direction.

III. Proper cooperation with the State and National Agricultural Agencies would do much to hasten the improvement of agriculture. Our most intelligent farmers should try to aid in the direction of the activities of these agencies. They have made many mistakes, and are still working in all respects to our best advantage from lack of information as to our problems or their relative importance. We are supporting these agencies by our taxation. They are directed by men who are anxious to do everything to co-operate with them in the working out of our problems and the dissemination of this knowledge among our farmers.

IV. Cooperation between our farmers for the distribution of knowledge of the best methods of farm procedure is necessary. This society is now almost the only agency we have for the distribution of the experimental knowledge which our own farmers have worked out. Many of our farmers are still proceeding along lines which others by careful and long continued experimentation proved to be unscientific and unprofitable.

If we could effectively bring about permanent farm tenancy through a fair lease system and through the provision of financial institutions from which an industrious tenant could borrow on long terms for the purchase of lands; if we could awake our people to the necessity of protecting themselves against the common preventible germ diseases; if we could put into effect intelligent cooperation between the farmer and the State and National agencies now operating among us, and could distribute the large amount of carefully worked out experimental knowledge which is already possessed by many of our best farmers; we would be a long ways towards the goal of better agricultural conditions which we are seeking.

We should then have:

(A) Better schools, roads and churches through a development of the cooperative and community spirit:

(B) Steady improvement of the soil, because our people would understand that they must rotate their land, use cover crops, and raise as much live stock as conditions will allow:

(C) We will have more generally in the South specialized crops—crops which take less labor and more brains and will turn out more money value than those formerly most generally planted:

(D) Rational fertilization will be better understood and more commonly practiced, and we will be saved an enormous drain from unbalanced fertilizers:

(E) The highest possible grade of seeds will be appreciated, and farmers will understand the importance of pedigreed breeding, and of producing their crop seeds under the very best conditions of soil and spacing, and that all planting seed should be separated before use—only the heaviest and most vital to be planted:

(F) We will understand that our farm products must be standardized, both as to quality, preparation and package:

(G) Better and fairer systems of marketing will be put into general effect through an awakening of our business men and farmers to the importance of mutual obligation and the realization by bankers, merchants and other business men that it is to their interest to see that each town provides the farmer with the best possible market for all of his produce, a market in which the interest of every seller will be scrupulously protected. The period of ultra individualism is rapidly passing and in its place we are entering an age in which the right thinking man feels his responsibility towards his fellow man, and towards the community at large.

If this cooperative spirit continues to develop and expand it will result in the successful working out of most of the social and economic problems that now confront us.[53]

VII

In late 1913 David went one night out into the country, to Swift Creek school, to attend an agricultural meeting. A close friend, Dr. W. W. Long, head of agricultural extension work in South Carolina, spoke. During his talk, Long stated that for some time he had wanted to establish practical agricultural instruction in the high schools of at least one county in the state, this to be a pathfinder for statewide adoption. But a year's program of this type of instruction in a county would cost about twenty-five hundred dollars and he had no such funds. Dr. Long talked on. David was sitting with Bright Williamson of Darlington. They consulted together and when Dr. Long had finished one of them stood up and said that between them they would underwrite the project for Darlington County. Dr. Long accepted on the spot, and then prevailed upon J. M. Napier to come to Darlington County and conduct the program. Mr. Napier pushed the work along very successfully to fill David's definition of a real need.[54] "About 97% of the boys who attend our county schools never go to college. They get no preparation for their life work besides that which comes from the home and the rural schools.... The vast field of practical knowledge accumulated in recent years by Experiment Stations and scientific farmers is a blank to them."[55]

53. Published in the *Hartsville Messenger*, August 26, 1915.
54. Recollection of Mr. J. M. Napier, Darlington, S.C.
55. D. R. Coker, Bright Williamson, and D. L. Lewis to "Editor the State,"

Similar work had been going on in other states,[56] and by 1915 the beginnings on the Smith-Hughes Bill to provide Federal help for agricultural education in the public schools had been made in Washington. On October 14, 1915 the *Hartsville Messenger* reported that "Hon. David F. Houston, Secretary of Agriculture and a member of President Wilson's cabinet, Dr. Bradford Knapp, head of the United States farm demonstration work, and Mr. W. W. Long, State Agent for the United States farm demonstration work and head of the Clemson extension department of Clemson College, were entertained last Friday and Friday night by Mr. and Mrs. David R. Coker." "Such important personages," as the paper summed these people up, were in Darlington County to inspect the outcome of Mr. Napier's work in the high schools, in partial preparation for determining the administration's policy toward Federal aid. They liked what they saw, and, as the paper reported, ". . . praised the work done by Mr. J. M. Napier."

It was no accident that David was at Swift Creek school when Dr. Long spoke. They were good friends, whose devotion to better agriculture was sufficient to allow them to differ bluntly on any particular subject and remain on good, or better, terms. There was a similar lifelong relationship between David and Mr. Napier. The correspondence between David and such men as these is one of the most wholesome chapters in the history of these times.

Next to the seed farm, David thought best of this Extension Service of all the organizations trying to help the farmer. It was a rounded organization that sought to supply and demonstrate the facts through which the farmers could farm better. He supported it at home and across the state. Most of all he supported it with the seed farm. As his work broadened to include almost all field and vegetable crops

---

February 7, 1916. This letter was written in support of a bill before the General Assembly of South Carolina "proposing a small appropriation for the teaching of agriculture in the rural schools."

56. U. S. Department of Agriculture, *Yearbook of Agriculture, 1940* (Washington: U.S. Government Printing Office, 1940), pp. 255-56.

DAVID COKER AND PEDIGREED SEED 159

grown in South Carolina, first hundreds and then thousands came each year to see the crops, to hear about seed breeding, and to get a wide variety of agricultural advice. This was the best demonstration farm in the state, and the extension people were welcome to use it as such, and did. After 1920, the State Experiment Station, largely because of this competence and size of the seed farm, discontinued its cotton breeding operations.[57]

This public nature of the seed farm had been all along a conscious characteristic. David enjoyed the work, but had no thought that it could break even financially. The breeding operations were carried on as part of the store's farming operations.[58] George Wilds had come in 1908 to help with the work,[59] and in July of 1911[60] David's first cousin, S. Pressley Coker, having done graduate work at Cornell, came as head breeder. In 1913 young Lee Wiggins, recently come from the University of North Carolina to be David's secretary, suggested that the breeding might carry itself as a separate entity. David was skeptical, both as a businessman and because he did not conceive of the breeding work as a commercial enterprise. He finally consented, and in that year Coker's Pedigreed Seed Company was formally established, as a partnership between David, the Major, and Joe Lawton, which was the way the store was held.[61]

VIII

So long as the farmer was to have a real stake in twentieth century American life, he had need to be a businessman in the market place. He was not a businessman and this was one cause of his individual poverty.

The individual farmer participated also in a collective pover-

---

57. U. S. Department of Agriculture, *Yearbook of Agriculture, 1936*, p. 701.
58. D. R. Coker, "Financial History and Structure of Coker's Pedigreed Seed Company." This typed manuscript, undated, was found in the 1929 files of Mr. Coker's papers and undoubtedly was written in that year (Mrs. D. R. Coker).
59. D. R. Coker, "Breeding Work and Status of Coker's Pedigreed Seed Company." Undated manuscript, probably written in 1929 (Mrs. D. R. Coker).
60. U. S. Department of Agriculture, *Yearbook of Agriculture, 1936*, p. 670.
61. Recollection of A. L. M. Wiggins, Hartsville, S.C.

ty, for, to use David's term, "the cotton industry" did not receive the advantages that normally accrue to the production of a large amount of wealth: good marketing facilities where the farmer had standing, promotion by buyers and converters of the farmer's products, cheap and convenient credit, discretion as to when and how to sell, the normal kinds of business services and information, and an equal position with respect to all other parts of this national economy. After the average cotton farmer had grown his crop, his control and positive activities came to a halt, and there was no one who took hold at that point and served him adequately.

David had received a fine object lesson in this situation in the unusual efforts required to establish the simple, physical equipment for an adequate long staple market in Hartsville, and to induce the mills to examine and use the staple cotton raised there. As usual, a large part of this situation can be attributed to cultural lethargy and ignorance. Still, again, money was required for positive action. Personally and through the store he had spent money to breed the seed. Most important, had he not been able to convert the staple length and the better grades into substantial profits during the first year or two, the staple industry would not have survived. To do this he went considerably beyond the bounds of good business practice, though in the outturn his dealings in staple cotton were profitable. This was his personal work and he could do it at Hartsville. But the lack of marketing facilities that would encourage farmers to raise better and specialized crops was general.

The farmer was aware of his own misery and knew a good deal of its causes. Since the Civil War there had been many efforts to improve the farmer's position in the market. A long roll of farmers' organizations—among them the Grange, the Farmers' Alliance, the Farmers' Union, the Southern Cotton Association, to name a few—had attempted to improve, one way or another, the situation. There had been some temporary success, and in some localities there had been relatively persistent success. In general, and particularly in the South, these attempts had foundered on the inability of the farmers to hold together and to secure and support businesslike management of the organizations.[62] During these years the Farmers' Union and the Southern Cotton Association were of no little consequence in the Hartsville area, but they failed for the stated reasons. David, along with the Major, had been skeptical of practical success and did not join, though they approved of the objectives. In the Spring of 1908 following the panic of 1907, he discussed the cotton outlook, saying that "the officers of the Southern Cotton Association and the Farmers' Union had a strong case early last fall when they advised the farmers to hold for 15 cents, and this price I think would have been realized before now if the business situation of the country had not been completely changed by the October panic. But the demand for 15 cents cotton should have been withdrawn when it became clear that the cotton goods situation was going from bad to worse and the true blue members of the associations might have been saved a big loss."[63]

Still, the problem remained. The existing system of merchants and bankers served the premises and needs of the one crop system very well. In the agricultural areas, as David pointed out, they depended almost exclusively upon the farmer, and were in a sense his business agents. Certainly they composed a reservoir of business experience and facilities. David's conclusion was that they might well serve the farmers in the interests of an improving agriculture, and with profit.

David had a feeling for integration of the several parts of the economy, for, of course, he had grown up in such a family integration at Hartsville where he had seen how one part might serve the other. Quite early in 1908, before he came fully to a consideration of the human and economic aspects of agricultural improvement, he had given the South Carolina mill owners a fundamental proposition:

62. Wilson Gee and Edward Allison Terry, *The Cotton Cooperatives in the Southeast* (New York: D. Appleton-Century Company, 1933), pp. 32-36.
63. D. R. Coker, "The Outlook for the Farmer," published in the *Hartsville Messenger*, March 26, 1908.

The fact that the careful breeder can within natural limits exaggerate and fix almost any plant characteristic might be taken advantage of by the spinners requiring cottons different from those here, to have bred for them in their communities, varieties exactly suited to their purposes. . . .

I am strongly of the opinion that a small farm, in charge of a plant breeding expert, would be a valuable adjunct to almost any mill that has to buy cotton at a distance. . . .[64]

During these years the mills were moving to the land of cotton, and he was proposing the next step—that they take an intelligently selfish interest in what was raised in the cotton fields. Here also was an idea that later became a major agricultural policy of private and governmental farm agencies: the specialization by an entire community in the growing of a single commercial crop, for a dependable and sizeable supply is always necessary for the establishment of a market.

By the time the staple cotton industry had been established at Hartsville, David had become increasingly aware of the dynamic relationship which might exist between the merchants and bankers, on the one hand, and the farmers on the other, to the benefit of both.

It has already been noted that by 1915, if not earlier, he was beginning to call on business men and bankers to know that their fate was tied to that of the farmer. This was true and logical, and susceptible of demonstration. There was beginning to appear, though, an undercurrent of grave concern that these several elements of the cotton economy could change their ways in time to establish themselves on a sound basis. Thus there was more hope than fact in his statement that "The period of ultra individualism is rapidly passing and in its place we are entering an age in which the right thinking man feels his responsibility towards his fellow man, and towards the community at large."[65]

As usual he spoke in plain language and specifically. He

---

[64]. D. R. Coker's speech to the South Carolina Association of Cotton Manufacturers, June 11, 1908, published in the *Hartsville Messenger,* June 18, 1908.

[65]. Speech before the Darlington County Agricultural Society, published in the *Hartsville Messenger,* August 26, 1915.

told the Florence, S.C., Chamber of Commerce that "I am not going to give you the usual kind of agricultural talk tonight. . . . I am not going to enumerate and praise the resources and prosperity of our section, yours and mine. It is not usual to point to shortcomings, and to tell the unpleasant facts about our country. The true friend of the people, however, will not shrink from this task. . . ." He went on to enumerate the details of agriculture's plight, ending with the statement that ". . . most of our farmers are still hopelessly tied to the wheels of the chariot of King Cotton." Then he said that ". . . I consider it to be the duty of the businessmen of the towns everywhere to see that the farmers are provided with fair and adequate markets for the sale of their products. Too many of our businessmen pay little or no attention to their town markets. . . ."

I believe that this and every other organization of its kind in the State should in cooperation with the government authorities make a careful study of the agricultural conditions, resources and possibilities of the section. After such a study has been made I believe that certain agricultural specialties should be decided on as most suitable for local conditions. Then every effort should be put forth to establish these specialities upon a profitable basis, educating the farmers in their production and affording high class marketing facilities.[66]

He was thinking primarily of the farmer and of a fundamental way through which the individual farmer could be established in the market and have the stamina to stay: for "I find that our farmers are quick to take on the new crops, but they fail oftener than not to succeed with them. This is often because they have not been educated in the proper methods of production and handling and have no adequate nearby market."[67]

In 1917 he wrote a banker that "the merchant and banker should realize that marketing is *his* problem . . . all farm problems are your problems, and this problem of marketing is

---

66. D. R. Coker, "Agriculture, Our Greatest Undeveloped Resource," Speech before the Florence, South Carolina, Chamber of Commerce, 1915 (Mrs. D. R. Coker).
67. *Ibid.*

especially your problem, for it is one that the businessman can handle far better than the farmer."[68] David was especially aware of the potential of the merchant's and banker's money. ". . . the right word at the right time to the farmer from the banker or businessman, will often accomplish more than a dozen bulletins or lectures from agricultural authorities."[69]

IX

The work of these prewar years was in the main hopeful work. Certainly David's local activities carried him along in the belief that real progress was possible within the existing framework of southern culture, though he was in no way unaware of the difficulties. Nor was he alone. There was a widespread and general interest in the improvement of the rural life of the nation, and there was special interest in the plight of the South. On almost every hand there was evidence of progress, industrial and agricultural, such as Professor Edwin Mims found in 1911 when he toured the South writing articles for Walter Hines Page's *The World's Work*. Professor Mims stopped in Hartsville and wrote in detail of what he saw there, as representing "the south realizing itself."

All this was true. Fortunately for his perception, but perhaps unfortunately for his peace of mind, David was all his life engaged in several occupations that gave him realistic insights into what was actually going on in the South. The store was such a place; so was cotton buying. These, still, were in the main stream, and in the two of them could be recorded the fates and fortunes, the regressions and improvements of the southern people. Most sensitive of all, perhaps, was the seed breeding. This was a new element that was basic to any long range improvement. Such improvement would carry an awareness of the value of pedigreed seed along with it. Seed sales, particularly cotton seed, increased each year. Yet neither these, nor the more important awareness of the value of pedigreed seed, were spreading like wildfire. Fundamental

68. D. R. Coker to B. H. Pringle, Jr., May 1917 (Mrs. D. R. Coker).
69. D. R. Coker, "The Relation of the Banker to the Farmer," undated manuscript, apparently written in 1915 (Mrs. D. R. Coker).

DAVID COKER AND PEDIGREED SEED

improvement was perhaps taking place, but it was slow and not yet certain.

In 1914 David took on another job that placed him in a strategic position to look at the South, particularly the rural eastern South. When the Federal Reserve System was established in that year David was named as a Class B director for the Richmond branch.[70] He was informed of his election by telegram, which came while he was away from Hartsville. His secretary read the telegram and then showed it to the Major. Major Coker read it carefully, then said, "Well, that's fine. We will have to consider this carefully. I am not sure that we can spare David." David was "spared," of course.[71]

For several months after the outbreak of war in Europe commodity credit in this country almost ceased to exist. Cotton prices dropped sharply as export markets dried up, and banks and merchants began calling in their loans from the farmers. Almost complete financial demoralization moved over the South.[72] All this was spread before David and the other directors at Richmond. Hundreds of banks, overnight, had come to the verge of bankruptcy or beyond, as the worth of their farm paper fled away.

Though there had been relative stability in the cotton economy since the panic of 1907, David had no particular illusions about the general prosperity of the South. Still, the extent of the demoralization surprised him, and raised great doubts that the southern economy could, of itself, sustain a long program of general improvement. Writing in 1915, he said that

> The state of affairs prevailing in this country last fall and winter revealed a condition which few of us had previously suspected. For some years our publicists, politicians and real estate boomers had heralded to the world that the South was in a condition of great prosperity and the impression was widespread that cotton farming was a most profitable pursuit. But, when we made the biggest crop on record and it was put on the market at a price which averaged fully 60 per cent of the five years average, we find that our

70. Recollection of A. L. M. Wiggins, Hartsville, S.C.
71. *Ibid.*
72. U. S. Department of Agriculture, *Yearbook of Agriculture, 1940*, p. 285.

country had not accumulated sufficient profits to stand up under the shock.[73]

"Accumulated sufficient profits to stand up under the shock" are the important words here. There was simply no increment of capital. Any chance economic breeze could wreck the farmer, the merchant, the banker. None of the three, mortgaged and indebted by one bad year, could afford to do anything but go more deeply the next year into cotton, hoping to recoup. Usually the slow progress toward balance, quality, diversification and cover crops was lost.

Certainly one thing was obvious: ". . . there has been no great profit in the raising of cotton at 11 or 12 cents and . . . the bulk of the returns from our cotton crops have been paid out for fertilizer, grain, provisions, agricultural machinery, mules, etc., the major portion of which came from other states. I believe that these expenditures and the large item for labor has practically consumed the money received from most of our cotton crop."[74] It was equally obvious that ". . . our country cannot continue to depend almost solely upon the cotton crop if it is going to advance in prosperity and culture."[75]

All this David had said before, in one way or another. But this large-scale demonstration of the frailty of the cotton economy added an increased urgency to his work, and to his public efforts for improvement. As, in 1915, wartime prosperity began to reach the South, there were again many optimists. David took the sober view. All along, as he did in 1917, he advised the farmer plainly to ". . . show prudence and patriotism, pay his debts, invest liberally in liberty bonds, contribute to the Red Cross and other charitable war agencies, respond to all other patriotic calls made on him by the Nation and State Councils of Defense, and put aside the balance for those emergencies which the future is almost sure to bring forth. . . ."[76]

73. D. R. Coker, "The Relation of the Banker to Agriculture" (Mrs. D. R. Coker).
74. *Ibid.*
75. *Ibid.*
76. *Coker's Pedigreed Seed Catalogue,* Fall, 1917.

X

Whatever else was true about southern agriculture, present and future, it required good seed, and would continue to require good seed. Good seed was, in fact, a dynamic element which would open up new possibilities and have considerable influence upon the course of southern agriculture. David did not lose sight of these facts nor allow the urgency he felt for the general situation to diminish the importance of the breeding operations at Hartsville. He was aware, also, that in part at least his growing stature as an agricultural leader had its basis in his being able to demonstrate the worth and practicality of good seed.

Even before he succeeded in bringing the Hartsville staple cotton to climax development in 1909, David had begun a main breeding project with another variety of staple cotton. Dr. Webber had established staple cotton breeding operations for the Federal government at Columbia, S.C., in 1900, and he and David had maintained contact. Dr. Webber had developed two promising varieties, the Columbia and the Keenan. In 1906 Dr. Webber was planning to leave the government service to go to Cornell to teach and carry on research. David visited him at Columbia while Dr. Webber was in the midst of turning his work over to assistants, and he and Dr. Webber walked into the fields to look over the breeding plots. Dr. Webber pointed out the plant that he considered the best in all the plots, and David asked if he might have the seed from a single boll from this plant.[77]

With my trained instinct to protect governmental rights I started to refuse this request, when the thought flashed into mind that I was leaving the Department and that in the change of management, ideas would necessarily change and much might be lost. I thus broke my unvarying rule and gave Mr. Coker one or two bolls from this very superior plant. It meant much to the cotton industry that I did so, as nothing ever came from the great bulk of the seed that I retained, while from the little handful of seed of this one plant that

---

77. Letter from Dr. H. J. Webber to J. C. Ware, January 3, 1936 (Mrs. D. R. Coker).

I gave to Mr. Coker came the Webber 49, the Webber 82, and the numerous strains that followed of the Webber cottons. The use of my name for this variety was, of course, Mr. Coker's doings, not mine.[78]

David began to breed this "little handful of seed" in the plant-to-row method, as he was breeding the Hartsville cotton. Two excellent varieties were achieved, introduced in 1910, and named the Webber 49 and the Webber 82 in Dr. Webber's honor. Both cottons were of slightly longer staple than the Hartsville cotton and had excellent uniformity and productiveness. The most important feature of the two new cottons was the fact that they both matured earlier for picking than did the Hartsville cotton. Early maturity lessened the risk from unfavorable weather in late September. More important than this, the early maturity lessened the boll weevil damage in August and September. By 1910 the boll weevil had caused great damage in the lower South, having virtually wiped out the staple cotton production in the Mississippi Delta country. The Webber cottons were widely adopted in the Delta and did much to restore the staple growing in that area.[79] The boll weevil had not yet reached South Carolina, but he was on the way year by year; he was well heralded though imperfectly seen, and was already a factor in the future of staple cotton in the Hartsville area.

In 1915 an important new direction in cotton breeding was taken when attention was turned to breeding short staple cotton,[80] what David later called a "bread and butter" cotton for the South. The object was to combine very early maturity, quality of fiber, and productiveness, with a uniform staple length of an inch or slightly more. The boll weevil was one reason for this departure; this in addition to the fact that nothing like the potentialities of quality and productiveness of short staple cotton had been reached, particularly in the early

---

78. *Ibid.*

79. Article by Dr. Webber published in the *Arkansas Gazette* (Little Rock), September 26, 1920.

80. George J. Wilds, "Commercial Cotton Breeding," address delivered at the Annual Meeting of the Georgia Agronomists, January 23, 1947.

maturing varieties, and the general cotton farmer needed a good cotton that he could grow without the special requirements of skill and markets of long staple cotton. Such a cotton was required also in any long range program to reduce the amount of land devoted to cotton. Several years were required before climax results were reached in this work.

Work continued of course on corn and the small grains, and by 1915 peas, velvet beans, and sorghum were offered for sale.[81] More important, perhaps, than any specific product was the continuing and widening process of meticulous breeding, year in and year out. There really is no finished product in breeding, certainly no stopping place. Any variety, such as the Hartsville cotton, will deteriorate over a period of four or five years through natural variation, through natural field crossing and through gin mixing with other seed. In a real sense, the variety has to be recreated every year; each year after 1909, for instance, plant-to-row tests were conducted on the Hartsville cotton, the best plants being rigorously selected and increased during the following years in carefully controlled increase blocks and fields. It was this "bred" seed that was sold year in and year out and not just haphazard reproduction from seed harvested in 1909. Beyond this, of course, the continuous breeding and selection not only maintained the variety at a high level but quite often it brought about improvement in one or more characteristics of the plant. Before the Hartsville cotton was discontinued in favor of the earlier maturing varieties of staple cotton in the 1920's, nine different strains of this variety were introduced, in addition to the original strain brought out in 1909. Each strain represented a demonstrable improvement over previous strains.

In the fall of 1914 the first catalogue, symbolizing the recent formal establishment of Coker's Pedigreed Seed Company as a separate entity apart from the store, was published. It was the beginning of a remarkable publication, whose primary, specific purpose was to explain and make the case for good seed to the southern farmer. There were twenty-two pages of

81. *Coker's Pedigreed Seed Catalogue*, Spring, 1915.

printed material and pictures in this first catalogue. Of the twenty-two, nine pages, including five of the first six, were devoted exclusively to explaining the reasons, necessity, and methods of seed breeding, and to unvarnished agricultural advice.

As it developed, the catalogue became a highly personalized instrument through which David gave general advice, reported new agricultural developments, summarized market information, and on occasion lectured the farmers. Throughout, "we make no special prices or reductions. We believe our seeds are worth what we charge for them, to one customer the same as another."[82] In 1915 the lead article of the Spring issue set forth the southern agricultural situation for the edification of prospective customers: most farmers ". . . are still living from hand to mouth, buying most of their provisions, fertilizer, labor and mules on credit at an expense which takes the bulk of a full crop at full prices to liquidate. Most of them cultivate the bulk of the land in cotton, and year by year the soil is depleted of its life-giving humus, and yields are only kept up by constantly increasing applications of expensive fertilizers."

It was into this situation that David sent his seeds. His plain speaking was not resented, perhaps because it was plain speaking, and certainly because of the tremendous amount of practical work that he had accomplished. The seeds could stand the test, and increasingly he took on a semi-public role. His letters on agricultural affairs were printed by the state newspapers in the same way as were those of official farm agencies, and motives were seldom sought behind "Dave" Coker's advice.

Shortly after this country entered the war, David was named by his good friend Governor Manning as State Food Administrator, and, shortly after, as Chairman of the State Council of Defense. Here, again, were jobs that offered wider perspective on the southern agricultural situation, and on the great upheaval of agriculture that war and postwar were to bring.

82. *Coker's Pedigreed Seed Catalogue*, Fall, 1915

8

The Major

I

HARTSVILLE, when the Major had turned his full attention there in 1886, was a cross-roads, a store, a church, a few neighbors whose barking dogs were heard faintly. There is neither remembrance nor record of what plans he may have had for himself beyond expanding the store and continuing his farming operations. Perhaps, once the railroad was secured, he would have built a cotton mill at Hartsville.

Whatever he may have intended, the children's maturity soon snowed him under. Ideas, projects, and problems all came fast and furious. The long struggle to make paper occupied the entire ten years of the 1890's, and gave him the most anxious moments of his civilian life. Then, when the technical difficulties were solved in the late nineties, he was still in a competitive, if profitable business, and for a good many years he conducted the business affairs of the Fiber Company, selling in a touch-and-go market. At the same time, he had much of the daily responsibility of the Southern Novelty Company. For a number of years he worked each day for several hours at the Fiber Company office, then walked across the yard to the Novelty Company office. All the while he remained in touch with the store, with the cotton oil mill, and he supported David in the seed breeding.

The capital for all of these activities was the Major's, directly or indirectly, but in many ways this was the least of his contributions. He set a stable base, not just for physical operations, but for the morale and encouragement of the children, whose ability and creativity were accompanied by sensitivity and, on occasion, temperament. The Major, so far as he was able, responded appropriately to the different needs of each child, from an apparently inexhaustible reservoir of spiritual and emotional resource. He stood virtually alone in the later years. He and his wife were very close, and Sue Stout Coker's interest in her family was paramount. She had brought them through the bad years after the War. But by the late 1890's her health was failing markedly.[1]

The Major's force did not come primarily from a desire for great achievement, though he was immensely proud of the several accomplishments. With or without this, he was committed—maturely, irrevocably, and without complaint—to standing steadfast at Hartsville, responsible for an orderly establishment in which, first and last, the everyday necessities and decencies of life were respected. This, after much hard and rich experience, was his perspective, and there was room therein for patience, understanding, and a sense of development. In August of 1900 he wrote his son James a letter, a letter in which much of a reticent, sometimes austere, man is revealed:

Aug. 15, 1900

My Dear Son:

Your last letter was forwarded to me at Asheville, N. C. where I went to see your Mother last Thursday. I took Jennie with me as your Mother needs some attendant. Anna came home Monday and I got back last night. Margaret was in Asheville, but did not like a city and I hardly know what she will do. They were all well, M—being not strong according to her usual habit. Your Mother seemed pretty well again but very feeble.

We are getting on fairly at the mill. Trade has been dull & prices low but trade is now picking up, and the paper machines are doing pretty well and could do much more if we had the stock. The ground wood is scarce because of very low water. No 2 Digester has been considerable trouble. In fact we have hardly

---

1. Conversation with Mrs. J. L. Coker, Jr.

averaged more than one regularly running Digester for a long time. We have managed somehow to keep going. It is pleasant to hear good news from Vivien & the children. We have had tidings from Will in Jamaica which are interesting and Susie is said to be improving.

Altogether we have much to be thankful for and my earnest wish is that you may all live happy and useful lives.

With much love to the grandchildren and to Vivien I remain as ever—

Your aff. Father[2]

Mrs. Coker died in 1904 and the Major knew that he was getting old, even though there was no evident falling off in his capacity to do several jobs well. "I have told my friends that when an old man slips down the hill he has a hard time to get up again."[3] Yet a sense of compulsion remained: ". . . whatever we old folks find in our hearts to contribute must be attended to without delay."[4]

He knew also that time and growth required that the younger people assume control. Giving over did not come easily, for a lifetime of being responsible had made the habit strong. In another context he wrote that "I would not put my complete dependence in any one person." He was proud of the boys, recognized their ability, but it was deep in his nature to check things himself. Until the end he liked for them to come in and tell him what was going on.[5] Yet for too long he had admitted the compulsion of plain facts, and he knew too much about nature to deny the principle of succession:

I am arranging to sell my stock in the Carolina Fiber Co. to my son James and to Howard Edwards and Walter Edwards. If we reach an agreement, the price they pay me will be $2000.00 per share which is too low by, say, thirty or forty per cent., the book showing about 2600 as of date January 1st 1906, but my purpose has been to give these boys the opportunity to manage the mill and I think the time has come for me to do it.[6]

2. Major Coker to J. L. Coker, Jr., August 15, 1900 (R. G. Coker).
3. Major Coker to Mrs. L. W. Lide, December 17, 1914 (Watson collection).
4. Major Coker to Major J. J. Lucas, January 12, 1910 (Watson collection).
5. From recollections of Mrs. J. L. Coker, Jr.
6. Major Coker to G. A. Norwood, October 25, 1905 (R. G. Coker).

This was in 1905. The assumption was that Howard Edwards would handle the business end, Walter Edwards to be Superintendent, with James continuing in his general engineering capacity, for James was not inclined to take over the daily administrative duties. Unfortunately, within a few days after this letter was written personal differences arose between the Edwards boys and Major Coker, and the sale was called off, the Major being forced to continue in charge of the Fiber Company.[7] As fast as possible, however, he transferred control to James, and to Paul Rogers, another nephew who had entered the company.[8] Similarly, as fast as young Charles developed as salesman and treasurer of the Southern Novelty Company, control of that company was shifted to him. But these things required several years, and the Major was quite active in the affairs of these companies until he was well past his seventy-fifth birthday.

All things considered, the Major kept up with the boys rather well. However he could get tired of the eternal movement and change. He wrote Will of the prospects of a silver plating enterprise that was being started in the Southern Novelty Company: "We have gone ahead on nothing but faith too often."[9] It was in 1906 that J. W. Norwood, son of the Major's former business partner in Charleston, proposed that the Major join him in a Mediterranean cruise. The unexpectedness of the proposal took his fancy, but he hesitated: "Do you think me crazy to leave my people here with 'the bag to hold' in the present circumstances?"[10] Yielding to the family's urging, he made the trip with no little pleasure.[11]

His interest in education was abiding. In 1894, almost all secondary education in South Carolina was to be had at boarding academies, or high schools, for there were then few publicly supported high schools in the state. That year the

7. Letters and memoranda pertaining to the controversy are in the Major Coker materials (R. G. Coker).
8. Conversation with P. H. Rogers, R. G. Coker and L. W. Vaughn.
9. Major Coker to W. C. Coker, August 6, 1907, (W. C. Coker).
10. Major Coker to W. C. Coker, February 15, 1906 (W. C. Coker).
11. Conversation with W. C. Coker.

Welsh Neck High School was established in Hartsville, on land given by Major Coker and in buildings largely given by him. The governing and originating body was the Welsh Neck Baptist Association, perhaps the strongest single organization in the upper Pee Dee country. The churches that composed the Association were committed to support the school, which was eventually located just across the road from the Major's home, on part of a great cotton field.[12] With the help of several good men, notably his son-in-law Joe Lawton, he looked after the school. He took a close interest in the teachers and students, in expenses, and in the never ending struggle to secure enough students. While the Association contributed some money, normally Major Coker met the annual deficit of two or three thousand dollars himself, or it was forthcoming from some part of the family.[13]

In 1908 the state began to move into high school education, ". . . wisely, as I think. . . . In every county we will soon see at least one State high school or a high school course added to the primary courses in our common school. This plan is so obviously the wise and correct plan from the point of view of those who have in charge the public school system of the State that it will surely be adopted and then the necessity for such a high school as we have had here will grow less and less as the state system goes into operation."

Now what are we to have in place of this Welsh Neck High School around which our affections have gathered for these many years? Shall we simply abandon our plans of educational work and for the building up of an institution of learning for this section. That would be in our opinion, a very unfortunate step.[14]

In the usual words in which his actions were conceived, it was decided ". . . that we must go forward and not backward; that we must make an advance and not a retreat. In place of a high school superceded in its usefulness by the new state

---

12. From recollections of Mrs. J. L. Coker, Jr.
13. Conversation with W. C. Coker.
14. Major Coker's speech at closing of Welsh Neck High School in spring of 1908 (Watson collection).

system our board have decided to establish a college for young women."[15]

As usual, also, the establishment of the college met a logical and specific need: ". . . there is at present better provision for the education of young men in colleges and universities in this state than for young women . . . and there is no such school such as we contemplate east of Columbia. . . ."[16] Over the Major's objections the new college was named Coker College, and began operating somewhat tentatively in the academic year of 1909-10 under a board of trustees elected by the Welsh Neck Association and by the other Baptist Associations in the State.

The Major proposed to endow the school substantially and to continue his support in other ways. But first he had a rather delicate situation to resolve. Without being in the least doctrinal about it he had for many years taken a prominent part in Baptist affairs, especially at Hartsville and to a lesser extent in the Welsh Neck Association and in the State. His wife Sue, daughter of a Baptist minister, worked ceaselessly, if modestly, for the church, and the Major was always considerate of her wishes. Together they had sustained a Sunday School at Hartsville in the early days, printing the lessons on a small printing press that young James had rigged up; Major Coker had supported the church as he had supported the Welsh Neck High School and other necessities of the community. These things he had done without involvement in doctrinal questions. Because of his position and natural reserve he was seldom pushed to the wall in regard to such matters, on which it is certain that he looked with considerable detachment. If necessary to ease a strained situation he would say something like "I have to confess . . . that I am not sufficiently educated in that line to appreciate discussions involving theological questions."[17]

It is unlikely that he was much surprised that ultimately

15. *Ibid.*
16. *Ibid.*
17. Major Coker to Rev. A. C. Wilkins, October 10, 1914 (Watson collection).

THE MAJOR 177

he had to face the perennial issue of fundamentalism. And, indeed, the question soon arose, with heat in some quarters, as to whether or not the new college would be denominational. Being "a great believer in 'religious liberty' and 'freedom of conscience' "[18] he had no intention of setting up a strictly denominational, or sectarian, school. He wanted a school conducted along accepted Christian lines of morality and behavior, and he had no objection to religious instruction, but it was to be no more Baptist than Episcopalian, and the school's first business was to be education, not religion.

Yet it seemed imperative that the support of the several Baptist Associations be held and increased if the college were to succeed, even though he was making preparation to give a substantial endowment. Legally the college belonged to the trustees chosen from the Associations, and he well knew that many of the Baptist preachers and laymen were dangerous opponents. If the Associations were alienated, so as to remove their support and be in active opposition, then the college would almost certainly fail.

He moved firmly and plainly, but at his age charged no windmills. He simply made his point through the endowment of $150,000 that he established in 1910. Rather than give the money to the college trustees outright, he set up a separate board composed of five members who would annually turn over the income from the endowment provided that the ". . . College is conducted as a non-sectarian institution, maintaining a good reputation and grade as a College for women . . ." Further,

That while Coker College for Women belongs under its charter to a body of Baptists, it is my special purpose in establishing this fund and creating this trust that all interested persons, of whatever religious views, shall be benefited thereby, therefore of the five Trustees under this Trust there shall always be two Baptists and three of other religious denominations.

It is proper for me to state that it is understood by me that a non-sectarian institution is non-sectarian in the sense that Wofford

18. *Ibid.*

College, at Spartanburg, S.C., and Furman University at Greenville, S.C., are now non-sectarian.[19]

There was some grumbling, and this stand may well have caused some money to be withheld in the beginning. Though irritated, the Major kept his patience. He thought a ". . . positive statement on the subject of Government will be all sufficient." Such a statement was that ". . . it is the fixed purpose of the College to be broad and non-sectarian in its work, for it is engaged in the work of Christian education for the good of all the people irrespective of denominational affiliation and its doors are open to welcome young women of every religious faith."[20]

The college held his close interest. Beyond doubt it was his delight to see girls come from the surrounding area to a school where none was before, and to see a large number attend on scholarships. His large sense of duty was in some measure fulfilled. He enjoyed the concerts, the plays, the bustle of school activities. The students and faculty paid him respectful attention. In his letters there remain a good many short, precise notes like the following:

If the day is suitable, I would like to have one teacher and six students (or seven students) go to ride with me this afternoon at 3:00 o'clock. Please advise me by phone number 21 at one o'clock and oblige.[21]

And then there is one as follows:

Coming home from our drive on yesterday I heard one of the girls say that she had lost her hat pin. As I understood, she valued it very much as a keep sake, so this morning I drove down to the place where you had your little picnic and my man, Robert, looked carefully in the straw and found the hat pin that I enclose herewith. I did not find out which one of the girls had lost it but you will know. Please return it to the proper owner and oblige.[22]

19. Major Coker to Dr. A. C. Henslee, July 25, 1912 (Watson collection).
20. Major Coker to Dr. A. J. Hall, April 25, 1914 (R. G. Coker).
21. Major Coker to Miss McBride, October 13, 1914 (Watson collection).
22. Major Coker to Miss Fort, October 30, 1914 (Watson collection).

He was not under the impression that he had bought himself a bauble for amusement, or an institution that would merely enshrine his name. He was forever conscious of the fact that Coker was a small college; that by definition it was committed to serving the educational needs of the girls of the area as cheaply as possible, and that its resources were not large as those things went. He did not interfere in the teaching, or the curriculum, or in the exercises. But he watched closely to see that things went orderly and well. He suggested fire drills, and the planting of a garden. "At this season of the year you know it is very important to have the College dormitories well screened. . . . Please . . . take some steps to relieve the girls of the nuisance of flies and mosquitoes in their bed rooms as well as in the dinning room and parlors."[23] "I want to tell you that I found the scuttle hole leading up to the roof open last week. . . . Evidently some young people had been going through it on to the roof. I had George close up this door, but I wish somebody could see that things like this cannot happen. It is a pity to have so fine a building injured by inattention or neglect."[24]

These were small items, it would seem. Certainly it does not appear that he ever became entirely sympathetic with the academic man's attitude toward such details. Perhaps there was involved also some of an old man's fussing. If so, he had reason. Not long before the above notes were written, Andrew Carnegie's private secretary had written a short letter turning down the college's request for library help, closing with the somewhat gratuitous statement that ". . . an institution which calls itself a college and with only 350 books cannot be in the grade which must have been reached before it can come within Mr. Carnegie's scope."[25] He was conscious therefore of the close relationship between small savings and educational vision, as appears in the following letter:

23. Major Coker to S. W. Garrett, March 27, 1912 (Watson collection).
24. Major Coker to S. W. Garrett, August 18, 1914 (Watson collection).
25. Major Coker to Rev. Joel I. Allen, January 30, 1911 (Watson collection).

June 24, 1913

Dr. A. J. Hall, Pres.,
Hartsville, S. C.

Dear Dr. Hall:—

Yours of June 23rd received. Replying to the same, I believe I called attention on yesterday to the uneconomical work that has been done on the Campus and to the failure to use to advantage our opportunities for providing a good vegetable garden for the College. It is hardly necessary for me to enlarge upon these matters. What we need on the Campus is an intelligent Janitor and such a man we may not be able to secure at present.

Your letter, however, opens the way for me to say that the greatest waste in College expenditure that I know of, I feel myself partly responsible for as I agreed to the expenditure. We could have saved on our building operations fifteen thousand dollars. Such a building as we could have erected for this reduced amount would have served our purposes a while and the money saved could have been invested to provide at once some things almost indispensable to a high grade College: for instance a better Library, teachers of high qualifications and other things that will, no doubt, occur to you. I believe it is well for us to consider economy (with efficiency) in the use of every dollar we have to spend. With kind regards,[26]

He was, of course, as Hartsville became a town, the dominant figure in the community, a position he naturally and increasingly shared with other members of his family. His actions and opinions had wide influence. Yet it was his nature, and by far his preference, to assume that other people were quite capable of managing their own affairs and of conducting themselves properly. It does not appear that he asserted himself for assertion's sake in the affairs of the town. He wrote "earnestly and respectfully" to the mayor about a street matter in 1911, and assured him that ". . . this letter is not written in any captious spirit."[27]

Yet he was quite capable of asserting himself to the limit on several matters that appeared to be within his responsibility, and to have importance in the general ongoing of community

---

26. Major Coker to Dr. A. J. Hall, June 24, 1913 (Watson collection).
27. Major Coker to F. A. Miller, August 2, 1911 (Watson collection).

life. One such matter was the question of public health. Will had brought home the information that flies and mosquitoes, breeding and feeding in places of filth and stagnant waters, carried the germs of the malarial and contagious diseases that took such a toll of health and life in the South in those days. Will remembers quite well that his information was received very coolly by at least one doctor who maintained to the end that miasmas were the cause of the fever.[28] Convinced, the Major began to take direct action. He went to considerable trouble and expense to see that his own land and properties were drained and cleaned up, that screens were put in and that all measures thought to be necessary were taken. He was equally insistent in regard to the whole town. He caused to be established, and became chairman of, the Board of Health. He pushed matters mercilessly. He insisted that doctors make reports as required by the state health authorities and he had no hesitation in placing a great deal of responsibility on the doctors for conditions in the town, as appears in the following letter written in 1910 which was one of many: "The time has come, I think, when the town should begin the fight against the mosquitoes. No doubt you have thought of this yourself. If you can start them off at work please do so."[29]

In his later years the Major mellowed considerably and got some quiet and satisfying enjoyment out of a good many small pleasures. He began to smoke cigars. It would seem that he ordered them variously as his fancy was taken by an advertisement or by friends' advice.[30] He maintained his interests in flowers and plants, birds and animals.

Your letter of the 28th of September received today. Sometime ago in many of the gardens near our dwellings there were bird boxes put up to accommodate Blue Birds and they were occupied by them every year to the great benefit of the gardeners. On one occasion in March some time ago a heavy snow with great cold occurred and the Blue Birds were nearly all frozen, or starved, I

---

28. Conversation with Dr. W. C. Coker.
29. Major Coker to Dr. William Egleston, March 9, 1910 (Watson collection).
30. See various orders for cigars in letters (Watson collection).

don't know which. The next year these boxes were occupied by English Sparrows and I have not seen many Blue Birds around the houses since that time. I see them in the woods and around the roadsides, but they do not nest near our dwellings as they once did. I think the Sparrows make themselves very disagreeable to other birds. Now one finds very few bird boxes, for our people do not care to be hospitable to the English Sparrows, for they are great nuisances.

The work your Society is doing for the protection of useful birds is very much needed. I will take great pleasure in recommending your work to others.[31]

The old wound in his hip and leg opened up in these later years, the healing came loose and there was a frequent discharge. He did not complain, and viewed it with some detachment. "I am thinking of going to Richmond, arriving there on Monday so as to let Dr. Johnston look at my wounded leg. I do not know what he can do, but he wants me to go and it will be some satisfaction to all of us to see if there is anything which causes the recurrence of my trouble."[32]

There was something: "From the X ray picture the surgeons determined that there were left in the old wound a good many particles of lead which were scraped from the bullet as it passed through the bone. These lead particles have been there for forty-six years and have not given me any trouble until the last few years."[33] There was an operation that was only partially successful. After forty-three pieces were removed it did not appear that he could stand the strain of further probing so the remainder were left in his leg.

His main direction was ahead, yet memories crowded in upon him and he sometimes glanced backward. Certain things had been kept alive: annually after 1885[34] the survivors of the old Hartsville Company met for an all day session, most times at the Major's house where a great feast was laid. In 1899 he published a history of the Company, written by himself

31. Major Coker to Miss Belle Williams, September 30, 1914 (Watson collection).
32. Major Coker to Dr. W. C. Coker, June 25, 1909 (Watson collection).
33. Major Coker to Frank R. Chambers, July 14, 1909 (Watson collection).
34. James Lide Coker, *History of Company G*, p. 5.

THE MAJOR 183

up to the time of his wounding, and it is a remarkably accurate record, set down in his usual plain statement, and impresses one familiar with other such works by its rare personal restraint.[35] Without ostentation in 1914 he paid a fertilizer bill for a relative of one of the men who had nursed him in 1863, being "... glad to render this service to one of my best friends, who, in my time of need, freely gave me the care and attention essential."[36] It is a matter of frequent remark at the store even today that there was always credit beyond the usual limits for members of Company E.[37]

Principally through his efforts and those of Bright Williamson of Darlington the Pee Dee Historical Society was established in 1909. The purpose was to gather and publish materials on the Pee Dee area. Care was taken that the affair did not degenerate into an antiquarian discussion. More than a dozen pamphlets were published, all valuable locally, and several, such as Edwin Charles Dargan's *Harmony Hall*, were useful contributions to general social history. The Major took a close and substantial interest in the work of Professor H. T. Cook of Furman, who wrote biographies of David Rogerson Williams and James C. Furman, as well as a general history of the Pee Dee country. Cook was a professor of Greek, and professional historians have had justifiable criticism for his work. Yet he did the work where it was not done before and has not been accomplished since; and these books are essential to any history of the area.

II

There was a generic quality about what the Major did at Hartsville. He returned there and placed himself completely on his own resource. He had returned to live. To live was to do first, and directly, that which lay at hand.

... there is work here for which I am responsible that demands from me everything that I can properly perform. Its demands are not small nor are they to be set aside ... so far as I can see, no

35. *Ibid.*
36. Major Coker to E. L. Wilkins, December 29, 1914 (Watson collection).
37. Conversation with A. L. M. Wiggins, Hartsville, S.C.

other person is charged with the work to which I am alluding. I must do what is laid upon me or it will not be accomplished.[38]

He did every day that which seemed necessary and required of him, insofar as he understood his responsibility. He did not apologize for what had to be done, nor soften his duty with explanation. It was a matter of occasional exasperation to the children that he taught them almost wholly by example. Yet, by example, he made what went on at Hartsville important and worthwhile, and so the children, growing up, developed the feeling that important things could be done at Hartsville.

For the Major, to live was also to "go forward," to take the plainly indicated next step, to respond always to life by not standing still. Whatever might reasonably be accomplished ought to be accomplished. This latter was an inner compulsion rather than an outer statement, and in his own terms. Its force appears in the setting of the times. In the same year that he turned completely to Hartsville, 1886, Henry Grady journeyed to New York, and there heralded the beginning of the "New South" of reconciliation, and of industry and commerce.

Twenty-five years later, in 1911, Edwin Mims came and stayed a while at Hartsville. He was touring the South for Walter Hines Page's *World's Work*, writing a series of long articles on the "New South," and he found that Hartsville ". . . so well suggests and presents in concrete form the forces that are reshaping the communities and commonwealths of the South. . . ."[39]

The irony here is double edged, at least. For the Major had never turned his back on the Old South, though he wrote that he was glad that the slaves were freed; indeed, before 1860 he was seeking, through science, to improve agriculture; he did not approve of secession; and as early as 1869 he was seeking ways to establish a cotton mill. What was accomplished ultimately at Hartsville was not accomplished in terms of a "New

38. Major Coker to James Lide Wilson, September 12, 1914 (Watson collection).
39. Edwin Mims, "The South Realizing Itself. Hartsville and Its Lesson." *World's Work*, Vol. 22, No. 5, pp. 14972-87.

South." He was merely being himself, and he had his father Caleb's capacity to stand aside and see the whole objectively, make terms where necessary, and to forge ahead where possible.

He never let down the bars on fundamental propositions. Even after considerable financial easement had been reached, it was not his impression that past achievements accomplished today's work. The process of care, foresight, attention to detail and honesty that had operated to restore life after the war did not cease because enterprises had grown larger; these qualities were, if anything, more important.

He had, indeed, seen how it was during the war and after. He had then a plain, long-remembered look at desolation. Life was to make a living, to scrape together sustenance, to re-establish the main lineaments. The day's work of necessity had to be sufficient unto each day, so that the next day could be met. Mrs. Coker said afterward that in these times "James made every edge cut." A small gain loomed large where there had been nothing before. Recovery was not sensational, but was, rather, the slow accretion of morale and materials through everyday care and foresight, through a daily recurrence to fundamentals, through economy and self-denial.

The adversity was important in making the man; it is no less important however that his efforts in adversity were successful. When he reached bedrock, that at least was solid. Desolation would not respond to complaint, but it would respond to work, foresight and care. Those things that lay at hand—the land, the store, cotton—if tended carefully could be depended upon to sustain life. He never forgot that disaster was close when fundamentals were ignored, nor that they were the basic components of large enterprise as well as small. There was also a progression. With care something could be left over, and by 1874 he had some money to put into the business in Charleston with George Norwood.

Becoming solvent, he expected to remain in that condition. His mature years extended from 1858, when he first came to

Hartsville, until his death in 1918. He was twenty-eight in 1865; sixty-three in 1900. He lived therefore in a time and place when the rules of personal solvency were perfectly clear, being those of private enterprise. These rules were a part of life as he found it and he accepted them. He took it to be his duty to attend to his own affairs promptly and efficiently; he expected others to do the same. Up to a point he clearly saw a close connection between personal solvency and character. Work was essential. Beyond that, the exercise of prudence and foresight, the payment of debts, the honest, efficient management of personal affairs, were of prime importance. Those matters were essential in the individual's discharge of his responsibilities.

He held himself to the mark all the way through. The possession of relative wealth did not cause him to lose sight of what went on underneath. Several small stories of his later life remain: If, as he rode along in his buggy, he saw an ear of corn in the road that had been carelessly dropped, he would stop and pick it up. Yet, at the same time, he was glad for David to be using in his experiments good land that would produce a great many ears of corn. The point being that here was an ear already grown and need not be wasted. Or, again, there is the story that, late in life, he lost an umbrella. He carefully computed the length of life that had remained in the lost umbrella and did not replace it until that time had expired. It was his habit to compute his personal accounts daily and carefully. Thus, one month when he received a statement from J. L. Coker and Company, he replied quickly: "I find that in making a subtraction showing the balance due me you have made a mistake against yourselves. Please correct and oblige."

He lived well, in the large but unpretentious house, but did not change his way of living appreciably as his wealth increased. He indulged the children. When they went off to school no restrictions were placed on their spending, and, in fact, he urged Will to spend more.[40] As a personal, family

---
40. Conversation with Dr. W. C. Coker.

matter he helped when there was sickness or other problems. Yet, tacitly, the children were aware that they were not expected to set up their way of life, as they moved out on their own, in excess of what they earned. It will be remembered that, after the Major had had his education at Harvard, Caleb Coker had insisted on a thoroughly businesslike arrangement in their joint conduct of the Hartsville plantation.

Money was no magic solution. In fact, the Major viewed it with distrust where it was won cheaply. His rule, to which there were exceptions, was not to make personal loans. In cases where money was not repaid when due, he was patient so far as the money itself was concerned, but insisted that the debtor put his affairs in an orderly shape so that at least a token payment could be made regularly. He received once an urgent appeal from the son of a man under whom he had served for a time during the war. The Major replied:

> You have possibly noticed that I have recently arranged to contribute a large amount to our College for Women at this place. This and other obligations will require all of my available resources and I have nothing to lend any one.
> Nevertheless I wish to do something for you and I suggest that you allow me to arrange with your creditors to pay them $1,000 on account. With this payment they will no doubt extend the balance due, so as to give you the time you require, say three more years.
> Your father and I were close friends while he lived and I am offering this to you because of that friendship and because I feel sure that you are a worthy son of one of the best and bravest soldiers I ever knew.[41]

The language was considerate, as usual, and he may well have wanted to make a more flamboyant gesture. But he would not allow himself the luxury, nor would he ever ease his own position with apologies or explanations. Nor would he intrude money where it was not wanted. He thought, but was not sure, once, that a niece needed money. He asked his

---

41. Major Coker to Major J. J. Lucas, January 12, 1910 (Watson collection).

daughter to find out, adding "make her understand that it will be a favor to me if I am allowed to help in any way."[42]

So long as a man kept his affairs in order, Major Coker did not equate achievement with making money. He agreed gladly for David and Will to devote their best energies to plant breeding and botany. From a money standpoint, and for his own personal help, he needed their full time at home in business affairs. However since their work was also worthwhile, he made no suggestion that they discontinue it. One of the few general propositions that he laid down was to advise his associates to be well satisfied with a moderate profit. By definition, almost, he guarded his credit closely, paid his debts, and acted with the utmost fairness and honesty. He was not naïve; he looked to see that others acted in the same manner as he, and always availed himself of the ordinary protection of notes and contracts. He could say no when necessary.

He had grown up in an individualistic world and had been much impressed with the new science and view of life that proceeded from Darwin. Yet he tempered his actions with a compelling sense of duty and community responsibility. He did not give up his personality, nor did he let it run wild. An agent for a reputable church agency wrote him for money in the later years, saying that "... by your energy, skill & economy with God's blessings you have gathered much of this world's goods. By giving this sum it will not impoverish you nor by withholding it will not enrich you."[43] This was the year in which the Major endowed the college, and he replied right shortly: "You do not know the circumstances in which I am placed and you are not in position to determine how I shall distribute what I possess. That responsibility is mine and I must follow the dictates of my own conscience. You must excuse me."[44]

Despite his accomplishments he had always been more

---

42. Major Coker to Mrs. R. F. Watson, July 14, 1914 (Watson collection).

43. From a prominent minister to Major Coker, November 19, 1910 (Watson collection).

44. Major Coker to a prominent minister, November 21, 1910 (Watson Collection).

interested in the process of accomplishment than in the ends themselves. As he passed seventy-five and headed toward eighty this became more apparent: "Time only will work out the problems that confront us."[45] He remained acute, but in these years just before and during the first World War, times were changing rapidly. When the outbreak of the war demoralized the commodity and money markets, there were many schemes for the relief of the farmers in the way of loans on cotton. "I fear we will not have any good results from the schemes of legislators, politicians and others."[46] Yet, as a last testament, he believed that ". . . our people intend to be honest, and, that being the case, suitable indulgence can be extended to them without great risk."[47]

45. Major Coker to C. C. Twitty, October 13, 1914 (Watson collection).
46. *Ibid.*
47. Major Coker to Bright Williamson, September 2, 1914 (Watson collection).

9

D. R. Coker and the Collapse of Southern Rural Life

I

THE WAR had opened darkly for the cotton grower. Short cotton averaged just slightly over nine cents a pound in 1914 on the Hartsville market, down from an average of thirteen cents in 1913. Staple cotton drew a premium, but it too was down an average of more than a cent a pound. With a large part of the European markets gone, prospects were not good.

Yet as the American economy hummed to wartime, domestic demand for cotton increased and cotton followed the other commodities, and all the rest of the economy, on and upward. At Hartsville, in 1915, short cotton sold for an average of twelve cents; for nineteen and a half cents in 1916; twenty-seven in 1917, twenty-eight in 1918, and hit a peak average of forty and a half cents in 1919. Paralleling, staple cotton also shot upward, until by 1919 inch and five-sixteenths cotton averaged over eighty-one cents a pound.[1] On March 30, 1920, Mr. D. R. Coker* wrote that "strict middling 15/16" cotton is bringing here today 40c, while strict middling 1¼" cotton is bringing $1. (I have bought these lengths and these grades at these prices today.)"[2] Across the South the 1919 crop sold for thirty-five cents a pound, and, though never before, brought in two billion dollars to the cotton farmers.[3]

1. *Coker's Pedigreed Seed Catalogue*, Spring, 1923, p. 3.
2. D. R. Coker to Albert D. Oliphant, March 30, 1920 (Mrs. D. R. Coker).
3. A. B. Genung, "Agriculture in the World War Period," *Yearbook of Agriculture, 1940* (Washington: U. S. Government Printing Office, 1940), p. 285.
    * David of the preceding chapters will hereafter be referred to as Mr. D. R. Coker.

The cotton farmers were not just thirsty. They were bone dry and parched. The years before World War I have since been called parity years; but as Mr. D. R. well knew, there was no fat and mighty little lean in these years. This great new cascade of money was a wonderful thing. Weathered men who had scarcely seen any money in years now had hundreds and thousands of dollars. Large farmers, who before had made a living, now in 1919 had twenty-five, fifty and even hundred thousand dollar crops. True, labor was up; farm machinery was up; feed was up; clothes were up; and the money was cheap money. But it did not seem so, and cash money in hand had been a long time coming. A great many mortgaged their farms and bought new lands at high prices to grow more cotton. Almost all contracted for labor at high figures, bought fertilizer and farm machinery at inflated prices. A good many also bought automobiles, clothes, and gadgets that had been long out of reach. Merchants and bankers extended credit freely and a large number began speculative ventures of their own.[4]

There seemed to be no limit on cotton prices as the spring of 1920 came around and the land was turned for cotton. The crop that went into the ground cost a lot of borrowed money; it went in at inflated prices and on great hopes.

The hopes were not good. That fall, at Hartsville, short cotton averaged seventeen cents, not half of the 1919 average; the long inch and five-sixteenths cotton averaged only thirty-two cents—this cotton that had often sold for a dollar and more a pound the year before.[5] As vivid as they are, the averages don't tell the whole story. By December, "This year, to the present, over 20,000 bales, practically all staples, have been sold here at prices ranging from 63c to 18c for the better grades, while short cotton has been bringing from 30c down to 12c."[6] The drop from good September prices had been fast and far. No farmer that autumn got what he had counted on; many,

---

4. Chester C. Davis, "Development of Agricultural Policy Since the World War," *Yearbook of Agriculture, 1940* (Washington: U. S. Printing Office, 1940), p. 299.
5. *Coker's Pedigreed Seed Company Catalogue*, 1923, p. 3.
6. D. R. Coker to J. W. Gaines, December 31, 1920 (Mrs. D. R. Coker).

pushed to the wall by debts, brought their cotton to market for prices that did not pay half the cost of growing.

As usual the situation with regard to selling or holding cotton was chaotic. The farmer was on his own judgment, and in general he distrusted tomorrow's price in favor of what he could get today. Crowded markets pushed prices down further. At Hartsville, in an attempt to salvage as much as possible for the farmers from the situation, the principal cotton buyers, who were dealing mainly in staple cotton, agreed not to bid on cotton except when they had specific orders from mills. This arrangement maintained a certain amount of competition among the buyers themselves and allowed them to pay a full market price rather than a lower, speculative, price.

Our market was closed here from October 16 to 26 inclusive and again from November 6 to 15th inclusive. On October 15 strict middling 1¼ cotton was bringing 30c and on October 27 it brought 34c. On November 5 it was also bringing about 30c, but the decline in the New York market and in the price of goods made it impossible to get orders except at lower prices and the market was reopened on the 16th at about 22c for strict middling 1¼. This grade is today bringing 23c.

During the last closed interval of this market I know of strict middling 1¼ cotton which sold as low as 16c to speculators in surrounding markets. If every cotton market in the South would remain closed when it had no legitimate orders the farmers would realize current values for their cotton.[7]

Great losses were, nevertheless, sustained in the Hartsville area, but "This immediate area is suffering less than any other in the south that I know for it has made a maximum crop in almost all of which is staple cotton worth 2c to 10c per pound more than short cotton."[8]

The Major had been dead now for almost two years, and this was the first crisis that the family at Hartsville had ex-

7. D. R. Coker to E. H. Pringle, Jr., November 26, 1920 (Mrs. D. R. Coker).
8. D. R. Coker to T. H. Price, January 10, 1921 (Mrs. D. R. Coker).

COLLAPSE OF SOUTHERN RURAL LIFE 193

perienced without him. In March of 1921 Mr. D. R. wrote his brother, Dr. Will Coker, in Chapel Hill, N.C., that

... The condition here in practically all of our businesses except the Cotton Company is very depressing. I think the C. F. Co. and the Novelty Co. are running about even now. The Fertilizer Company will sustain a big loss on high priced raw materials and probably a considerable loss on carried over accounts, besides from now on business will probably be cut in half. The steady decline in oil mill products will probably not allow the Oil Mill to come out even. The Seed Company has, I think, sold about one fourth of their seed and will have to borrow around $100,000 to carry them until next fall. J. L. Coker and Company have a heavy carry over of debts from last year and sales are running about 60% of last year. The Cotton Company has thus far furnished J. L. Coker and Company with most of the money they needed to borrow—about $40,000.[9]

The Bank of Hartsville, like the store, was heavily involved in farm credit and its position also was alarming. All told, the situation presented a considerable test of family solidarity. While the holdings of each member of the family in all of the enterprises were substantial, each one had his main responsibilities: James to The Carolina Fiber Company; David to J. L. Coker and Company, the Coker Cotton Company, and the Pedigreed Seed Company; Charles to the Southern Novelty Company; and Joe Lawton to The Hartsville Oil Mill and The Hartsville Fertilizer Company. As Mr. D. R. wrote his brother in the letter quoted above, "All of us here have been under a severe strain . . ." but, he added, ". . . are doing the best we can under the circumstances."[10]

The best under the circumstances was a great amount of mutual help. The situation worsened after the date of the above letter before it improved, but support was brought up wherever it was needed, and all of the enterprises were able to survive. Perhaps the most concerted support was given to the bank, which became and has continued as a symbol of family

---

9. D. R. Coker to Dr. W. C. Coker, March 19, 1921 (Mrs. D. R. Coker).
10. *Ibid.*

interest and cooperation. Hartsville, for the most part, has been spared the terrible losses of bank failures.

The crisis was met, but there was a difference. In earlier times J. L. Coker and Company, the Major's "old milk cow," had been the stable element. Now it was a borrower, not a lender. Its profits had come from agriculture. However the farmers to whom credit had been extended could not pay up. As late as February 2, 1921, Mr. D. R. wrote that ". . . our collections have been very poor, only about twenty-five per cent having come in thus far."[11] There had been other bad years for cotton farmers, but this terrible blow of 1920-21 was decisive. The resilience was gone: the foreign market for cotton was seriously curtailed, the boll weevil was expected to appear in full force on the 1921 crop in South Carolina, and almost every farmer's future was a shambles of debt. It was the beginning of the end of the old cotton economy.

Pushed to the wall, and with the future dark, J. L. Coker and Company took the first necessary step in liquidating the older ways: for 1921 it could not extend farmers the usual, long-term credit. Customers of long standing would be accommodated as necessary, but the rule would be that "all credits in the future will be made on a strictly banking plan."[12]

Mr. D. R. had been wary of the wartime prosperity. Even so, he had had this hope: that the farmers through thrift and caution, could skim off and keep enough capital to clear the boards of debt and come even with the game. To this end he spoke neither softly nor privately: "There is abundant evidence that many of our people are engaged in a perfect orgy of money spending. I was told today of a large plantation upon which the tenants had each made a net profit of from $500.00 to $1500.00, and that all of these tenants together could probably not raise $300.00 in cash today."[13]

As prosperity continued after the end of the war and

11. D. R. Coker to W. C. Coker, February 2, 1921 (Mrs. D. R. Coker).
12. Advertisement in the *Hartsville Messenger*.
13. "Open Letter to Farmers," 1917 (Mrs. D. R. Coker).

through 1919 he remained both wary and hopeful. In December of 1919 he sent to the state newspapers an article titled "Danger Signals" in which he warned again and in detail of the artificial nature of wages, capital profits, commodity prices, interest rates and speculative returns. Yet amid these danger signals he saw some moderate hope that a successful descent from inflation could be made: "The South is apparently winning her strenuous fight for fair prices for cotton. The people of the State are in the best financial condition in their history. Let us all pull together to conserve the financial resources we have recently accumulated and go steadily forward in our struggle for economic independence."[14] In that same December of 1919 he predicted with amazing accuracy the fall of cotton prices late in September of 1920.[15] Yet, as late as July of 1920 he thought it possible that ". . . agriculture in this section is on the eve of becoming permanently more profitable."[16]

Perhaps his private hopes were more sanguine than those he expressed in public, for when the clearing dust from the crash showed that the South was in worse shape than ever, his disappointment was complete. Writing publicly of the situation in October of 1920 he laid the blame where it seemed to fit: "Our people have made enormous profits during the past three years. If they had chosen to hold on to a fair proportion of these profits they would have been completely free from outside financial dictation and need not have been under the compulsion of selling a bale of the present crop until satisfactory prices were forthcoming. Instead . . . they spent their profits and have gone into debt to the very limit of the ability of the banks to finance. Hundreds of millions of dollars have been drawn into the South to finance this crop, whereas our own resources should have been conserved for this purpose."[17] In his view, this period of prosperity was the first time since

14. "Danger Signals," letter to Governor R. I. Manning that was circulated to the state newspapers (Mrs. D. R. Coker).
15. D. R. Coker to J. Adger Smyth, Jr., December 4, 1919 (Mrs. D. R. Coker).
16. D. R. Coker to S. P. Stoney, July 21, 1920 (Mrs. D. R. Coker).
17. "The Cotton Situation—Its Causes and Remedies," letter sent to the *State* and *News and Courier,* dated October 19, 1920.

the Civil War that the South had had the opportunity to accumulate sufficient capital to break the ceaseless chain of the farmers who ". . . owe the merchants and the bankers who in turn owe the jobbers, the large city banks, and the Federal Reserve Bank."[18]

It was not just the loss of a certain amount of money that made the situation tragic. It was also the condition to which the South was returning. Return to normalcy meant merely ". . . that our labor employed in cotton production will have to re-enter a condition of practical slavery."[19] Complacency in certain quarters somewhat removed from the situation irritated him considerably: "It is all right to talk about the South taking its loss and liquidating but the fact is that there has not been sufficient demand to take care of the small amounts of cotton coming on the markets. . . . The tenant farmer has already taken his loss and in many instances has been left to shift for himself in mid-winter with practically nothing to do."[20] He was saying that an era was over, that the breaking point had been reached.

He went to England in June of 1921, and, directly and bluntly, told the august, formal World Cotton Conference, that "The cotton world must be made to understand that the South has only been able to raise cotton in the past at prices under fifteen cents per lb. by paying wages only sufficient to maintain the average laborer and his family in a condition of dire poverty. . . ." He then read the great of cotton a balance sheet for the average landowner and tenant in South Carolina. The landowner lost money; the net profit to the tenant for the year's work was $194.[21]

II

Mr. D. R. had done his thinking on seed breeding before the roof fell in, and work was already well underway. In

---

18. *Ibid.*
19. D. R. Coker to J. W. Norwood, November 27, 1920 (Mrs. D. R. Coker).
20. D. R. Coker to Theodore H. Price, January 10, 1921 (Mrs. D. R. Coker).
21. This address, published in pamphlet form, was entitled "How Can the Quality of the American Cotton Crop Be Improved and the Supply Kept Adequate to the Demand?" (Mrs. D. R. Coker).

COLLAPSE OF SOUTHERN RURAL LIFE 197

cotton the need was clear: "I have my breeding force actively at work in trying to produce a *bread and butter* cotton for the South which will run about 1-1/16 staple, high percent of lint, very early in maturing, very high in production, and with seed of high oil content."[22]

The strategy of such cotton was powerful and simple. It did not require the skill in cultivation of long staple cotton, and therefore could spread among the generality of farmers. It would mature early enough to escape the worst of boll weevil damage. It would produce more per acre, and its consistent "inch" staple length would command a premium. Thus fewer acres would produce as much or more lint and greater money return. This was the only realistic way of releasing the much abused southern land for soil recovery and diversification.

The need for this cotton was apparent in 1915 before the wartime boom, when the search for a "bread and butter" cotton had been first undertaken. It was no less true when Mr. D. R. stated the program in July of 1920 before the crash; it remained true after the crash. Mr. D. R. had estimated that perhaps as long as ten years would be required to breed such a cotton. The plight of the agricultural South after 1920 did not lighten the prospects for what lay ahead, nor offer a hopeful future for such hard, creative work. He could, in fact, be discouraged. His brother James came into the seed company office one day in 1921 and found him depressed and moody. Prospects for the seed company were dark and Mr. D. R. informed his brother that he expected to go along with the seed company financially to the bitter end. "Well, David, if you go broke on this thing, then I will too."[23]

As with the long staple cotton earlier, this work on short staple cotton was a tedious process of selection. It was not until 1926 that a first climax was reached when the Pedigreed Coker-Cleveland Strain Five was introduced.[24] This cotton,

22. D. R. Coker to B. E. Geer, May 7, 1920 (Mrs. D. R. Coker).
23. Conversation with A. L. M. Wiggins.
24. *Coker's Pedigreed Seed Catalogue,* 1926.

which came to be known as Cleveland Five, was "inch cotton," a cotton trade way of summing up staple lengths of comparable mill use that run from 15/16 of an inch to 1-3/32 inches. Bred to a uniform staple of 1-1/16 inches under average Hartsville conditions, Cleveland Five consistently made usable inch cotton under varying conditions of soil, weather and cultivation. It was productive, matured early, and was highly storm resistant. In 1926 the South Carolina Extension Service estimated that about 20 per cent of the South Carolina cotton crop was inch cotton.[25] By 1928, when the first official figures were published by the U. S. Department of Agriculture, a third of the state's crop was in this category. By 1932 over 60 per cent of the cotton raised in South Carolina was good inch cotton, and drew a premium of from one-half to three cents a pound for staple length.[26]

The value of this cotton is almost incalculable. Cotton men today on the whole will say that the general raising of the average staple length of the bulk of the crop to around an inch or slightly better has been worth, across the years, about one cent a pound to the farmer. As he looked at the situation in 1932 Mr. D. R. was somewhat more conservative in regard to the contribution of the Cleveland Five up to that time: writing about the two Carolinas he thought that

> ... it is conservative to estimate that the two states have during the past six years produced, and the Carolina mills have consumed, at least one and one-half million bales, which . . . would have been bought from the west.
>
> I estimate that the mills have paid the farmers an average of at least ½c per pound premium for this cotton over local short staple prices, and that they themselves have secured this cotton at least ½c cheaper than they would have had to pay for western cotton of equal length. I am quite sure that I am within the facts when I say that the farmers and the mills of the Carolinas have received between five and ten million dollars during the past six years that

---

[25]. "Report of Committee on Cotton Production, Atlantic Cotton Association." Mr. Coker was chairman of the committee. The Association met in Greenville, S.C., April 16, 1934 (Mrs. D. R. Coker).

[26]. *Ibid.*

they would not have received but for our work of cotton breeding. This takes into consideration only the length and spinning quality of the cotton and not the excess yield which the new varieties are making over the average of the shorter staples.[27]

There was a corollary, of course, to a bread and butter cotton. This was something to take the place of land that might be released. The main emphasis was on small grains, principally oats, that would hold the soil in winter, enrich it with humus, and provide feed for livestock. This was the second major part of his breeding strategy.

By 1920 improvement had been made in the Fulghum oat, increasing its yield considerably. But the South grows oats in the winter, harvesting in the spring to make way for the summers' corn and cash crops. An oat that could withstand the winter's cold was required, and the Fulghum could not do this.

At first it was hoped that a cold resistant oat could be isolated by saving and reproducing those plants that survived in a field that was severely damaged by cold. After some cost and disappointment along this line, it was decided that hybridization offered a better prospect. In 1921, Mr. J. B. Norton made numerous crosses between the relatively heavy yielding Fulghum and several cold resistant varieties. Mr. Norton, a man whose life was the study of growing things, had come to the Pedigreed Seed Company in 1920 from the U. S. Department of Agriculture. One of his crosses, between the Fulghum and a Grayside oat, showed such promise that all others were abandoned. A large number of plants from this cross were in plant-to-rows in the winter of 1923-24. That winter was very severe. Approximately 97 per cent of the Fulghum checks were killed, but a number of selections coming from this cross came through over 90 per cent and made splendid yield records. From this hybrid, by continuous selection, testing and elimination on yield and cold resistance was bred the Norton oat, which was introduced in 1927.[28]

27. Typed manuscript written by D. R. Coker in 1932 (Mrs. D. R. Coker).
28. George J. Wilds, "Commercial Oat Breeding," speech before the annual meeting of the Georgia Agronomists, January 22, 1947.

Cold was not the only problem. Immunity to disease also had to be bred into otherwise good oats. In the spring of 1924 a low yielding oat, Ferguson's Navarro, that was immune to smut disease was crossed with the cold resistant, good producing Norton oat. Breeding this oat for high yield, cold and smut resistance was a long and tedious process. By the time the decade came to a close there were over a hundred selections from this work under test that showed excellent promise, but it would not be until 1935 that a climax of these efforts would be reached in the very excellent Fulgrain oat.

III

The seed breeding was a clear line of hopeful work running through a decade that, otherwise, became for Mr. D. R. a social and economic nightmare. For whatever kind of prosperity returned to the remainder of the country after the collapse of the early twenties, there was no real recovery in the agricultural South; there were only desperate attempts to recoup in a deteriorating situation where there was no margin of profit. Almost all of Mr. D. R.'s fears were fulfilled, but none of his moderate hopes that the rural South had maintained some part of its war and postwar advance. It was a decade, and more, of increasing collapse, of worry and tension, of the leaching away of many hitherto stable positions around which the region's life was built: good farmers—men who held large families and tenants and communities together, who had weathered a life's seasons of cotton growing—tried over and again to move along with a new crop of cotton, but found everything mercurial and insubstantial, and looked on puzzled and hurt as profits and land, tenants and children, and finally hope, were drained off. Merchants and bankers, somehow symbols of a going cotton economy and always symbols of personal fortune and status, grasped desperately at crumpled, brittle paper whose value fled always just beyond their finger tips. Tenants were cast loose with less than nothing by the irresponsible or the completely bankrupt, else they clung to the

COLLAPSE OF SOUTHERN RURAL LIFE 201

old places, sharing what there was in a Saturday's doling out of meat and meal.

Proposals for remedy appeared, some fairly radical, for the need was vital and personal. Mr. D. R. could not "... conceive that any American citizen should really want another American citizen to try to raise his family in a condition of abject poverty and ignorance."[29] Failing the awakening of a better conscience in the world, he could, when he let himself go to old friends, contemplate with some satisfaction "... a prompt exodus from the farms which would very quickly bring the world to a realization that it must pay the agricultural producer more for his products or go naked and starve."[30]

Generally, these proposals looked to a voluntary reduction of cotton acreage, and to a voluntary cooperative marketing of cotton. Mr. D. R. did not see in these programs any real incentive to the balanced, diversified farmer, but his main serious objection was simply that these proposals would not work. He had "... little confidence in the efforts to reduce acreage by agreement, because a very large proportion will not agree."[31]

... Frankly I do not feel that cooperative marketing as a general proposition in the South is going to be a very great success until the general average of education among our farmers is considerably raised. As long as members are comparatively uneducated and unfamiliar with business methods it will be easier for self-seeking or politically minded men to get control of the organizations and use them for their own profit. Even if the correct type of management is secured it may be subjected to great annoyance by lack of business knowledge of the members.[32]

Yet of course something was needed. Partly because of his experience and the success of staple cotton around Hartsville, and partly because of his acquaintance with European agriculture, he began to work toward community, or small area, development, generally known as reclamation projects.

29. D. R. Coker to Hugh MacRae, January 22, 1921 (Mrs. D. R. Coker).
30. D. R. Coker to Dr. W. H. Mills, May 4, 1921 (Mrs. D. R. Coker).
31. D. R. Coker to W. A. Stuckey, January 20, 1921 (Mrs. D. R. Coker).
32. D. R. Coker to Dr. W. H. Mills, May 14, 1924 (Mrs. D. R. Coker).

These reclamation colonies were to be pathfinders and examples for the generality of farmers. State financing was required, but this was denied by the Legislature of a poverty-ridden state. Nor was it possible to obtain Federal sponsorship on a south-wide basis.

The deterioration of southern agriculture and rural life continued, and many people were rapidly approaching starvation in the midst of potential plenty. By 1925 it was true that "the majority of our people have not been prosperous since the spring of 1920, and nearly all are disappointed at the present year's crop outturn, which . . . will net little or no profit."[33]

The next five years were worse. In the Hartsville-Darlington County area a virtual climax, beyond which things could not get much worse, was reached in the crop years of 1928 and 1929. In both years there were almost complete crop failures due to weather. On September 22, 1928, Mr. D. R. wrote that "I have never known a worse condition of discouragement and depression among the farmers. Share croppers in large numbers are threatening to quit their crops unless full picking wages are paid them. They can hardly be blamed for this, as they have no equity in their crops and their families must live."[34]

By November of 1928 there had been

. . . fifteen bank failures in this and the two counties adjoining, North and South, within the past month. One bank out of eight is open in Chesterfield County and three out of eight in Darlington County. Nothing could more clearly evidence the prostration of agriculture, for these bank failures are all due to a persistent absence of farm profits for the past nine years. A large part of the land in this section is under mortgage to these failed banks and under present conditions it is unsalable at any price.[35]

This was a current situation. Attuned to it in many directions, he did not have to wait for a stock market's crash or a decennial census to know what was going on.

33. D. R. Coker to William E. Gonzales, November 20, 1925 (Mrs. D. R. Coker).
34. D. R. Coker to I. O. Schaub, September 22, 1928 (Mrs. D. R. Coker).
35. D. R. Coker to W. M. Garrard, November 15, 1928 (Mrs. D. R. Coker).

COLLAPSE OF SOUTHERN RURAL LIFE 203

The next year, 1929, was no better, especially around Hartsville where storms and wet weather and the boll weevil ruined the crop again. By November of 1929 ". . . a very large proportion of the farm population of the County—probably one-third—is without adequate means of subsistence. Many are on the point of starvation. . . ."[36]

IV

After these many years of effort, and with this result, Mr. D. R. was forced to a fundamental conclusion. Convinced of the necessity of a complete readjustment of southern agriculture, he became at last convinced, if reluctantly, that "there is no agency at present which can or will do this work except the National Government."[37] The condition of poverty, long endured, required relief.

In 1929, as a member of a committee, Mr. D. R. wrote an appeal to President Hoover for Federal help in the establishment of the reclamation projects. Writing this for a specific purpose, he explained the need in terms of the general national situation:

Southern rural rehabilitation is not exclusively a southern problem. Its solution will affect the prosperity of the entire Nation. Agricultural prosperity is so important to the welfare of the Nation that your Committee believes that similar steps, after demonstration in the South, might well be undertaken in most or all of the other states.[38]

No substantial help was then forthcoming, but he did not fold his hands. The structure was falling in on itself, and he knew it, but he threw every resource at his disposal into holding what there was and building for the future. He would not quit. Almost every year he fought the fight for Extension Service funds in the legislature of a poverty ridden state. J. L. Coker and Company, as the depression deepened, began to sell

36. D. R. Coker to Hon. A. H. Gasque, November 30, 1929 (Mrs. D. R. Coker).
37. D. R. Coker to Hugh MacRae, April 9, 1929 (Mrs. D. R. Coker).
38. Address to President Hoover by Committee of Seven States, 1929, written by D. R. Coker, undated (Mrs. D. R. Coker).

the ingredients of boll weevil poison at cost. He carried on ceaselessly the struggle that he had begun in 1921 to have adopted a cheap and simple method of boll weevil control that might be used by tenants as well as large planters. Day in and day out he wrote and talked, to newspapers, to magazines, to friends, to farm groups and city groups, to school children, and always that ceaseless personal meeting with farmers who came to Hartsville.

In 1929 he made a tremendous effort to lift Darlington County by its bootstraps. He organized, financed, and conducted a large five-acre cotton contest in which a hundred Darlington County farmers participated. The best seeds were furnished as well as expert supervision. The fates were unwilling, for this was one of the years when wet weather caused a virtual crop failure. On the whole the contestants fared better than the average Darlington farmer, but a sensational success was required to make the case, if at all, and in the outturn Mr. D. R. took a substantial financial loss along with his disappointment.[39]

In all adversity he gave his best energy and efforts to the Pedigreed Seed Company and there they were needed in full measure. Insofar as it was the pre-eminent institution of its kind in the eastern South, the seed company was a heart trying to pump blood into a body whose functions were halting, often irrational, and in some places atrophied. The survival of the seed company was purely an act of faith, first, of Mr. D. R., and also in considerable measure of the Hartsville branch of the family.

This was his life work and he stayed with it. On several occasions he was urged to run for Governor by highly responsible people who had reason to estimate his chances correctly. Nothing was or is certain in South Carolina politics, but no one was better or more favorably known to the farmers in this rural state, and also to the manufacturers and business men. Undoubtedly, as have all the Cokers, he would have found it

39. D. R. Coker to S. H. Schoolfield, January 30, 1930 (Mrs. D. R. Coker).

difficult to canvass the voters. However, on the basis of the public need, he might well have acceded but for the fact that "I have gained a position of some influence in the State by my agricultural work and my willingness to spend much of my time in advising the farmers. I have a considerable clientage which I feel I am serving usefully and I feel sure that if I stood for public office many of these men would no longer follow me."[40]

The seed company had not been established to make money, and, indeed, Mr. D. R. was never able to look on it as primarily a business proposition. It became a big operation and it had, therefore, at least to break even. After its incorporation in 1913, modest profits were made until 1921 when heavy losses were sustained. The next two years showed small profits but operations were in the red for both 1924 and 1925. It appeared that only substantial expansion would take care of the high capital costs of breeding and this was accomplished. Following this, operations were profitable in a modest way through the spring sales of 1928. Severe losses were sustained on farm operations that fall, and in succeeding years, as the depression deepened, deficits mounted.[41] As early as 1926 Mr. D. R. had begun to cast about for ways to perpetuate the seed company as a public service, well aware that the breeding of seed could not expect to fare well until southern agriculture righted itself. For the next several years he made efforts to have the company endowed, but without success.[42]

Left on his own, his decision was to stick, and he threw everything into the hopper.[43] By January of 1932

the Pedigreed Seed Company has seen the worst year of its history. The statement indicates a loss of about $48,000.00. . . . The writer has thrown his entire financial resources behind the two com-

---

40. D. R. Coker to Dr. Elison A. Smythe, June 2, 1925 (Mrs. D. R. Coker).
41. "Financial History and Structure of Coker's Pedigreed Seed Company," typed memorandum by D. R. Coker in his papers of 1929 (Mrs. D. R. Coker).
42. See "The Coker Foundation for the Advancement of Southern Agriculture," by A. L. M. Wiggins, under articles and speeches, 1929 (Mrs. D. R. Coker). Also, letter to Hugh MacRae, September 20, 1928; letter from Frank Chambers to D. R. Coker, December 13, 1926.
43. Conversation with A. L. M. Wiggins.

panies, and is personally carrying a major percentage of the Seed Company's finances. At the present moment, they owe me about $94,000.00, forty thousand of which I am borrowing on personal collateral and the balance of which represents all the money I could scrape together during the year in dividends and sales of stocks.[44]

At this same time the seed company also owed J. L. Coker and Company in excess of $100,000.

Mr. D. R. naturally assumed the largest part of the burden, but it was in part also a family affair, if for no other reason than that all members of the family owned stock in both the seed company and in the store. "The majority of our stockholders in both companies concur with me in the position that we must maintain the stability and credit of our companies and of the Bank at all hazards, and I have been tendered such financial assistance as may be needed by several of them. As stated above, my entire resources are at the disposal of these businesses, as I would not care to own a dollar's worth of property if either of the institutions with a long and honorable reputation of usefulness would have to come to an end. I am drawing no salary from any of them."[45]

V

The times were bitter and gray. When the decade changed its numbers Mr. D. R. moved out of his fifties and into his sixties. He still wore his full, close cut beard that was now shot with gray. There were before him no completely well years, but he moved firmly and forcefully, the years of his work cloaking him about in a distinguished way.

The spirit was there, and did not diminish. As late as the year of his death he wrote an old, old friend to come for a visit at the "high tide in our home garden and at Kalmia." He promised a week-end filled with flowers and growing plants, and the glories of the new grains. Then "we could

---

44. D. R. Coker to Will and Susie, January 27, 1932 (Mrs. D. R. Coker).
45. *Ibid.*

COLLAPSE OF SOUTHERN RURAL LIFE 207

spend Sunday morning, while the regenerate are attending to their religious duties, in making private and unprintable comments on the times and the state of the nation."[46]

Yet now at the turn of the decade lean faced men walked the streets, and down the dusty roads, and when they met there was no need to talk for with "five cent cotton and ten cent meat, how in the world can a poor man eat?" It was like this as he came to his sixties. After a full thirty years of living the parable of good seed, he saw not just the South but the whole nation was falling in on itself. And so he sought once more to understand the whole. He worked too hard to be a Jeremiah. But having spent his health and risked fortune on works, he responded out of his vast experience with something of an elder's intuition: "Like Sampson, I fear our present civilization is pulling down the temple upon its own head and will destroy itself."[47] "I refer to the rapid improvement in the chemical and mechanical processes which are rapidly reducing the amount of human labor required per unit of manufactures."[48]

Few yet realize that the tremendous urge for cheap mass production is improving industrial and chemical processes more and more rapidly year by year and is throwing out labor at a more rapid pace than it can be absorbed anywhere else in industry. The same process is becoming more and more evident in agriculture as great bodies of land are being mechanized.[49]

He was trying to state the problem, searchingly, not in a formal way but as the occasion arose when he wrote his friends, or as he formulated specific programs. He was an agrarian for all his other interests and knew it: "My thesis is that we have but one problem; i.e., the saving of the civilization of our state. I should say that nine-tenths of this problem is rural and agricultural. The bankers, manufacturers, merchants, professional men, churches, schools and the state government can-

46. D. R. Coker to Judge Henry C. Hammond, April 21, 1938 (Mrs. D. R. Coker).
47. D. R. Coker to D. D. Wallace, May 30, 1934 (Mrs. D. R. Coker).
48. D. R. Coker to John T. Roddy, December 6, 1930 (Mrs. D. R. Coker).
49. D. R. Coker to Hugh MacRae, April 7, 1931 (Mrs. D. R. Coker).

not be saved unless rural life and agricultural profits are improved. I shall work along this line as long as I see hope of success or as long as I am physically able to proceed."[50] With all this he well knew that ". . . nothing can be done to stop the advance of science and its utilization."[51] Nor would he want it so. Few men had used science so well, or seen it work with such beneficence as he. Even as he deplored the apparent effect of mass production, he wrote that "agriculture today needs more than at any time in the past to utilize and profit by the work of the scientist."[52] He embraced happily all new developments of farm machinery, and often spoke feelingly of releasing the farmer, and his family, from the drudgery involved in much of farm work.[53]

It was not science or its physical children that caused his concern. Rather, it was those great impersonal forces of the new urban and industrial world that a man immersed as he was in country life was at a disadvantage in understanding. These forces seemed, first, to debase the balance of a sound rural life in the total society, and then to come crashing down of their own weight, carrying everything before them. In the crisis, he tended first to recur to a level of life that was somewhat less grandiose in material achievement, but more balanced and self-sufficient in the earlier American style. "Under present conditions the farmer and his laborers are in a safer position than those engaged in industry because the former class has shelter and usually fuel for the gathering and can produce (certainly in this section) the basic foods required for the sustenance of life, while millions of industrial laborers are idle and on the verge of starvation."[54]

What was the end? He could sustain no mood of resignation. In one of the clearest, most crystal-like and predictive passages of his career, he wrote in November of 1932 that:

50. D. R. Coker to Hugh MacRae, October 1, 1930 (Mrs. D. R. Coker).
51. D. R. Coker to D. W. Gaither, June 8, 1931 (Mrs. D. R. Coker).
52. "Report of the Committee on Agriculture, 1931," South Carolina Council, 1931. Mr. Coker was chairman of the committee and wrote the report.
53. Conversation with J. M. Napier.
54. "Report of Committee on Agriculture, 1931," South Carolina Council, 1931.

The great opportunity for Southern agriculture is in providing homes and a good living for the surplus population of the North and West, most of whom are now without means of support. Five to ten acre farms should be laid out in the South along our new improved roads by the millions. Part of the family would cultivate a garden, an orchard and a few acres of grain and forage and would look after a cow, pig and chickens. This would provide the bulk of the family food budget while one or two members of the family would work in the nearby town or city and provide the small additional revenue necessary. This type of agricultural development would encourage the movement to the South of industrial plants and provide the South with most of its manufactured products, which can be made and distributed here at much lower costs than in the North because of lower real estate costs, the greater purchasing power of money here, cheapness and abundance of food and a pleasant and healthful climate.[55]

In a paper of broader scope, he had previously asked "Why should not factories be built alongside rural railroads, interurban lines and our splendid paved roads on lands costing only a few dollars per acre and the laborers live within a few miles on two to ten acre farms, going to work on local trains or in automobiles or buses?"[56] It was a question framed both as a program and to state a way of life. It was the new integer of progress as he saw it, in the darkest days when social calamity and personal tragedy bore heavily upon him.

Whatever else, of one thing he was certain: ". . . the so-called educated and intelligent are calmly, nonchalantly and carelessly *sittin* on the bomb, unconscious that an explosion will occur unless prevented by intelligent and strenuous activity on their part."[57]

VI

Mr. D. R. worked to line up the South Carolina delegation for Governor Roosevelt of New York and went, in that critical summer of 1932, to Chicago as a delegate at large pledged to

55. D. R. Coker to Earl S. Haines, November 2, 1932 (Mrs. D. R. Coker).
56. "Report of Committee on Agriculture, 1931," South Carolina Council, 1931.
57. D. R. Coker to Rutledge Smith, November 28, 1930 (D. R. Coker).

Roosevelt's support.[58] Mrs. Coker, who knew the candidate from New York, made a seconding speech to Roosevelt's nomination at four o'clock one morning. Mr. D. R. came home pleased with the course of the convention and was assured that Governor Roosevelt ". . . is a gentleman in every sense of the word and is allied with the best and soundest men in the Party. . . ."[59] Of greater importance, he felt that "the Democratic standard bearer . . . realizes what few of those now influential governmental leaders seem to have sensed, i.e., that the agricultural and rural life of the Country must be reestablished on a sound and profitable basis if our American civilization is to survive."[60]

There was some responsible editorial mention and advocacy of Mr. D. R.'s being named Secretary of Agriculture, and a good many southern leaders stirred themselves in his behalf. Mr. D. R. held himself available but made no efforts. It is likely that he would have been a strong candidate except for two factors. It is doubtful that the President-Elect intended to appoint other than a midwesterner to Agriculure. Further, Daniel C. Roper had claims to consideration for cabinet membership. Mr. Roper was a South Carolinian by birth and Mr. D. R.'s father-in-law.

That fall and winter of 1932-33 was a time for searching for programs to fulfill the hopes of the new administration. Hugh MacRae got together a group of southern leaders to meet candidate Roosevelt in Atlanta in September, to discuss the needs of southern agriculture. Mr. D. R. was unable to go, but he sent along to Mr. MacRae a brief statement of a general program. He began by stating that "we must have a policy of financing bona fide farmers for the purpose of buying land and building homes, and we must create better conditions both by the reduction of their tax and tariff burdens and by a system of direct adult education which will permit the prompt and

---

58. See letter to Jas. M. Baker, May 13, 1932; also letter to H. B. Harris from A. L. M. Wiggins, June 25, 1932 (Mrs. D. R. Coker).

59. D. R. Coker to Judge Henry C. Hammond, September 10, 1932 (Mrs. D. R. Coker).

60. D. R. Coker to Hugh MacRae, September 2, 1932 (Mrs. D. R. Coker).

profitable improvement of agricultural production."[61] He then went on to lay out the ways of achieving these ends. All that he said had roots in the thirty years of his work. His main object remaining the individual farmer, he asked for government funds, advice and some supervision so that the farmer could be established soundly on his farm.

Yet there was a difference—quite simply, in the fact that the program was presented, and that it located the initiative in the national government. He knew the dangers well, and feared that we will ". . . end up by all working our fingers to the bone to support an enormous horde of government workers in semi-idleness."[62] The terrible, senseless, tragic poverty of southern agriculture that he had toiled with for thirty years had to come to an end, regardless.

In the outcome, the programs having major support proposed to create with government funds artificial minimum prices for stated commodities. He did not feel that such a program went to the heart of the matter, but, again, he would not resist what would help the farmer. He felt bitterly that the years of protective tariffs had ". . . made the North immensely rich at the expense of the South and West and although labor in protected industries is receiving five to ten times as much as labor in agriculture."[63] He told his business friends quite frankly that if such a program "is the only thing that offers any hope of raising the prices of wheat and cotton to points where the producers of these commodities can live, it will probably be applied and the rest of the country will have to make the best of it."[64]

He was in fact in a torment that would never be resolved in his lifetime. One of his most balanced and thorough statements of the general agricultural situation was the "Report of the Committee on Agriculture, 1931," of the South Carolina Council. Here he reaffirmed, for instance, that "many farmers who have not had the opportunity of a college education are

61. *Ibid.*
62. D. R. Coker to G. H. Milliken, December 27, 1932.
63. *Ibid.*
64. *Ibid.*

real scientists in certain lines, have developed superior methods by experimentation and observation and sometimes have originated varieties of economic plants and animals which are superior and valuable." This, and other similar points, were from his earlier days. But, as for a solution, he went this far in the other direction:

It should be manifest to all that it is the duty of government not only to insure the safety of its citizens and the protection of their property but also to insure to them an opportunity to labor and earn a subsistence for themselves and families.

He knew how far he had gone, and it was not easy. He explained it, saying, "the plain fact is that the tariff is transferring vast sums of money, rightfully belonging to the farmer, to the pockets of the manufacturer. The farmer cannot be placed in his rightful competitive position until the tariff is radically revised in the interests of agriculture." He also paid his respects to the basic tenets of his faith:

When Thomas Jefferson and his co-workers were forming the Government of the United States it naturally never occurred to them that a time would ever come in this Country when a man who was willing to work would find it impossible to find a place to work and earn the minimum necessary livelihood for himself and dependents. History today, however, is recording the fact that six millions or more of our able-bodied American citizens are unable to find employment and that they with their families are consuming their accumulated savings, depending on charity or are suffering for the necessities of life. This situation follows closely upon the greatest period of prosperity and wealth accumulation that this Country has ever seen.[65]

VII

Mr. D. R. and the new Secretary Wallace established good relations from the first. They had in common their interest in seed breeding and their zeal for agricultural improvement. For all practical purposes, Mr. D. R. went along in support of the New Deal farm program. But the manner of his going

65. "Report of Committee on Agriculture, 1931," South Carolina Council, 1931.

along, the reasons for it, his doubts and reservations, are all pertinent to the history of the man and of the time.

The establishment of the Triple A was the first move of the new administration in agriculture. It was done hurriedly to meet the needs of the crop year of 1933 that had already started when the administration took office. This act was based on the assumption that, in the crisis of a nation in depression, overproduction was the basic problem of agriculture. Simply, this act sought an across-the-board reduction of specified farm products, among them cotton, the object being to raise prices. The farmers received benefit payments for their acreage reduction, as well as the increased prices.[66]

On its own merits, this program did not recommend itself to Mr. D. R. His papers for 1933 have been imperfectly saved, and it is unlikely that he wrote much, in view of the seriousness of the situation, in respect to his objections. But he did have some serious doubts. This program did not deal directly with the urgent problems of ownership, education, new cash crops, and diversified farming. An across-the-board reduction of cotton acreage offered no differential incentive to the good farmer; in fact, the good farmer was penalized for past progress. It was not a long-range solution to successful farming except on the assumption that the government would maintain farm prices at an artificial level year in and year out. It was a program that of necessity would be centralized in Washington.

He had, in addition, a personal objection. Under the Triple A regulations the Pedigreed Seed Company farms were considered ordinary farming operations. Acreage reduction would apply there as elsewhere. Cotton lint was secondary to the production of seed, but its sale helped to defray the expenses of the seed. Thus the seed company could either reduce its output of cotton seed, take a severe loss from the payment of penalties on cotton produced in excess of quota, or increase considerably the price of seed. Considering that the seed com-

---

66. H. E. Shiver, B. F. Buie, and Inman F. Eldredge, *South Carolina Raw Materials* (Columbia: The University of South Carolina Press, 1949), pp. 38-39.

pany was operating at a loss as a public service, none of this made sense, then or now. Mr. D. R.'s first reaction was not to join the program. Yet he knew that under the circumstances this was the nation's program for at least a year, that there was no possibility of any other program, and he was vitally aware that some move had to be made. It is unlikely that he ever considered any public disapproval; he committed himself personally to the program when old and trusted friends advised him that his participation would ease the inevitable adoption of the program in Darlington County.

Having joined the program he complied fully and undertook a sympathetic interest in its progress. But, apparently as must all elders, he suffered some irritations in the dawning of a new day. It was a long way from Hartsville to Washington; and a far cry from the easy and informal relations with the state extension people that had become habitual with him. Southern agriculture had passed from the semi-public and public hands of such as he and Dr. Long into the new, growing bureaucratic structure in Washington.

It was, indeed, a long way from Hartsville to Washington, or from Omaha or Austin to Washington, and along this new distance in American life there was much confusion. He sought to keep the way open, characteristically trying to bring the responsible individuals at either end into close and continuing contact. Locally, the great brunt of the program fell on the extension service man in each county, the County Farm Agent. He was the man, and his office the place, where the farmer met the program, received his allotment, had his crops checked, drew his benefit checks, made his complaints. Time and again Mr. D. R. sought to present the problems of the County Agent to appropriate officials in Washington. In general, replies were polite and respectful, but inconclusive.

In fact, there was something approaching tragedy in this situation, where the Jeffersonian agrarian and the New Deal agrarians could not bridge the gap that lay between them. Mr. D. R. was not well during these years. A heart condition had for several years past put a severe restriction on his hours

COLLAPSE OF SOUTHERN RURAL LIFE 215

of application. Replying to a request for an article on the cotton farmer's problem in 1938, he would ". . . see if I can get together an article. . . . However, I have been confined to my home for practically the entire time for more than a month and my mind may not function on the call as well as usual."[67] Characteristically, he resolved both the personal and general situation like this: "My policy is to dig in and wait, meanwhile trying to develop better and more profitable agricultural products for the benefit of the eastern south."[68]

VIII

There was satisfaction a-plenty in that direction. In these middle years of the thirties, which were the last years of his life, the small grains that had been sought for so many years began to appear in the breeding plots at Hartsville and in the fields across the eastern south. It will be recalled that the Norton oat that was bred in the twenties had the qualities of cold resistance and a good yield, but it lacked resistance to smut and rust diseases that annually took a heavy toll of the southern oat crop. The problem during the middle and late twenties and the thirties was to breed resistance to these diseases into a heavy yielding, early maturing, cold resistant oat. Stated simply, the problem was to develop a bread and butter oat comparable to the Cleveland Five, or the later Coker 100, cotton.

As early as 1924 Ferguson's Navarro, a very poor yielding but smut immune oat, was crossed on the good yielding Fulghum. Later, in 1927, the Navarro was crossed on several of the best Norton strains. A large backlog of breeding stock came from these crosses and during the late twenties and early thirties extensive testing and selection was carried on. A good many promising strains began to emerge and in the fall of 1935 the excellent Fulgrain oat was introduced, combining high yield and early maturity with cold and smut resistance. This oat moved quickly across the cotton belt.

67. D. R. Coker to Dr. Clarence Poe, November 21, 1938 (Mrs. D. R. Coker).
68. D. R. Coker to Col. John F. Bruton, August 31, 1935 (Mrs. D. R. Coker).

Even before the Fulgrain was introduced, a number of oats having rust resistance had been brought in for crossing with the Fulgrain antecedents. By the winter of 1936-37 there were ". . . 11,000 head selections from such crosses in 4th and 5th generation head-to-row test; 600 of the most promising of these were saved and the next winter (1937-38) planted in yield, cold, smut and rust tests."[69] The ingredients for success in regard to rust resistance were in these test plots.

These then were the grains that Mr. D. R. urged Secretary Wallace to come and see. This was his repeated invitation to farmers and friends, and he was bestowing his greatest gift when he asked people to come and share his delight. Here was both symbol and reality of an improving southern agriculture, the basis of a new day captured out of years of breeding: "We are taking millions of acres out of production of cotton and tobacco. Can we use it more profitably than by planting a large portion in oats and wheat followed by forage crops of legumes?"[70]

He was perhaps most proud of the grain breeding, but there were also during these years of the middle thirties great new developments in cotton. As good as the Cleveland Five cotton had been, and its relative the wilt resistant Clevewilt, breeding for a better bread and butter cotton had gone on continuously. In 1937 the Coker 100 cotton was introduced, and here was a bread and butter cotton de luxe, an early maturing, highly productive cotton having a uniform 1-1/16 to 1⅛ inch staple that met the largest mill demand. Patterned after the Cleveland Five, it exceeded it in every respect.[71] Its great adaptability made it a practically universal cotton in the Carolinas, with substantial plantings in other states of the eastern South.

During these years great strides were made in long staple cotton. The Wilds long staple cotton, which had been intro-

69. George J. Wilds, "Commercial Oat Breeding," address before the annual meeting of the Georgia Agronomists, January 22, 1947.
70. *Pedigreed Seed Company Catalogue,* Fall, 1938.
71. George J. Wilds, "Commercial Cotton Breeding," address before the annual meeting of the Georgia Agronomists, January 23, 1947.

duced in 1928 after almost a decade of breeding and which was the successor to the Deltatype Webber, produced new strains of exceptional length, strength, and fineness of fiber that equalled the best of the Egyptian long staples for many purposes. Mr. D. R. proudly showed these to his friends among the fine yarn spinners.[72]

As he enjoyed and worked with the new breeding developments, he did not forget that a long road lay behind and that he had been over it. He remembered especially that others had been over the road also; and perhaps with less reward than he. On November 21, 1938, Dr. Clarence Poe, editor of the *Progressive Farmer,* wired him for nominations for that magazine's annual award to the "Man of the year in service to southern farm people." Mr. D. R. first mentioned George Wilds, who "like clockwork . . . has furnished to southern agriculture year by year for a number of years increasingly valuable strains of our basic crops and besides he has worked out methods of handling the soil and of culture which have added additional increments to those of higher yield and better quality due to the breeding of superior strains of seed."

And then he went on to say that

A considerable number of men in the Extension Service in South Carolina deserve consideration in this connection. The AAA has simply worked them to death. Here and there all over the state they have been falling out of line simply because of exhaustion and nerve strain. These men have borne the brunt of the agricultural program. They have worked days, nights and Sundays. Old Bill Tiller of Chesterfield County, the oldest County Agent in the state in point of service (and probably in years also) has been in and out for several years. He pulls himself together, however, and goes right back at it as hard as ever. Only two months ago he had a severe breakdown but is back at work again.

J. M. Napier of this county is another who has worked beyond any limits of reasons and is now in bed from a nerve trouble caused from overwork.

These splendid fellows and many others in the Extension Service

72. D. R. Coker to W. K. Kenyon, August 27, 1936 (Mrs. D. R. Coker).

deserve the encomiums of agriculture, but instead of praise they have, in many instances, had only blame.[73]

Three days later, on November 24, he talked informally as he had done countless times to a group of farmers who had come to go over the seed farm. This time a record was kept; it covered five closely typed pages. His closing remarks were: You can't try everything I have told you today, but if something I have said appeals to you you can at least try it and see whether it proves successful with you. Nobody can tell you everything there is to know about anything. If someone can answer every question you ask right off the bat you'd better get your hat and leave right away. If some of you asked me a half dozen questions about farming, probably by the time you got to the third and fourth I'd tell you I didn't know, that we had no experience along that line. We have found out some things about farming and are glad to pass them on to our customers. This work began about 1901 and we not only breed seed but we try to find out the best agricultural practices. We have no secrets, we are glad to tell you anything we have found out. But the more any farmer investigates for himself the more knowledge he has and the more unsolved problems he has.[74]

IX

Mr. D. R. died in his sleep on the night of November 28, 1938. Dr. J. E. Mills, a distinguished chemist working then at the Sonoco plant in Hartsville, had come to call late in the afternoon. Dr. Mills found his host lying back on a couch before an open fire. They talked of many things. Finally, Mr. D. R. reached down and picked up several stalks of ribbon cane that lay on the floor. "Dr. Mills, we tried this new cane last year and it turned out fine. We can increase it next year and sell it, and I suppose make some money on it. But I believe that I know a faster way of getting it out than that. I am going to send it out free to some good farmers that I know over the state, with the stipulation that they pass it along next year without charge. I believe that this is the way it will be worth most to the farmers."[75]

73. D. R. Coker to Dr. Clarence Poe, November 21, 1938 (Mrs. D. R. Coker).
74. In D. R. Coker papers, 1938 (Mrs. D. R. Coker).
75. Conversation with Dr. J. E. Mills.

10

C. W. Coker and Industrial Development at Hartsville

I

THE VICISSITUDES of agriculture and rural life during these years from 1900 to the 1930's were accompanied in the South by the growth of industry.[1] This was true at Hartsville, where the industries that the Cokers had so laboriously, and so modestly, established were growing, though not without troubles and tribulations that were often equal to those of D. R. Coker at the Pedigreed Seed Company.

There was required here, of course, both expansion and improvement. The somewhat epic pioneering efforts that had established the Carolina Fiber Company, and from which success had grown the Southern Novelty Company and the Hartsville Cotton Oil Mill, were not negotiable in the competitive market, though the Cokers had learned much from their mistakes. Even the southern markets could not remain at a competitive advantage to them, for many sorts and kinds of industry were coming to the South, and if the Cokers could make paper from pine, and then make textile cones from the paper, others could, too, and would. In the personal sphere, expansion and improvement, it seems, required the capacity to take on industry as a way of life, to be devoted to it, in the way that D. R. Coker was devoted to agriculture and James to engineering.

1. Francis B. Simkins, *A History of the South* (New York: Alfred A. Knopf, 1953), pp. 326-43.

II

The Southern Novelty Company had been established in 1899, primarily to make paper cones on which cotton yarn could be wound. No more than five thousand dollars had been required to establish this industry which was another reflection of the Cokers' tendency to develop and extend what lay about them.

W. F. Smith had come down from the Pairpont Corporation in New Bedford, Massachusetts, as a man experienced in the manufacture of cones. With James Coker, Jr., apparently taking a close technical interest, Mr. Smith directed the operations of cone manufacture. These first operations took place in an unused tobacco warehouse in Hartsville. The cones, as was then the custom, were made on small hand operated machines that were run by women operators. About eighteen of these machines were set up in the warehouse.[2]

By modern standards these cones were fairly rough articles, though they suited the needs of the times very well. Within a short time the cone making was transferred to quarters on Black Creek adjoining the Carolina Fiber Company, which was furnishing the paper from which the cones were made. Shop and other facilities of the Fiber Company were used at first, and there was in general a close relationship between the two companies.

Even before coming to Hartsville, Smith had long had in mind the construction of an automatic cone making machine that would eliminate the hand labor and would speed up operations and reduce the cost of cone making. The Pairpont Corporation had not been especially interested in this development, however, and this seems to have been the main reason for Smith's desire to come South with the Cokers. They encouraged his efforts along these lines, and within a few years of his coming he had perfected and patented an automatic cone making machine. This machine was built at Hartsville, in what was by then the Southern Novelty Company machine

---

[2] Local sources, principally L. B. Stogner, Hartsville, who was present and active in these affairs at the time, supplied this information.

shop, largely by L. B. Stogner from Mr. Smith's drawings and instructions.[3]

The building of these machines, and their installation at Hartsville, was the first of several critical developments that have made sustained and expanding manufacture of cones, and other paper products, possible. For the time and place, the Novelty Company gained a good competitive position, particularly with reference to supplying southern textile mills. Even so, the fundamental nature of the cone making business remained, namely, that if the Cokers could go into it virtually on a shoe string, others could also. Such papers of Major Coker for this period that survive show clearly that competition was one of his greatest worries. The year 1908 seems to have been a particularly disturbing one with regard to possible competition. In July the Major wrote that "a friend of mine from Columbia, S.C. tells me that a party in that city . . . is making an effort to get up a company for the manufacture of paper tubes.[4] In August the Major heard from a New England friend that another experienced cone maker from New England ". . . says where he is figuring in the South is at Mobile and the capital is all ready. . . ."[5] The next month he heard again from New England that ". . . parties connected with the Talladega Light, Heat & Power Co. of Talladega, Ala. were very anxious indeed to go into the Cone business."[6] Others, also, endeavored to construct different and better cone making machines. The gentleman who hoped to set up business in Mobile ". . . allows he has a machine ready on paper that will take a blank and complete all trimmed ready for shipment, case and all for $1.00 per M."[7]

While all these moves presented a constant threat that on occasion became a reality, the main company with which the Major had to concern himself was the Pairpont Corporation of

3. *Ibid.*
4. Major Coker to Thos. A. Tripp, July 6, 1908 (Watson collection).
5. Copy of letter written by Arthur F. Salmon, sent to Major Coker by Thos. A. Tripp (Watson collection).
6. Thos. A. Tripp to Major Coker, September 26, 1908 (Watson collection).
7. Copy of letter written by Arthur F. Salmon, sent to Major Coker by Thos. A. Tripp (Watson collection).

New Bedford, Massachusetts. As the general manager of that corporation wrote the Major in 1908, ". . . the fact remains that you and ourselves are the only practical Cone makers in the United States...."[8] The Novelty Company apparently licensed the Pairpont Corporation to use the cone making machines, charging a royalty for the privilege.[9] The two companies worked out a sort of gentleman's agreement, whereby each would stay more or less in his own territory.[10] This was a somewhat uneasy agreement that eventually fell by the way. The Pairpont Corporation was an old and conservative firm, and seems to have wanted, at all costs, to keep the Cokers pacified and happy.

The greatest hazard, perhaps, lay in the dependence of the Novelty Company upon the southern textile industry. This was a period of expansion in the textile industry of the South. Many of the mills were operating on a close margin, and they were quite sensitive to every slight turn in business conditions. There were prosperous times, but there often were times when, as the Major wrote Smith in 1908, "there is nothing doing in the South and our orders to the Novelty Company are very small."[11] To relieve some of this dependence on the textile industry, an attempt was made in 1907 to integrate a silver plating business with the Novelty Company, but this failed.[12]

III

The Major's youngest son had been associated with the Novelty Company almost from the beginning. This was Charles Westfield Coker, named for the young Charles who was killed at Malvern Hill in 1862. Born at Hartsville in 1879, he was the last child and considerably

---

8. Thos. A. Tripp to Major Coker, May 20, 1908 (Watson collection).

9. Rough copy of a proposed agreement, in Major Coker's hand, for the use of these machines (Watson collection). See also Major Coker to Thos. A. Tripp, February 14, 1914 (Watson collection).

10. See, for instance, Major Coker to Thos. A. Tripp, May 4, 1909 (Watson collection).

11. Major Coker to W. P. Smith, July 25, 1908 (Watson collection).

12. Conversation with A. H. Rogers, Society Hill, S.C., who was active in the Novelty Company at the time.

younger than the other sons who remained at home. He began as the company's first treasurer and salesman, and then increasingly took on additional responsibilities from the Major. Mr. Smith was in active charge of manufacturing until his death before the First World War. By the time of the Major's death in 1918, when he became president, Charles had been in effective management for several years.[13]

In 1921, in a memorandum to his salesmen, Charles stated a major controlling fact about the cone and tube industry. "... the cone business is so limited that if all the cones in the United States were manufactured in one plant, the entire value of the product of the plant would be much less than the entire value of the average cotton mill in the United States."[14] In large part tied to the fortunes of the textile industry, and requiring relatively little capital investment, it was a hazardous, competitive activity.

Business was good during the war and immediate postwar years, but the Novelty Company suffered severely in the recession of the early 1920's. So much, that there was serious consideration among the stockholders of selling the company. It was not without difficulty that Charles convinced some of the stockholders to hold on. That he was the youngest son was of no advantage to him.

Charles was not merely hanging on. He felt that he had in mind the basic elements necessary for the development of the Novelty Company. "Quantity production of cones is the only way to bring about price reduction."[15] The reason was clear. "On January 1, 1921 our prices will be reduced to $4.50 base and on tubes to $3.00 base."[16] On this basis, a cone sold for a little less than half a cent, a tube for not quite a third of a cent. "For these prices to show a profit it will be necessary for us to market not less than 60,000,000 cones during the year and 40,000,000 tubes. However the profit will be very small

---

13. Sketch in catalogue (Sonoco Products Company).
14. Memorandum to salesmen, January 1, 1921, p. 2 (Sonoco Products Company).
15. *Ibid.*
16. Memorandum, "Selling Program for 1921" (Sonoco Products Company).

unless we can increase our sales to 100,000,000 cones and approximately 50,000,00 tubes."[17]

Quantity production would not do the job of itself. Quality production was required, for the simple reason that the cones and tubes, in use, virtually became a part of the textile machinery. Yarn was wound and unwound on them at high speeds. To do this, it was required that the cones fit their holders accurately, that their surface finish be uniform, that they be strong enough to take the high speeds and the handling of storage and shipping. No matter how cheap the price, few mills could afford to use inferior cones. It was obvious that, as the textile industry raised its standards, so also would the quality of the cones have to keep pace. To his salesmen in 1921, at the same time that the above reduction of prices was announced, Charles said that "It is our purpose not to let up on quality in the least. In fact our plans contemplate an improvement in the quality of all the goods we sell. Our Solid Wound Tube Department will be enlarged and improved and the prices reduced on these to 75c a thousand linear inches per number."

Quality and quantity, linked together, were key concepts, but they were hardly decisive in the American industrial picture of the early 1920's. All industrial concerns were achieving both, or going out of business. Charles went beyond these elements, in a largely personal way, and herein lay his important contribution. Of all the Cokers of his generation, Charles felt and accepted most completely the changes in life being wrought out by the growth of science, industry, and urban living. This was not merely a matter of perception of the new. James and David grasped the new, and worked with it all the days of their lives. Yet for James the technical job was the main thing; for David, the problem was to bring about change in southern agriculture, coupled with an allegiance to the human aspects of the older ways. Charles was younger; his early working years were spent in selling and in general business execution.

17. *Ibid.*

INDUSTRIAL DEVELOPMENT

There was already industry at Hartsville when he came to maturity, and during his formative years the struggle was on to establish the Fiber Company.

Whatever the reason, he was tremendously impressed with the fundamental change of the way of life sweeping over modern America. He did not like it in every respect, but he saw its better side and there was challenge in it for him. He committed himself to this new world, problems and all. In March of 1920 he dictated some rough notes for a talk he was to make in Hartsville. No doubt he qualified and refined these statements, but they reveal the central mode of his thinking.

The World War has completely revolutionized our lives. We have suddenly found ourselves facing new social and economic problems, which require a complete reorganization of our relationship to our political, educational, industrial and religious activities. Our old ideas have completely changed, our habits of thought have changed, our modes of living have changed. This evolution has been so sudden that we have not yet got ourselves together. We are still dazed and we find ourselves groping in the dark for light. Our methods of doing things are now antiquated. Methods which a year or so ago were efficient have become inefficient. In a short period of five years we have passed from one period of the world's development into an entirely new one, and these periods are as widely separated from each other as tho a thousand years had elapsed.[18]

With respect especially to industry, he saw clearly just what was the moving cause: ". . . that wonderful storehouse of science, the 'Open Sesame' of which is the laboratory and shop. The chemist and engineer must make these treasures available for practical every-day use of man."[19] The vital integer was what he called "Industrial Research." In the final analysis this was now the inescapable requirement of a successful industrial concern. Coming home directly to the situation in South Carolina, it was evident to him that "There are a good many industries in this state who probably have identical prob-

---
18. Rough draft memorandum, March 5, 1920 (Sonoco Products Company).
19. *Ibid.*

lems, and some of these concerns are now working along parallel lines, each duplicating the expense of the other in their endeavor to solve problems common to all. If we could but join hands in establishing a central research bureau to which we could submit our problems our chances for solutions would be greatly enhanced."[20]

This was not idle hope, and it was precisely here that Charles was definitive. In 1916 he had hired C. K. Dunlap, a young graduate in Civil Engineering, then teaching in the Hartsville public schools. Dunlap came as a production man, but soon it was obvious that he had unusual talents for making new and better machines, and for working out improved processes of manufacture. So Charles took him off production work, provided funds and equipment, and set him free to work full time at improving and inventing.

Dunlap's first work was in the plant itself, studying and changing production machinery and processes. There were improvements to be made in the production line. Most important, however, virtually all of the machinery to make the cones was built especially for the purpose at Hartsville. This was Dunlap's primary job, one where there was constant room for improvement, given the ability and encouragement. Charles supported Dunlap fully. It was in this way that a continuous application of science and inventive ingenuity was secured for the manufacture of cones and tubes at Hartsville.[21]

There was, though, another step. For whatever internal improvements were made in the production process of cones and tubes then in use, Charles grasped clearly that Sonoco Products Company—the name was changed in 1924—was a service industry. Its product was whatever the textile industry needed. And, again, he was aware that the textile industry was dynamic: "Changes in manufacturing processes and changes in machinery have been so revolutionary that before they can be fairly set going there have been other more modern methods and machinery invented to still further improve the

20. *Ibid.*
21. Conversation with C. K. Dunlap and C. W. Coker.

product or increase production." Research at Sonoco was, therefore, essentially research on the new and changing needs of the textile industry. Policy, then, was for Dunlap and others to stay in close touch with the new needs, giving service and advice on improved uses of current cones, and seeking new developments where necessary.

One of the new developments from this policy took place in the middle twenties, when Sonoco was able to fill a major new need in the cotton knitting industry. Textile equipment makers produced a creel from which the coned yarn could be furnished at high speed to the knitting machines. When these creels were first put into use, it was found that the yarn quite frequently hung on the nose of the cone, thereby interrupting operation to such an extent that it began to look as if the creels could not be used. Dunlap set to work on the problem and developed a way of treating the noses of the cones so that the yarn would not hang there.

Of all such developments, the most significant came early in the Depression, a short time before Charles died an untimely death. It was during the twenties that rayon fiber came into great use. This posed a hard problem for the cone makers. Cotton yarn, being relatively rough, wound easily on the cones then in use. The smooth, fine count rayon yarn, however, slipped and tended to bunch up on the standard cone surface. A new type surface was needed. Dunlap put in a lot of work on the problem, trying both physical and chemical means of treating the paper to obtain the proper surface. Various new shapes and sizes of cones were tried. Finally, Dunlap stopped in a textile mill in Philadelphia. There he talked to a venerable worker, asking him what was the best winding surface he had ever known. The old man replied that chamois skin was the best to his knowledge. Dunlap then returned to Hartsville to attempt to put a surface resembling that of chamois skin on the paper cones. After considerable effort, he found an abrasive that buffed the cone in such a way that the result was a soft, slightly fuzzy surface. This was tried in the mills and proved eminently successful. This cone was named the velvet surface cone and produced in quantity.[22]

There were other such major gains. A chronic problem concerned the dying of yarn. The normal practice was to unwind the yarn from the tube on which it came from the spinning machine, wind it on a special tube, dip it into the hot, chemically active dye, and then rewind it on another tube or cone. Much would be saved if a tube could be developed that would not give way under the action of the dye. In the late twenties, such a tube, the Dytex and Super Dytex, was developed.

> The development of this tube represents about two years of careful study and experimentation carried on by Messrs. Dunlap and Biggs; both in our plant and in the plants of our customers. It represents time, thought and energy and the aid of chemists employed by us to help in this development. . . . This tube eliminates two processes in winding and back winding, better dyeing results from the use of this tube because the dye liquors have no chemical effect on the tube. Deposits of rust and aluminum salt on the yarn package will be entirely eliminated because there is no metal to rust or erode and then last, but not least, the cost of this tube to our customer is less than one-tenth the cost of the metal tube now in general use.[23]

There were other developments—so many and so important that by 1930 Charles could write that

> . . . every new development in the last ten years of any consequence, in paper cones or tubes for the textile trade or in the art of making these articles have originated with us.[24] We have, of course, had to co-operate very closely with the builders of winding machines—representatives from our plants have visited plants of the builders of the winding machines and in turn representatives of all of the winding machine people in this Country have visited our plant and we have established a close and cordial relationship with them,

---

22. The story of these technical developments is based upon conversations with C. K. Dunlap, Hartsville, S.C.
23. Undated memorandum, apparently to salesmen, p. 2 (Sonoco Products Company). The year is certainly 1930 or 1931.
24. *Ibid.*

with the result that any problem that has to do with a paper carrier is promptly submitted to us."[25]

This was not merely by accident, nor solely because Dunlap and others had been successful in their development work. Charles saw the thing as an unbroken whole, from conception, to production, to sales. He told his salesmen that "The time is past when the salesman can discuss the weather and politics with a prospective customer and expect to get orders. The up-to-date salesman is a technical man and must discuss technical problems with his customer and the man who fails to keep abreast of the times in this direction becomes as obsolete and as useless as a jacquard loom in a new spinning mill."[26] He then went on to make his point clearly, and to compass the total: "When I tell you that we have spent over Sixty Thousand dollars in the past two years in an experimental way, you will realize the importance which I attach to the development of those products which are now ready to market."[27]

These policies of the 1920's were cumulative. Their clear consequence was that the Depression was a time of continuing growth and opportunity, when Sonoco became pre-eminent in its field. The single most important factor, perhaps, was the velvet surface cone for rayon, but this was part of the total process that was coming to full fruition.

Charles grew up exceedingly well to the new facts of industry in a world of agriculture. His main energy and purpose were directed toward a total functioning, toward a smooth operation, toward the success of the whole. As important as he considered the matters of research and production, he did not neglect the selling and customer service aspects. He learned that, year in and year out, quality was fully as important as price with the textile trade, and resourcefulness and reliability equally as important. He told a meeting of salesmen in 1931 that "I want each of you to saturate yourself with the history and policies of the Company in order that you may build up

25. *Ibid.*, p. 3.   26. *Ibid.*, p. 4.
27. *Ibid.*, p. 5.

on a factual basis the confidence and good-will of the people we serve in the Company you represent. Platitudes do not answer the purpose unless backed up by past performance and so I am of the opinion that history is far more convincing and compelling than a mere statement of the purposes of the Company."[28]

He became, in short, an industrial executive, and can be distinguished from his brothers as such. James was essentially an engineer, where both his genius and his pleasure lay. He could function as an adequate business man when necessary, but it required effort. David was a good executive, but, like James, gave his best to seed breeding and agricultural improvement. It is indicative of the way in which Charles paced himself that he wrote his sales manager in 1929 that "I am particularly anxious that you take a broad view of the responsibilities that go with the position of Sales Manager. As far as possible you should pass on to your staff the execution of details. Supervise them rather than burden yourself with the execution of numerous time-and-thought consuming details thus leaving yourself free to give study to and making plans for the extension of your sales and the supervision of your staff and sales force."[29]

In considerable degree he took his own advice. Sonoco was a relatively small organization during most of the time he ran it, there being about 100 employees in 1925. He had matured there and gave it his full devotion. So, of course, he watched things rather closely and was in daily contact with what went on. He had the happy faculty, though, of picking good, young people to bring to work, and of putting them in the right jobs. Dunlap was among the first but there were others, a half a dozen or more whom he engaged during the twenties and who grew in their jobs. As often as not their potential was not visible to the naked eye, but he followed his judgment and was seldom wrong. He asked for hard work,

28. Memorandum to salesmen, 1931, p. 1 (Sonoco Products Company).
29. Memorandum to C. H. Campbell, May 13, 1929, p. 1 (Sonoco Products Company).

and got it, and he established the policy, not always with the full agreement of his Board, of paying these people exceptionally well, and of making stock in Sonoco available.

In fact, he set wage rates throughout the mill that were the highest in the entire Hartsville area, even when the type of work and product are taken into consideration. This, again, was a conscious decision on his part, a piece with his total conception of the industrial organization. He had that indefinable something called charm, and could wander easily and naturally through the relatively small plant, calling every person by name, stopping to chat here and there, his hat appearing in his hand when talking to a woman worker. It was no pose, and his presence was felt throughout the mill.

In the years when Sonoco was growing, both before and after the First World War, it was the custom in the South for mill companies to build houses near the mills, standardized and rather unattractive houses. This was perhaps necessary in the beginning, because the bulk of the new workers came from rural areas and transportation was inadequate. But it led to a rather rigid separation of the mill town from the remainder of the community. A few such houses were built near the Fiber and Novelty Company plants, but quite early Charles had this stopped, on the grounds that he did not want the usual separation to grow up in Hartsville, certainly not with respect to the people working for him.

Charles' sense of change in the world about him into which he was born was not limited to industry. In an almost tactile way he felt it in every area of life. "Someone has said that change is an immutable law, and eternal adaptation the price of survival." With some exaggeration, but with essential truth for the long run, he wrote that "The old social system has been torn asunder, and we are facing the necessity of reorganizing our social and economic life to meet new conditions which are developing day by day."[30] His meaning was clearer when

---

30. Notes for speech, "Faith in Others," undated but probably in 1930 or 1931, p. 9 (Sonoco Products Company).

he said that "... there was a time when the population of the State was so sparse and contact with one's neighbors was so seldom that social problems of more thickly settled communities did not affect us, but now with the advent of better school systems, automobiles, quicker means of transportation, and thickly settled communities, these problems have become acute and are demanding solution."[31]

Given this increased frequency of social contact, "We are learning that every individual is responsible for the health, happiness and general welfare of every other individual in a given community."[32] He was reacting to the condition of the unfortunate, produced in part by the new changes, and yet left uncared for. He was reacting also to the senseless failure in South Carolina of communities, counties and the State to move forward in such areas as public health and prison reform.

So his interests turned to the field of public welfare—to the awakening of what he often called a "social conscience." This was needed to match the changing conditions of life, especially in South Carolina where an almost totally rural state was moving toward towns and cities and industrial employment. The care given unfortunates under earlier conditions by family and community was no longer being provided. An individualistic state, generally poverty stricken, found it difficult to commit itself to new services for the indigent, the orphaned, the criminal; for public health facilities and personnel; to an objective appraisal of the meaning of illiteracy, social disease and race to the social adequacy of the whole state.

As a successful industrialist from a well-known family, Charles did much to make the case for public welfare activities in South Carolina. He served on the Board of Public Welfare. As president for two years of the South Carolina Conference of Social Workers, he inaugurated a large-scale effort to initiate in each county of the state a public welfare movement. The instrument was the County Councils of Social Work, one for each county. "Those interested in social work in South Caro-

31. Speech draft, undated, p. 2 (Sonoco Products Company).
32. *Ibid.*

INDUSTRIAL DEVELOPMENT

lina, realizing the grave danger of neglecting our social welfare, have come together in conference and agreed to undertake to organize in each County, County Conferences for the social welfare...."[33]

These Councils, broadly based, had as their first job the stock-taking of the problems and needs of the county. Stock-taking required analysis and facing up to facts. "Our ignorance as to our own social and economic conditions makes it advisable to survey our own communities before we can arrive at a conclusion as to what the true condition is. There are no agencies in our State charged with the responsibility of making an unbiased study of the local social and economic status of any given community. Therefore, if this work is to be done soon, if we are to know ourselves and our communities, we, of a necessity, must use voluntary agencies."[34] The scope of this stock-taking was not limited. It would include feeblemindedness, health, taxation, pauperism, crime. In the setting, it was a fairly comprehensive plan. "Some have called this 'Plan Visionary.' If this is visionary, we certainly need vision in South Carolina."[35]

Charles was aware, of course, that both work and demonstration were required. "... there must be a small beginning and if the idea has merit, it will grow and draw to it the aid and talent of those who have always responded in all patriotic undertakings." Making the case concrete, he pointed out that

Two years after the establishment of a County Health Unit in Darlington County there was a reduction in

      Still Births amounting to 26.4

      Infant Mortality of 55.9

      Pneumonia 27.8

      Typhoid Fever 80

Whereas in two adjoining Counties who had no Health Units, over the same period of years, there was an increase in Still Births of from 1% to 16% and in the same two adjoining Counties there

---

33. *Ibid.*

34. Speech before the Fifteenth Annual Meeting of the South Carolina Conference of Social Work, Hartsville, June 4, 1925. The *News and Courier* (Charleston, S.C.), June 5, 1925.

35. *Ibid.*

was an increase in typhoid fever of 50% and 55% respectively, and in a third adjoining county, a decrease of only 18%, as compared with Darlington County's decrease of 80%.[36]

Talking to one group, Charles illustrated ways of starting: "Local Taxation. The County Budget. Pauperism, its causes and costs, and the proper care of the Indigent. Feeblemindedness, its effect on our social structure, and methods for lessening this evil. Crime, its causes and prevention. Juvenile Delinquency."[37]

A mental hygiene survey in your schools will probably indicate that between two and three percent of your school population is mentally defective. It would probably indicate that each mentally defective is costing your School Board at least $40.00 or more per year than a normal child. It would therefore be immediately apparent that special classes for these sub-normal children would effect a considerable money saving. Certainly enough to pay for special teachers, specially trained for this purpose and when consideration is given to the fact that sub-normal children so trained are more apt to develop into self-supporting, self-respecting and law-abiding individuals, than if they are forced along through the regular grades doing indifferent work and failing, year after year, to make their grades, becoming discouraged and developing the feeling that society is against them.[38]

"We believe that most criminals are mental defectives, and that we should recognize criminal tendencies as a mental disease, rather than moral degeneracy."[39] He worked strenuously for the improvement of prison facilities in South Carolina. Of the state penitentiary at Columbia, he endorsed a report to the Governor stating that the "... plant is inadequate, out of date, and entirely unsuited to its purpose.... Very little can be done to give the prisoners the proper amount of recreation and exercise, or to provide for them educational facilities,

---

36. Undated speech draft (circa 1925), pp. 3-4 (Sonoco Products Company).
37. *Ibid.*, p. 5.
38. Undated speech draft (circa 1925), p. 4 (Sonoco Products Company).
39. Speech before the Fifteenth Annual Meeting of the South Carolina Conference of Social Work, Hartsville, June 4, 1925. The *News and Courier* (Charleston, S.C.), June 5, 1925.

until the institution itself is either remodeled or a new prison erected."

He strongly advocated vocational training in the prison and that ". . . the superintendent of the penitentiary conduct an employment bureau for released prisoners. To turn a man loose on the State with a criminal record behind him and no employment is an invitation for him to drift back into crime. We believe that the time has come when South Carolina should make adequate provision for her unfortunate derelicts and offer them an opportunity to reform."[40]

Charles' efforts along these and other lines were cut off suddenly in 1931, when he succumbed to a heart attack at the relatively early age of fifty-two.

IV

For a good many years after 1900, the Carolina Fiber Company was the financial backbone of the family at Hartsville. It was quite profitable, even in a close and competitive market. The rigors of the 1890's had taught the Cokers a great deal about paper making, so that, when full operation was finally achieved, they proceeded economically and efficiently. The first dividend was paid in October of 1899, a good one of 6 per cent. Similar dividends were paid for a number of succeeding years.[41] Increasingly, Paul Rogers, a nephew of Major Coker, took over the duties of the business office of the Fiber Company, with James giving special attention to the engineering and production end.

By the 1920's, however, a major change became necessary in the Fiber Company. The paper that was being made by the sulphite process from southern pine was a brown water glazed wrapping paper, commonly known as butcher's paper, since its main use was in the wrapping of meat. By the twenties other processes of paper making had been developed whereby a softer, white wrapping paper was being made cheaply. This type of paper became fashionable with butchers and house-

40. Draft of report to Governor McLeod, undated (Sonoco Products Company).
41. Minute book of the Carolina Fiber Company (R. G. Coker).

wives, thereby virtually putting the Fiber Company's paper off the market.[42]

The situation in the early and middle years of the twenties is pretty well described by the following letter which was sent to the stockholders and directors on December 22, 1924:

For the first time in some years this Company is not in position to pay a dividend on account of its not making an appreciable profit for the year.

At no time during the year have we been able to market our product at a profit due to the general depression in business, to the large importation of Wrapping Papers at very low prices during the first half of the year and to large additional tonnage of Wrapping Paper coming on the market during the year, chiefly Kraft from Southern Kraft Mills.

Since it did not appear that these disadvantages could be overcome through the continued use of the sulphite process on southern pine, James decided that a shift to a new process was required. He chose the semichemical process, a way of making paper that had been developed in 1920 by the Forest Products Laboratory at Madison, Wisconsin, and which existed under an open patent. This process, as its name implies, converts wood to pulp through a combination of mechanical and chemical pulping. It is used to reduce hardwoods, and the shift from pine to hardwoods was part of the decision that James had to make.

James' son, Richard Gay Coker, came to work in the Fiber Company during this changeover and participated in making the new installations. The new departure, however, did not solve altogether the Fiber Company's problems. Competition from larger companies was severe, and the Fiber Company had a very hard time during the depression. Paul Rogers, who became president of the company on James' death in 1931, introduced the making of nine point board, which was used as the middle sheet in cardboard shipping boxes. This development helped to some extent, and the Fiber Company was able to come through the depression, though not as the moneymaker it had once been.[43]

42. Conversation with R. G. Coker.   43. *Ibid.*

11

Scholars and Scholarship

NOT ALL of the grandchildren of Caleb and Hannah Coker remained at home. Among those who left, an astonishing proportion became highly distinguished scholars. This chapter presents a brief account of the lives of these scholars (and of one medical doctor), not as a definitive treatment, but as a measure of the full flowering of the family.

EDWARD CALEB COKER

To Captain Coker and his first wife were born seven children, of whom four were sons. (Mary McIver Coker died in 1883; in 1885, two years later, Captain Coker married her sister, Lavinia McIver.) Of the four sons, only the eldest, Allen remained at home. The other three—Edward, Robert and Francis—on finishing college entered teaching, first in secondary schools, and ultimately in colleges and universities.

The oldest of the three academic sons was Edward Caleb Coker, born December 19, 1873, in the home the Captain had built near Camp Marion. During his first four years at school, Edward attended St. David's Academy at Society Hill; then, when the family moved to Darlington, he attended the St. John's Academy there. He went to South Carolina College at Columbia in 1890 and remained there through the school year 1891-92. The next year he spent at the University of Virginia. His college attendance was interrupted for two years, when he returned to Darlington as Principal of St.

John's Academy. In 1896 he returned to the University of Virginia, receiving the Bachelor of Arts degree in 1897.

From 1897 through 1901 Edward was Superintendent of the public schools in Marion, South Carolina. He held a similar position at Greenwood, South Carolina, from 1901 until 1906.

Edward's major subject in college had been mathematics. In 1906 he went to Winthrop College (the state normal school for girls) at Rock Hill, South Carolina, as professor of mathematics. He remained at Winthrop until 1924, when he moved over to the University at Columbia as professor of mathematics and astronomy.

Edward remained at the University until his retirement, in 1948, as Emeritus Professor. In conjunction with his teaching at the University, he was able to establish an Observatory. He also took the lead in the development of an Arboretum, and was generally and consistently active over the years in the beautification of the campus.

Edward Coker was a quiet, friendly man, spontaneous in good cheer. He was primarily a teacher, one who held the respect of his students, and often their affection. He died at Florence, South Carolina, on March 28, 1956.

WILLIAM CHAMBERS COKER

Of the Major's sons only one left Darlington County. This was the third son, Will—William Chambers Coker, born in Hartsville on October 24, 1872. A tall handsome man, Will had the capacity to excel in business. After he had graduated from South Carolina College in 1894, he went to Wilmington, North Carolina, to work in the Atlantic National Bank. This bank was operated by the Cokers' old friends and business associates, the Norwoods, the Major holding some stock. Will did well in the bank, so well that by 1896 he had become a vice president.[1]

However, by 1897 he had decided that this was not quite his cup of tea. He wanted to go back to school to do graduate

---

1. Conversation with W. C. Coker, August 10, 1948.

work in botany, and so he went to Johns Hopkins in 1897. His decision is understandable, in the same way that David's interest in seed breeding is understandable. Observation and endless discussion of natural history was an everyday affair in the Coker household.

Certainly Will's consuming interest in botanical study was related to the fact that his father had studied in 1856-57 at Harvard in this and allied fields. The transfer of content from the Major to Will was not great, nor would it have been in character for the Major to have had much to say directly about what he had done at Harvard. Rather, what was important was the existence in the family of the idea of study at an advanced level. What Asa Gray, Agassiz, and Horsford, devoting their lives to scholarly work in science, had done was of value—it was worthwhile. The scholar's life, then, had standing in the family. From the Major, also, Will received much of his predisposition to accept the scientific state of mind. The Major had an early copy of Darwin's *Origin of the Species*. Will read this. He was well acquainted, of course, with his eldest brother James' work and talk on things scientific, and he was at home when the first beginnings in making paper were undertaken. Will grew up using, as boys do, the books, microscope, and apparatus and materials that the Major had brought from Harvard. The vacuum jar, for instance, was useful as a way of killing insects. In time, also, Will was allowed all the room he required on the piazza for work tables and collections.[2]

Entering South Carolina College in 1891, he played tennis on the varsity team, took an active part in the Euphradian Literary Society, and worried his parents because he obviously was not spending enough money to keep body and soul together. He also was a "Highly Distinguished" graduate. The Major learned of the distinction only from the commencement program. He said to Will, "This is gratifying," and for the

2. *Ibid.*

first time in Will's memory, put his arm about the boy's shoulder.³

Entering Johns Hopkins in the fall of 1897, Will completed his formal course work by the following June, and then began his research. His thesis was "On the Gametophytes and Embryo of Taxodium." It was, as Couch and Matthews have said, "a classic in seed development." During this time he made contact with Dr. Webber, out of which friendship the seed breeding at Hartsville developed. Following the custom of the times, Will, finishing at Johns Hopkins in 1901, went to Europe for a semester in Strasburger's laboratory at Bonnam-Rhine, Germany.

In the fall of 1902, Will came to Chapel Hill, to teach at the University of North Carolina. To drive off in all directions at once has not been characteristic of any of the Cokers. None, however, had more singleness of purpose than Will. He entered completely into academic life, and into the life of Chapel Hill. A bachelor until late in life (he married Louise Venable in 1934) and of considerable independent means, his work—steadily and consistently, rather than hurriedly—was the main thing. In the way of Johns Hopkins scholarship of that period, he marked off his areas of professional botanical interest carefully and firmly, and followed them through a lifetime. He set himself in motion as a scholar, apparently left all doubts behind, and let nature take its course.

Will had the family's predilection for bringing into some kind of orderly array the things that lay close at hand. Within a year of his coming to Chapel Hill he had published a list of the woody plants of the village. This taxonomic interest in woody plants was appropriate to a state and region beginning to want to know about themselves, and Will maintained it throughout his life. In 1916 he published with H. R. Totten *Trees of North Carolina,* followed in 1934 by *Trees of the Southeastern States.* (The latter book has had three editions.) Partly at the suggestion of the Major and also to finish some

---

3. John N. Couch and Velma D. Matthews, "William Chambers Coker," *Mycologia,* XLVI, No. 3 (May-June 1954), 374.

boyhood work, Will completed and published in 1912 *The Plant Life of Hartsville, South Carolina.* Because of its elements of ecology, this work was significantly ahead of its time.[4] The Major took a close interest in his work, and showed remarkable patience as Will proceeded deliberately in the scholar's way. He got a great deal of vicarious enjoyment out of Will's life of study and research. It was a wonderful fruit from all of the hardship that had followed after his year at Harvard. He did not consider it frivolous; indeed, he once told Will rather pointedly that it was his "duty" to accept an offer from the University of Texas, for the facilities for work were clearly better there than at Chapel Hill. Yet, of course, Will's work was outside of his province, and Will was living at Chapel Hill. They did not deal in daily affairs. The consequence was that the Major relaxed quite a bit with Will, as with one not immediately concerned. On occasions he would write Will about some trouble at home, not so much seeking an answer as unburdening his mind. He would write, also, of those events which, in his old age, gave him particular satisfaction.

The University of North Carolina in 1902 had special need of a man such as Will—that is, of a young man of character and high scholarship who had come to stay. The University was just beginning to move forward after having been forced to give most of its energies to survival, following the Civil War and Reconstruction. Today, in the mid-fifties, it is one of the leading universities of the land. Most often, the beginning of its growth to this present position is dated at the accession of Edward Kidder Graham to the presidency, in 1914. The first period of growth, in both size and stature, is usually placed in the administration of Harry Woodburn Chase, 1919 to 1930.

A major source of this development in the University was in a remarkable group of young men who came to Chapel Hill around the turn of the century and later, many selected by President Venable, as young men with promise. Louis R. Wilson has made a roll of these men. There was, it appears in

4. *Ibid.*, p. 375.

retrospect, a decade and more of incubation, when these men were planting themselves firmly and soundly in their disciplines. Will was one of this company.

There was no Department of Botany when Will came to Chapel Hill in the fall of 1902. He was officially a part of the Department of Biology. There was no laboratory, or equipment for his work. Dr. Henry Van Peters Wilson, Chairman of the Department of Biology, gave him a microscope. In an odd corner was a small number of sheets of leaves collected some years before by W. W. Ashe. The organization and development of a Department of Botany became for Will, therefore, the main framework of his work, inseparable from his own research and teaching.

One of his first jobs was a happy meeting of necessity and accident. Adjoining New East, which housed the Department of Biology, was a swampy five-acre tract, of no particular use except for skimpy grazing for the President's cow and horses. As Will and President Venable walked by it one day, President Venable suggested that Will take it over and see if he could not improve its looks.[5] Will drained the plot as well as possible, and began planting in it with a view to developing a collection of living plants of botanical interest and of use in teaching botany, as well as for an ornamental garden for the University. The plot soon came to be known as the Arboretum, a designation to which Will objected because both its size and soil made it unsuited for plants requiring greatly different growing conditions. Yet, whatever its botanical limitations, this Arboretum, commonly known as Coker's Arboretum, figured significantly in the University's life, for it represented growing, natural beauty, and a certain persisting relation with Nature that has been a major characteristic of the academic village. In 1903 Chapel Hill was indeed "academe among the trees," a small, leisurely institution. During the next half century of Will's tenure there, it was to grow into a large university. It could not remain, of course, completely as it was, in appearance and atmosphere. But it retained a

5. Conversation with W. C. Coker, August 10, 1948.

remarkable amount of this earlier natural beauty, on and off the campus. For this, much credit is due to Will's work.

For not only did he develop the Arboretum, and the grounds of his own home. He was also named the first chairman of the faculty Committee on Buildings and Grounds at the University in 1913, and remained chairman until 1945. His influence on the planting of grass, shrubbery, and flowers, and on general landscaping was paramount during this period, and he was among the most influential in the design and layout of new campus buildings. In a University that normally had only scanty funds for campus beautification, he was able through his own funds to make many things possible that otherwise would not have been. For a number of years Will provided landscaping services for many of the high schools over North Carolina.

There was also another job corollary to his main work that Will took on not long after he came to Chapel Hill. This job also had influence on the scholarly growth of the University. In 1904 he became editor of the *Journal* of the Elisha Mitchell Scientific Society, and, again, remained in this capacity until his retirement in 1945. Under his editorship, the *Journal* became a full-fledged scientific publication in a state and region where such journals were few and far between.

By 1908 a separate Department of Botany had been created, and moved, along with the Department of Zoology, to the newly constructed Davie Hall. The Department grew apace with the University over the succeeding years.

According to two of his most outstanding students, Will took his rank in botany largely on the basis of his research on fungi. As they have related:

> In spite of his prodigious researches on the higher fungi, and the high quality of these as taxonomic contributions, Dr. Coker's fame as a mycologist rests largely on his work on the Saprolegniaceae; began in 1908 and reaching its climax in the publication of "The Saprolegniaceae," in 1923, a work which has had world-wide influence in stimulating researches on the aquatic fungi.[6]

6. Couch and Matthews, "William Chambers Coker," p. 376.

Indeed, the Department of Botany at the University of North Carolina was for perhaps twenty years the center in the nation for the study of aquatic fungi.

In addition to work on the aquatic fungi, Will also carried on an extensive work on the Clavarias, Gasteromycetes, Amanitas, Hydnums, and Boletes. Will demonstrated the existence of sexual phases in some lower organisms in which sexuality had previously been unknown. This work was related to the later development of certain highly valuable drugs. One of Will's students, working in his laboratory, established the occurrence of water molds in soils, many of which cause plant disease. It was thus made clear that plant diseases are not always brought into a particular plot, but may be there already in the soil.[7]

Professionally, Will was open to criticism on the grounds that he attempted too much. His enthusiasm for nature was great, and his state and region were relatively unchartered. He may have attempted to cover more botanical fields than was feasible.

Will Coker was an eminently successful teacher. He insisted that the students be brought face to face with good and fresh laboratory materials. From this point he took it to be his job to stimulate the students to contribute as much as possible to their own instruction. Often graduate students worked alongside Will, at adjoining tables. Among the first of such students was H. R. Totten, who became the second full time staff member in Botany, and a lifelong collaborator with Will. Will's first assistant was H. A. Allard, who went on to later distinguished work in the field of viruses and (with Garner) discovered photoperiodism in plants. Another early and distinguished student was John N. Couch, who succeeded Will as Chairman of the Department. Other students included Lindsay Olive, Velma Matthews, Leland Shanor, Budd Smith, Kenneth and John Raper, and Alma Whiffen. Alma Holland Beers was for many years a close assistant and collaborator.

Will's methods in the general undergraduate botany course

[7]. From conversation with John N. Couch and Alma Holland Beers.

were somewhat unconventional. Usually he began with the low forms of plant life and progressed to the more complex. The stages in this progression were never quite the same, for a walk from his home to classroom might cause him to select an entirely new topic for that day's lecture from the one originally planned, and for which an assistant had provided and arranged materials.

Will retired from the University in 1945; but he did not quit work. Several articles were published, and at his death he had filled four large fascicles with notes on shrubs of the Southeastern states, along with over four hundred drawings.

Will Coker held on to a close interest in the family's life in Hartsville. In the bachelor's way, he did not make as many trips home in his young years as were actually planned. But there were a good many. He and the Major were rather frequent letter writers. And, of course, he was always deeply concerned with, and interested in, David's work in the seed breeding. They discussed these matters a great deal, and Will gave his share of financial support to the Pedigreed Seed Company in the hard times, early and late, and urged other members of the family to do so.

As he grew older, Will's concern for Coker College increased, so much so that the College became his principal philanthropy in the later years. One of his favorite Ph.D. students, Velma Matthews, went to teach Botany and Zoology at Coker. In the late 1940's Will gave the money for the construction of a new science building, and lived to witness its dedication. In the early years at Chapel Hill he had bought many hundreds of acres of wooded and run-down farm land on the outskirts of the village. Most of this was used as wild life refuge, and as a source of botanical study. As the village grew outward, it became necessary to develop much of this property for residential purposes. The money received from the sale of these lots went to Coker College, and, at his death in 1953, a major portion of his estate was left to that institution.

SARAH COKER

Sarah Coker was a warm, delightful, life-loving person. Born in 1881 at Society Hill, the sixth child in Captain Coker's family, she went to Hollins College in Virginia in 1898, where she remained for two years. An excellent student, her degree was in classical studies. She returned home for a year, and then taught in the public schools of Florence for one year.

Adventuresome and with a desire to be of some service to people in need, she was not satisfied to remain at home. In 1902 she went to Philadelphia and entered the Woman's Medical College of Philadelphia, a bold step for a young lady from the rural South. She was graduated with her medical degree in 1908.

After she had interned, still curious about the world and anxious to serve, she joined Dr. Wilfred T. Grenfel in 1910. Grenfel, an English doctor who had done much medical service in the London slums, headed a medical mission to Labrador. Sarah went to the station at St. Anthony's. The cold was intense, living conditions primitive and hard. Many of the ordinary conditions of medical practice were not present. Once, operating in a bleak and remote part of Labrador, it was suddenly necessary that another blood vessel be ligatured—and the supply of ligatures was exhausted. Sarah quickly yanked a hair from her head and completed the ligature successfully.

Sarah could not withstand the severe elements, and no doubt she worked too hard. She developed pneumonia and pleurisy. Recovering, but weak and her lungs scarred, she came home, advised to attempt little work for at least a year. She could not remain inactive, though, and in a short time went to the Virginia State Teachers' College at Farmville, Virginia, as Resident Physician.

What was feared happened, for within a year she developed tuberculosis in her weakened lungs. Seeking cure, she went finally to Albuquerque, New Mexico, where her health improved greatly. So much so that she opened an office in Albuquerque and began again to practice medicine, specializing in pediatrics. She then became Medical Director for Child Welfare Service in New Mexico. Unfortunately, the Director of the Child Welfare Service became ill and for a long period Sarah was called on to fill both jobs.

It was too much on a weak body, and a general breakdown in health followed. She died in a Philadelphia hospital in 1923.

ROBERT ERVIN COKER

Robert Ervin Coker was the third son of Captain Coker, born at Society Hill on June 4, 1876. He went to the University of South Carolina in 1892, but stayed only for that year. The next year he went to the University of North Carolina in Chapel Hill, graduating there in 1896 with a Bachelor of Science degree and with membership in the highest scholarship fraternity.

Robert stayed on at Chapel Hill the year following his graduation as graduate assistant in Biology and received his Master of Arts degree in 1897. He worked under the incisive, dedicated Henry Van Peters Wilson, one of the great men of the University, of whom Robert later wrote affectionately that "in argument with Dr. Wilson it did not pay to be either vulnerable at the start or queasy in the rejoinder." With finances at home not of the best, Robert spent 1897 teaching in a private school in South Carolina. For the following two years he was principal of the public schools at Goldsboro, North Carolina.

In 1901 Robert again took up his graduate studies in Biology, going as his cousin Will had done to Johns Hopkins, where science was having one of its major American developments. There was soon another interruption in his purely academic studies, but one more to his liking. In 1902 he went down to Beaufort, on the North Carolina coast, to work in the double capacity of Custodian of the United States Fisheries Biological Laboratory and Biologist of the North Carolina Geologic and Economic Survey. This was a job of scientific investigation, with emphasis on the economic development of biological life in the abundant sounds and bays of North Carolina. His task, simply, was to determine whether or not oysters could be profitably grown. Funds and facilities were limited. But he produced an answer. Oysters could be grown in abundance and with profit if all of the factors in the situation were put into the proper relationships. These factors were the whole complex of animate and inanimate life and forces involved—man (his morals and laws), oysters, all manner of life in the sounds and rivers, the winds, the tides, and the shifting ocean floor itself. To produce oysters commercially, each of these factors was essential. Robert therefore took the whole approach and did not confine himself to the purely technical side.[8]

Indeed, the first recommendations were designed to change the laws of North Carolina covering private oyster cultivation. The conditions of man and oyster required that the private individual be allowed to lease and stake off sizeable beds, cultivate them every year, and have unassailable rights to the fruits of his labor. These conditions did not then exist. The consequence was that there was relatively little development of private oyster beds—the bulk of the oysters being taken from natural beds open to all. Under such conditions no more than a thimbleful of the potential was being developed and used. Correction for these matters was suggested by a manuscript which was submitted to appropriate members of the North Carolina General Assembly in 1905. The result was some improvement in legislation, but not all that Robert recommended. Permanent results, therefore, were modest. Over the two year period, Robert conducted experimental plantings of oysters in selected areas in Pamlico Sound, under varying conditions. Results were not uniformly good, but the conclusion was that ". . . with the natural conditions in Pamlico Sound and elsewhere as they are, the cultivation of oysters is quite practicable."[9]

[8]. Robert E. Coker, *Oyster Culture in North Carolina,* The North Carolina Geological Survey, Economic Paper No. 10 (Raleigh: E. M. Uzzel and Co., 1905).

[9]. Robert E. Coker, *Experiments in Oyster Culture in Pamlico Sound, North Carolina,* North Carolina Geological and Economic Survey, Bulletin No. 15 (Raleigh: E. M. Uzzel and Co., 1907), p. 70.

He then added, "The problem is before the state. Will it allow the oyster industry to continue to decline until its value is negligible? Or will it pass such simple and practical laws providing for the leasing of bottoms, that enterprising and intelligent planters may proceed to take up bottoms and lay the foundations of an industry which should increase ten-fold the value of the oyster to the state."[10]

Robert returned to Johns Hopkins in 1904, and in June of 1906 received his doctorate. Though awarded the Bruce Fellowship for the following year, he accepted an offer from the government of Peru which entailed work similar in principle to the work on the North Carolina coast. For where North Carolina was concerned over increasing the growth of oysters, Peru was concerned about the guano industry—the increase of the guano-producing birds along the coast and the extraction of guano deposits. This, also, involved a consideration of a situation of interrelated parts, human and nonhuman.[11] In addition, Robert was to study and advise on marine fisheries. The adoption of recommendations made by Robert and others led to immediate improvement in the guano industry. The number of birds increased at least three-fold, and the deposition of fertilizer from 25,000 tons to 125,000 tons annually.

Along with the work Robert was able to make a rich collection of materials of natural life, particularly of marine life. From much of this collection Robert and others were able to write articles which, taken together, constitute a sizeable volume. As a climax to this two years' work, Robert represented Peru at the Fourth International Fisheries Congress, held in Washington, D.C., in 1908, and presented a paper on his work in Peru.

Shortly thereafter, Robert joined the United States Bureau of Fisheries as Scientific Assistant. In 1910 he went as first Director of the United States Fisheries Biological Laboratory,

10. *Ibid.*
11. See, for instance, R. E. Coker, "Regarding the Future of the Guano Industry and the Guano Producing Birds of Peru," *Science*, XXVIII (July 10, 1908), 58-64.

at Fairport, Iowa.[12] The laboratory was charged with fish and mussel investigation in the Mississippi Basin. Again, this work centered on the total life conditions in particular relation to conservation and commercial use of water life. The most important single undertaking was to study the conditions under which fresh-water mussels could survive and increase, mussels being the basis of the button industry. In 1915 he returned to Washington as chief of the Division of Scientific Inquiry of the Bureau.

In 1922, Robert came back to Chapel Hill, to his alma mater, as Professor of Zoology. In considerable degree, of course, Robert's work up to this time had been directed by the jobs at hand. It is obvious that what he had done was to his liking, for in the greater freedom of university work he continued along essentially the same paths.

The area of his interest was water life, or, more accurately, the complex of animate life, life forces and processes centering in and around bodies of water. Though his first work on the North Carolina coast was with salt-water life, his interest in intervening years had turned to fresh-water life. At the University he carried on work in both fresh- and salt-water life, introducing course work in hydrobiology, and, later, in oceanography.

Of specific researches in water life there were many over the succeeding years. His most persisting work, and through which he made his greatest scientific contribution, was in the study of copepods and Cladocera.[13] These are small aquatic crustacea, existing in characteristic form in both fresh and salt water. As one of the more numerous forms of the larger group of plankton, the copepods and Cladocera occupy a strategic place in the process through which the photosynthetic energy of the sun is brought to the use of the economically important fishes. The copepods and Cladocera eat vegetable matter in the water. They, in turn, are eaten by larger water

---

12. R. E. Coker, "The Department of Zoology, University of North Carolina," *Bios*, XVIII, No. 4 (December 1949), 220-21.

13. *Ibid.*, p. 221.

life, which, in turn, is eaten by the carnivorous fishes. A knowledge of the details of the life of these tiny-sized fish is thus a prerequisite to the understanding of major scientific and applied problems. His work on the types, combination, and growth was recognized as a strong forward step that has led to many further results. One result of the work, as an example, demonstrated that the body form and size of some of these small creatures are quite plastic and depend in certain respects on environmental factors such as temperature. Spines and major changes in shape are results of the environment, although only the ability to make these plastic deformations is inherited. Broad implications as to the nature of growth processes and the classification of small organisms have resulted from the work.

The essential nature of his work is to be characterized in other than a recitation of the study of individual organisms. Himself friendly, comfortable looking and with wide-ranging interests, he has had a persisting interest in the total life situation. He has focused on the vegetable and animal life of a lake or pond, studying the mutual relationships and responses through which life actually goes on. He has been interested in the community of natural life. This area of work is formally known as ecology. This particular interest derives in part from his interest in the application of biological knowledge to practical affairs. In addition, there is involved an integer for strict biological science. The ecologist ". . . knows that certain fundamental biological phenomena manifest themselves only in the large. Some one has to face such problems. . . ."[14]

Specifically, "Ecology, in contrast to other divisions of biological science, is concerned not so much with the particular plant or animal or part of a plant or animal, as it looks or behaves in the laboratory, but rather with organisms as they actually live and engage in the battle for existence among others in the real world. . . . No organism moves or has its

---

14. R. E. Coker, "Functions of an Ecological Society," *Science*, Vol. 87, No. 2258 (April 8, 1938), 312.

being except as part of a complex and in connection with the so-called outside world."[15]

Natural community life is not a matter of ". . . mere summations and aggregations of unrelated individuals like the several beans in a bushel."[16] Rather, there is involved ". . . some sort of organization in which individuals or species are but minor or major units of function. The ecologist is concerned with the structure and activities of these larger organizations—that is to say, with the composition and conditions of maintenance and operation of communities."[17]

Ecology, as such, is a relative newcomer in biological science. As a science of the total life situation, it lacks the precision of better developed branches. Virtually by definition, its subject matter cannot be brought into the laboratory, except only approximately. As something of a pioneer in formalized ecology, Robert has aided in its establishment among all biologists. In 1936-37 he served as president of the Ecological Society of America. On the occasion of his presidential address he noted to his fellow ecologists that it is ". . . perhaps not unnatural for the outsider to criticize, to say: you have not set up an experiment under the strictest conditions of control. Your only answer is that you know it, but you are going ahead just the same."[18]

This was advice from an inveterate builder, a man with a rare facility for bringing diverse elements together. From 1926 to 1929 he was chairman of the Committee of Aquiculture of the National Research Council. From the work of this committee, and his direction, there developed the Limnological Society of America, a national scholarly organization of those engaged in the study of fresh-water life. Robert was president of this society in 1937. This later became the American Society of Limnology and Oceanography.

In 1935 Robert succeeded Henry Van Peters Wilson as chairman of the Department of Zoology at the University of North Carolina. Until Robert's coming in 1922 "Froggy" Wil-

15. *Ibid.*, p. 311.
17. *Ibid.*
16. *Ibid.*
18. *Ibid.*, p. 312.

son had been for twenty-five years the department's only full-time faculty member. In 1927 C. Dale Beers joined the staff. By 1935 it was time indeed for growth, given the increase in the student body and the University's growing stature. By the time that Robert retired in 1947 the full-time staff had grown, and the offerings and enrollments in Zoology had been greatly expanded, in both the elementary and more advanced subject areas. To house the expansion in staff and students, Wilson Hall was built, and occupied in 1940.

In 1940, since Robert was 64 years old, this building was mainly for his successors. Wilson Hall could have been viewed as something of a fitting climax to a productive career. It developed, however, that Robert lived to and through the mandatory retirement age in a vigorous and productive fashion, and during this period accomplished much.

It will be recalled that Robert interrupted his graduate work at Johns Hopkins in 1902 to go to Beaufort, North Carolina, where he worked under both federal and state auspices on the development of marine industries in the bays and sounds and along the coast of North Carolina. His particular interest was the development of oyster production on a substantial scale. His analysis of the situation at that time, and his recommendations, were sound. However these latter were only partially adopted. Over the years some erratic advance in the industry was made. Research activities involving federal and state governments and academic people were maintained in the Beaufort-Morehead City area. Over-all, however, the great potential of North Carolina's coastal areas for the development of marine industries was not realized. Robert, along with others, continued to hope that there might be such development, and over the years he had done some work along this line.

In 1944 there began under Robert's direction a decisive step in the realization of this potential. In that year President Frank P. Graham of the University asked for proposals from the faculty of special research projects for which he might seek funds from sources outside the University. President Graham specified that there be a project in marine biology.

Robert's response was that ". . . the best possible project relating to marine biology was an Institute which would attempt to apply not only the biological but also other sciences and economics to the interests of the marine fisheries."[19] The central idea was to join, under the main auspices of the University and its Department of Zoology, the interests of science to those of the economic development of marine fisheries. Whatever their substantive relationships, these two interests are difficult to reconcile.

Robert undertook to effect this reconciliation. The first step was to draw up a beginning plan of the Institute. "It was not much, frankly; it dealt in generalities, by necessity; but it could serve as a basis of discussion."[20] The "basis of discussion" proceeded through numerous committees, emerging as a proposal, first, to conduct a survey of fisheries resources, and, second, to establish a permanent Institute of Fisheries Research for the continuing development of these resources. With funds provided variously by an anonymous friend of the University, by the General Education Board, the Knapp Foundation, the N.C. State Department of Conservation and Development, and the General Assembly of North Carolina, the survey was conducted, and the Institute was established in 1947. Dr. Coker was the first Director of the Institute. Dr. Harden F. Taylor was named Executive Director of a special survey of Marine Fisheries of North Carolina.

The Institute has moved successfully down its several roads. It has already made substantial contributions to the oyster and shrimp industries. In 1950 the Institute planted an oyster bed approximately one square mile in area. When this small bed was opened to public exploitation, it produced in the first year a return of $142,000 to local oyster fishermen, dealers and packing house workers. This was a vivid proof of the Insti-

---

19. R. E. Coker, "Establishment of the Institute of Fisheries Research," mimeographed manuscript in the University of North Carolina Library.
20. *Ibid.*

tute's value to virtually all skeptics. A large-scale planting operation, under supervision of the Institute, has been undertaken. Similarly, recommendations of the Institute for changes in the regulation governing shrimping have increased the income from these activities by from a half to three quarters of a million dollars. Yet, of course, the Institute's stock in trade is basic scientific knowledge. Up to the limit of resources, studies are continuously under way on the underlying and determinative factors of marine life, particularly in the bay and sound areas of North Carolina. "Studies on the effect of environment on the feeding of oyster and growth rate," is an example.

The road to the dissemination and use of Institute knowledge and recommendations has not been altogether without rocks. Persistence without impatience has brought success in this field also. State agencies and an increasing number of commercial fishermen are convinced of the general soundness, reliability and economic value of the Institute. Through all of this Robert has been a major figure—counseling, advising, exerting constant pressure for moving forward.

In his semi-retirement, Robert, in addition to his work with the Institute of Fisheries Research, has written two books capping his lifelong study of water life. The first of these, in 1947, was *This Great and Wide Sea*,[21] a wonderfully written work on the seas of the earth and the life therein. It is a summary book, sound for the scholar and intelligible to the layman. Language, thought, and pace, match the oracular movements of the seas—describing the whole in all of its massive movements, seeing also the thousandfold varieties of life at all levels and in all processes. Characteristically, the theme was interaction and response. For this work he received the Mayflower Award in 1947. The second volume was on freshwater life, titled *Streams, Lakes, Ponds,* published in 1954.

Robert has not been appalled by the fact that there may be an ultimate mystery of organic life. "I see no basis whatever

21. R. E. Coker, *This Great and Wide Sea* (Chapel Hill: The University of North Carolina Press, 1947).

for discouragement or disillusionment in the idea of a finite intellectual world. . . . Even within a finite sphere there is ample room for all the perambulations we need or wish to undertake during the period of our physical existence."[22]

There is a certain paradox in the nature of organic life. Protoplasm has a basic instability—". . . it is simply inherent in protoplasm to be reorganizing itself at all times. Stability in protoplasm spells death."[23] Yet, in the persisting paradox of life itself, protoplasm has an approximate stability. There is, in a sense, stability through change. "Any protoplasmic body might be regarded, as someone has said, as a vessel through which streams of matter and energy are flowing; but the matter and energy in passing participate in a definite organization determined in great part by the vessel."[24] Protoplasm is inadequate as a basis of life. It is not self-contained, but must interact with outside materials and forces. "All manifestations of life, as we now know them, are in the nature of responses to the addition of oxygen and other changes in the environment."[25]

In organic science, at any rate, man's greatest question will always be, "Can life be created, by man, in other than the normal reproductive way?" From the biologist's point of view, the affirmative answer would mean the creation of protoplasm. The chemist would not only have to bring the elements together, but in such a way as to "introduce into his combination of materials both a condition of instability enduringly characteristic of his particular protoplasmic product, but enduring indefinitely only through the power of reproduction from isolated parts—parts that become self-continuing and self-producing wholes." And more than this, this synthetic protoplasm must respond to its environment. Robert could "conceive of the complete analysis of protoplasmic substance and the *partial* reconstruction of protoplasmic behavior, but while keeping an open mind, I go no further now."[26]

22. R. E. Coker, "Some Philosophical Reflections of a Biologist," *The Scientific Monthly*, Vol. 48 (January and February, 1939), p. 64.
23. *Ibid.*, p. 65. 24. *Ibid.*, p. 66.
25. *Ibid.*, p. 67. 26. *Ibid.*, p. 67.

SECOND GENERATION AT HARTSVILLE. *Upper left,* James Lide Coker, Jr. (Champlain Studios, New York). *Upper right,* David R. Coker (courtesy of Mrs. D. R. Coker). *Lower left,* Charles W. Coker, Sr. (courtesy of Charles W. Coker, Jr.). *Lower right,* Joseph J. Lawton (James T. White & Co., New York).

SCHOLARS. *Upper left*, William Chambers Coker. *Upper right*, Edward Caleb Coker (Palmers Studio). *Lower left*, Robert Ervin Coker. *Lower center*, Francis William Coker (Alburtus, Yale News Bureau). *Lower right*, James Harvey Rogers.

JAMES HARVEY ROGERS

The sixth child of Caleb and Hannah Coker was Florence, who married John Terrel Rogers. One of the children born to John and Florence Rogers was named James Harvey, born at Society Hill in 1886. This boy attended St. David's Academy at Society Hill, and then went on to the University of South Carolina, where he received the A.B. degree in 1906, the B.S. and M.A. degrees in 1907. From South Carolina he went to Yale, where in 1909 he received another bachelor's degree; another master's degree in 1913; and the doctorate in 1916.[27]

This array of degrees ought not to suggest that Rogers was a budding pedant. The opposite was the case, for Rogers boldly followed his intellectual interests. Originally interested in mathematics, he went to the University of Chicago in 1913-14 to study higher mathematics. While there he enrolled in his first graduate course in economics, taking work under Alvin Johnson. Thus intrigued, he spent the following year at the University of Geneva where he went especially for the purpose of studying under the eminent economist and sociologist Vilfredo Pareto. It was after this year that he came back to Yale for his final degree in economics.[28]

Scholars in several fields will note essential paradoxes, if not contradictions in Rogers' training. Alvin Johnson was not the most likely economist to attract and keep a burgeoning mathematician's interest in economics. Professor Johnson did not lean toward the strict quantitative and mathematical approach to the study of economics, but rather to the historical approach, with great emphasis upon the shifting social framework. He was ever alert to the application of academic economics to practical affairs. Pareto, on the other hand, had in his early work pursued the virtually pure mathematical approach to economics, in the realm of abstract theory. Yet Pareto, himself, was by 1914 discouraged with this direction of work, in part because there was no evident way to test theory

---

27. Arnold Wolfers, Edgar S. Furniss, Walt W. Rostow, *James Harvey Rogers, 1886-1939* (Stamford, Conn.: privately printed, 1940), pp. 1-2.
28. *Ibid.*, p. 13 ff.

against reality. Moreover, Pareto had become convinced that economic matters could not be explained in terms of only economics. He had turned to his broader and monumental work in general social science. Pareto maintained, however, his disinterest in the solution of current problems.

It seems clear that Rogers came out of this diverse training with a personal synthesis of method and goal. He maintained his liking for the mathematical approach, for the formulation and statement of economic theory in mathematical equations rather than in largely non-quantitative and historical terms. As Rostow has related, Rogers "... was permitted dramatically to judge the merits of the two approaches. Walras had written to Professor Johnson agreeing with a recent article he had written, but urging, in fifteen pages of formulae, that Johnson's verbal analysis could be more profitably stated in mathematical terms. When shown the correspondence, Mr. Rogers sided with Walras."[29] Yet, Rogers did not confuse method with substance; he would not permit publication of his thesis at Yale on the grounds that it was essentially a mathematical exercise.

Nor was he inclined to engage in theorizing and mathematical construction without reasonable prospect that theory and formula could be tested against empirical fact. Though not so apparent until later, there was in him a strong strain of interest in current economic problems. It became characteristic of his work to formulate economic theory in testable mathematical terms, then apply the theory to the empirical situation, with a view to amending theory as necessary.

After completing his graduate work at Yale he went to the University of Missouri to teach. During the First World War he served as statistician with the Council of National Defense. He returned to Missouri, spent the years 1920-23 at Cornell, and then returned once again to Missouri.

His special field of work was monetary analysis. "It was the branch of economics which most nearly approximated the physical sciences in the refinement of its terms and the opportunities it offered both for empirical verification and ap-

29. *Ibid.*, p. 14.

plication."[30] Three of his major works appeared during the 1920's. Each in its own way was the application of a mathematical formulation to empirical data. The first of these three works was *Stock Speculation and the Money Market*. This book was essentially an attempt to trace out the quantity and flow, under stated conditions, of money used for speculation. One purpose was to determine whether great speculative activity attracted and occupied large funds that otherwise would have been put to productive use. He found that ". . . large increases in speculative activity required no diversion of new credit to the stock exchange."[31] Further, speculative activity could be expected to vary in the direction of general business conditions.

His second book of the twenties, *The Process of Inflation in France*, surveyed ". . . movements of the whole French economy in the war and post-war years,"[32] from a monetary perspective. This work was something of a *tour de force* with respect to method and to revealing the interrelationships of an entire national economy.

His third major work of the period was the chapter "Foreign Markets and Foreign Credits" in the book *Recent Economic Changes*. Here Rogers entered the area of international finance, once again expressing abstract concepts in quantitative terms. His central purpose was to discern the consequences of the new economic position occupied by the United States in the period following the First World War. The new position, of course, was that of creditor to the rest of the world. This nation during this period exported capital which, in part at least, stimulated the export of goods. One result was greatly increased inflow to the United States of gold. Ordinarily, it was to be expected that commodity prices would rise in reaction to the increased supply of gold. Rogers pointed out that this had not happened, and that there was inherent in the situation the possibility of a speculative stock exchange boom. He noted that the nation's high tariff structure would

30. *Ibid.*, p. 7.   31. *Ibid.*, p. 20.
32. *Ibid.*

probably not allow any material change in the direction of gold. He did not predict the world depression that was soon to follow, though this was at least in part indicated by his analysis, largely because there were no inflationary tendencies at that time.[33]

The onslaught of the Depression had great effect upon Rogers' work. He conceived it to be his job, as well as that of others, to bring the best of his knowledge to bear on the problems of the Depression—that is, to formulate plans for action rather than to hew closely to academic analysis. This frame of mind reflected the coming to the fore of two currents of thought that had never been completely absent. One, of course, was the application of economic analysis to current problems of the day. The other was the inclusion of non-economic facts as major elements in the economic situation. This was the course followed by Pareto—an awareness that forces which, at least by economic standards, were irrational, were an essential part of the economic situation.

So it was that Rogers left the essentially scholarly analysis of limited economic matters, and moved in the direction of a broader, less exactly defined, survey of the general economic situation. He aimed to reach the layman. In 1931 there appeared the book, *America Weighs Her Gold,* an effort to present policy recommendations in understandable, even polemic, terms. Rogers did not embrace reform with illusions; his state of mind was grim. In introducing *America Weighs Her Gold,* his first sentence read: "So largely determined is the course of human events by the strange characteristics of the human animal himself, on the one hand, and by the complicated environment in which he lives, on the other, that the intervening field of rational control is indeed narrow."

If this conclusion be true, the balances in which human affairs are weighed are largely beyond the control of the weighers. Indeed, in the ruthless course of events certain things are weighed, found wanting, and discarded without our knowledge of how and why. To a considerable extent, we are innocent and often dismayed specta-

33. *Ibid.,* pp. 21-23.

tors. Only here and there are the inaccurately observed and distorted weights even recorded, and then usually by nearsighted and biased observers.[34]

Usually the "... helpless weigher (can) do little more than record the vague and uncertain results which his limited capacities and crudely developed technique allow him to observe. In the mad rush of events which characterize the present-day operation of the capitalist machine under a pseudo-democratic control, such is the unenviable position of the study"[35] of the current emergency. Yet, in the narrow field where rational study and control were possible something might be done, and this was his object in writing, what was for him, a new type of book.

In *America Weighs Her Gold* Rogers made a number of sweeping recommendations for changes in the economic policies of the United States. Most of these recommendations were fundamental, and they were aimed at restoring the total economy. First, he advocated a lowering of tariffs, which had just been raised. "Aside from the political corruption which it has engendered in our national politics throughout more than a hundred years of our history, and aside, too, from the glaring domestic injustices which, since its inception, it has created and maintained; on it can now be laid the blame for a very important part in the extraordinary maldistribution of the money metal, in the recent drastic and decline in prices, and therefore in the world-wide depression."[36] He pointed out that for our now mature industries high tariffs were really no longer an aid but a hindrance; in the same way, bankers who in recent years had made great foreign loans, were now belatedly becoming aware that goods must flow in the international market for these debts to be paid.[37] Rogers went on to point out that even to the mid-western farmers "... the ingeniously contrived hoax seems at last to have become transparent."[38] Further, the

---

34. James Harvey Rogers, *America Weighs Her Gold* (New Haven: Yale University Press, 1931), p. xi.
35. *Ibid.*, p. xiii.
36. *Ibid.*, p. 193.
37. *Ibid.*, pp. 194-95.
38. *Ibid.*, p. 196.

working man is "... gradually learning that our high protective tariff, which from time immemorial has been pledged to keep his dinner pail full, not only is responsible for prolonging and aggravating the present unparalleled depression, but is likewise at least indirectly causing the migration of a highly important portion of American industry itself."[39]

Rogers recommended also the adjustment of war debts as economically desirable. At the same time he did not think that adjustment should not be without its other uses: "The United States with its enormous productive capacity is going to find itself with high and increasing customs tarriffs on almost every side. Under such circumstances, tariff concessions, perhaps in the form of reciprocity agreements, will prove of utmost importance."[40] He thought that the war debts should be used as a means of bargaining in tariff adjustment.

His next policy recommendation was in the field of money and credit, where he urged that the Federal Reserve System take steps to increase the supply of both. He pointed out that the great inflow of gold should have increased money and credit, which in turn might have mitigated the Depression. But the banks of the System "... in the past two years, have played the part of gigantic sponges continually soaking up the ever inflowing golden flood."[41] The result was that what might have been, under the circumstances, a beneficial inflationary effect was not achieved.

Finally, Rogers addressed himself to the gold standard. "Among the most illuminating anomalies of our so-called civilization is the gold standard. To the rationally inclined, that the weight of anything should be chosen and continued as a standard of value is strange enough. That it should be the weight of a substance which at the time of its choosing was usable only for ornament is stranger."[42] His disrespect for what he called his Golden Majesty was monumental. "In spite of long suffering and poverty, his Majesty's aristocracy and their cohorts are just as loyal as ever. Temporarily, against

39. *Ibid.*, p. 196.   40. *Ibid.*, p. 201.
41. *Ibid.*, p. 207.   42. *Ibid.*, p. 209.

their ponderous importance, in the ruthless balances of experiences, mere common sense is of inconsequential weight."[43]

This book appeared before the American public in the depths of the depression, in 1931. Its style, its cogency, its firmness, and the standing of the author—all these combined with the economic desperation of the times to give it a wide reading. It was ". . . in the best tradition of economic pamphleteering: the tradition that stretches continuously back to Ricardo and Tooke and the mercantilists."[44] Nor was its force dissipated by wide notice. It was on the basis of this book, and of succeeding works in the same vein, that Rogers was brought into the inner circles of economic advisers to President Roosevelt. Even casual students of the period will perceive that these recommendations, to a greater or lesser extent, subsequently appeared as public policy. It is not accurate, of course, to attribute all of this effect to Rogers; he was, however, among the more influential.

These and other measures secured some early relief from the Depression. But in 1937 there appeared an economic recession, with the unemployment figure still at 10,000,000. Permanent recovery had not been achieved by the measures adopted. This was not heartening, and it turned Rogers' interest to the reasons why.

His version of the reasons appeared in 1938 in another book addressed to the general public, *Capitalism in Crisis.* Rogers turned even more to forces that were not primarily economic, or only partly so, to explain the state of affairs. There was the unwillingness of investors, individual and private, to invest in wealth-producing areas. Pump priming by government spending had not induced sufficient private savings and profits into circulation to keep the economy prosperous. This he felt was more a psychological than an economic problem. Rogers was concerned also over the failure of more than a token spirit of cooperation to grow up between business and government. In a modern economy this was essential, especially that busi-

---
43. *Ibid.,* p. 210.
44. Wolfers, Furniss, and Rostow, *James Harvey Rogers,* p. 25.

ness look with sympathy upon the necessary governmental economic measures. Labor, also, must be included in this sphere of cooperation. Rigid prices on goods under complete or partial monopoly had retarded the recovery of the whole economy. Business must either ". . . adopt the original Ford plan of passing on to consumer a very large share indeed of all economies (as well as monopoly profits) of production; or else it must *spend* or *distribute* its earnings promptly."[45]

It was to such reasons as these that Rogers directed his attention; this book, therefore, was more an attempt at persuasion than an attempt to state specific action steps.

There was also in the book another element worth noting. The larger context of his arguments was the danger to the survival of democracy of protracted economic depression. Since the earlier book of 1931, totalitarianism had become a more urgent problem. Over and over again, Rogers pointed out that economic emergency had been at the root of the rise of these regimes—that they had gained power first through restoring some measure of economic order and prosperity. He was in 1938 more concerned with this danger than he had been in 1931. And, in a sense, the basic theme of the book was "How can democracies be persuaded to take those public economic measures necessary to restore their economies in time to prevent a totalitarian development?"

By 1939 war loomed in Europe. Should war come, Rogers felt that the United States would need every leverage of economic power that it possessed. One such leverage was the great supply of gold held in this country, on the basis of which loans might be made to certain South American countries. He went to South America in the summer of 1939 to survey this situation, and while there was killed in a plane crash.

Thus was cut short not only a period of public service, but also a lifetime of fruitful teaching. Rogers was an excellent, exacting teacher. When he left Missouri in 1930 to return to Yale to teach, many recent graduates of Missouri enrolled in

---

45. James Harvey Rogers, *Capitalism in Crisis* (New Haven: Yale University Press, 1938), p. 177.

the Yale Graduate School. A group of his former students organized themselves as a study group in New York. He brought zest, hard work and encouragement to his students.

FRANCIS WILLIAM COKER

Francis W. Coker was born at Society Hill on November 1, 1878, the fourth son of Captain Coker. Growing up there, at Springville, and at Darlington, he went on to the University of North Carolina in 1895, graduating *cum laude* in 1899. For two years he taught Latin, mathematics, and American history at the Webb School in Bell Buckle, Tennessee. He then went to Harvard for a year, studying philosophy. George Herbert Palmer and George Santayana were among his professors. Having previously become interested in the significance of biological ideas for philosophical theory, he took a full term of biology during this year at Harvard, and spent the following summer at a biological laboratory at Cold Springs Harbor, Long Island. That fall he went to the Miller School, near Charlottesville, Virginia, to teach, being assigned work in physics and botany on the strength of his recent and, to him, meager, science study.

When he came home to Darlington in the summer of 1903, he was tired and somewhat discouraged. His father, Captain Coker, advised him to remain at home for a year, doing some outdoors work, and generally improving his health, while he took stock of just what academic direction he really wanted to take. On reflection during that year, his interests turned to political science. He found that by far the broadest development of this subject at the graduate level was at Columbia University, and there he enrolled in the fall of 1904. His concentration of work was in political philosophy under William A. Dunning, but there was a rich dispersion: public law and jurisprudence under J. W. Burgess, John Bassett Moore, F. J. Goodnow, and Monroe Smith; medieval intellectual history under James Harvey Robinson; sociology under Franklin Henry Giddings; and the history of economic theory under E. R. A. Seligman. On completion and publication of his dissertation, *Organismic Theories of the State: Theories of the State as Organism and as Person,* he received his doctorate degree in 1910.

In 1907-9 he taught at the University of Missouri, did teaching and preceptorial work at Princeton in 1909-11, and then went in 1911 as Assistant Professor of Political Science at Ohio State University. He was Professor of Political Science at Ohio State from 1914 until 1929. That year he went to Yale University as Alfred Cowles Professor of Government and head of the Department of Political Science. He retired from Yale in 1947.[46] A quiet, purposeful man, friendly and approachable, he was at all three institutions a constructive, building force.

When, after his year at Darlington, Frank Coker turned to political science, he chose wisely. Especially in democracy, he found a life's consuming interest; on it he has bestowed a loving, though not altogether uncritical, respect. His interests, writings, and teachings have ranged rather widely, but always the central tendency has been toward an inspection, a catalogue, a partial analysis of democracy, particularly American democracy, and between the lines, a marveling at its existence.

Yet he has been, first and last, an impeccable scholar, a master of articulated political philosophies. It has been a mark of his writing, and pre-eminently of his teaching, to present clearly, fairly, and completely, varying and opposing sides, preserving in the doing something of the essential nature of intellectual freedom and of the democratic process. His major work, *Recent Political Thought,* was a thorough and accurate examination of the main relevant backgrounds of modern political philosophies, of the prevailing forms of government and their underlying doctrines, and of current political problems and tendencies.[47]

In this work, a major portion was given over to the exami-

---

46. Biographical data from letter to author, May 5, 1955.
47. F. W. Coker, *Recent Political Thought* (New York: D. Appleton-Century Company, 1934).

nation of democracy. Meticulously, he laid bare the attacks on democracy, and its evident shortcomings. In the figure of "the serious advocate of democracy"[48] he concluded that "There appears to be nothing in science or history to indicate that the predilections of the democratic theorists are unsound."[49] There are limitations. Democracy ". . . is unrealizable in an unsuitable social milieu. . . . It presupposes also that the citizens have enough intellectual and moral vigor to withstand persistent deception by demagogues and to apply some discriminating judgments to the policies of their chosen leaders."[50] Moreover, effective democracy should be representative: "General popular voting should be confined to the decision of basic issues—the popular election of only a few, most important, policy-determining officials, or the acceptance or rejection by popular vote of only the most fundamental measures. . . ."[51] And, lastly, ". . . democracy needs free and informed discussion of governmental affairs. The people do not govern merely by having a right to choose their governors. They must have also the opportunity to understand and criticize what these officers are doing."[52] In sum, ". . . democracy is not so much the right of each to have his ideas adopted as it is the right and opportunity of each to have his ideas heard and to hear the ideas of all others."[53]

As to the persisting question of leadership, of securing good leaders and some of the best, ". . . the democrat believes that no other method is better than the democratic method for identifying and bringing to the top the men of high political character, and that democracy, more nearly than other forms, confines these men to their function of leadership and prevents them from becoming dictators."[54] The mature democrat does not assume that all men are of equal ability, equally fit to govern and to lead; rather, he can find no grounds for locating superior ability in these matters in any special group, be it selected on intellectual, educational, economic, or biologic

48. *Ibid.*, p. 373.   49. *Ibid.*, p. 372.   50. *Ibid.*
51. *Ibid.*, p. 373.   52. *Ibid.*   53. *Ibid.*
54. *Ibid.*

grounds. Leadership developed through the democratic process is as efficient and as wise as that developed in any other way, and it has the advantage of bringing ". . . peculiar benefits, of a moral or spiritual sort, to the rank and file. To treat men as equals makes them more cooperative in spirit and more active in efforts to mitigate inequality."[55]

Frank Coker, over the years, has queried democracy in the United States on four major problems: the problem of locating political control, that is, of who should have ultimate authority; the lines to be drawn between governmental authority and individual liberty; the nature and limits of property rights and their relation to the actual realization of political rights; and the problem of political change to meet changing circumstances. These areas overlap, of course, and they include many questions of scarcely less importance.[56] Looking at each in turn, he has felt that "The main trend has been towards a more general acceptance of the ideal values of democratic government, freedom of opinion, equality before the courts, and free economic enterprise."[57] Yet he has not been unmindful that "there have indeed been notable repudiations of the ideals themselves; warnings of the practical incompetence and of the intellectual and spiritual tyranny and barrenness of democracy; disparagements of free speech, assembly, and association where these liberties appear to endanger the preservation of other traditional values; and denials that private property promotes free enterprise."[58]

Of these four basic problems, in Frank Coker's lifetime, two have been of critical interest in American life. One has been the question of the nature and limits of property rights. The underlying current on which this question has been carried has been the growth of corporate business and industry, the concentration of the ownership of wealth and capital goods in the hands of relatively few concerns. "When we adopted our

55. *Ibid.*
56. F. W. Coker (ed.), *Democracy, Liberty, and Property* (New York: The Macmillan Company, 1942), p. 11.
57. *Ibid.*, p. 11.
58. *Ibid.*, p. 12.

Constitution, some 90 per cent of the free inhabitants of America owned the properties upon which they worked."[59] Currently, as an example of the change, "A hundred large corporations own over a half of our total manufacturing plants. . . .[60] Thus the vast majority of Americans have lost their property rights, in the sense of rights of an individual over the materials and instruments, including land, with which he labors for a livelihood."[61]

The critical issue growing out of this development, of course, has been the extent to which the government ought to regulate and control the growth and power of this corporate structure, so as to protect the basic political and economic rights of the vast majority of Americans. A related issue is the wisdom of the government's taking positive action in the direction of the national economy—such as public works, the control of credit, the development of farm price supports—so as to mitigate inequalities of the "free" operation of market forces as they presently exist, and to guarantee a minimum level of national prosperity. These questions appeared with special force at the onslaught of the Depression, and continued in the actions of the New Deal and the subsequent defense requirements.

Without attempting the final answer, particularly regarding the primarily economic questions, Frank Coker has meticulously sought to identify the present situation in its context of the total of American development. He has pointed out over and over again the fact that governmental action with respect to economic affairs has never been absent, and usually it has been conscious and purposive. In his presidential address before the American Political Science Association in December of 1935, he said that "Our federal government has generally rendered whatever aid our expanding industrial and commercial capital-

---

59. F. W. Coker, "Income Stabilization and the American Political Tradition," *Income Stabilization in a Developing Democracy*, ed. Max Millikan (New Haven: Yale University Press, 1953), p. 90.
60. *Ibid.*, p. 92.
61. F. W. Coker, "Property Rights as Obstacles to Progress," *Annals of the American Academy of Political and Social Science*, Vol. 185 (May 1935), 135.

ism has seriously needed—in the way of protective tariffs; land grants to railways; aids to the development of foreign markets and protection of foreign investments; creation of favorable credit conditions; and intervention of federal courts, in behalf of large employers, in labor disputes that can be related to interstate commerce."[62] To object to governmental interference on purely historical grounds has no basis in fact.

As to the danger of the encroachment upon political, civil, and individual liberties by the state through its entry into the economic sphere,

Recent experiences in our national policy supply us with reasons to believe that political and civil rights can be kept generally as secure in a society whose government helps direct its economic development as in a society that leaves the controls predominantly in private hands. While we have been modifying some of our economic liberties, we have at the same time been making more secure some of our other liberties. This is shown in recent decisions of the United States Supreme Court in cases initiated or participated in by executive agencies. These decisions have helped to establish freer voters' participation in nominations and elections, freer communication of ideas, and fairer court trials through a fairer selection of juries, a more effective right to assistance of counsel, and a stronger protection against compulsory self-incrimination. While our government, during a decade and a half, has been applying new forms of economic intervention we have retained substantially unimpaired our rights to talk, organize, campaign, and vote in efforts to prevent, repeal, or extend the aids and regulations.[63]

62. F. W. Coker, "American Traditions Concerning Liberty and Property," *American Political Science Review*, Vol. XXX, No. 1 (February 1936), p. 3.
63. Millikan (ed.), *Income Stabilization in a Developing Democracy*, p. 105.

12

New World at Hartsville

I

THE GENERATIONS changed at Hartsville in the 1930's. To tell of what happened on the other side, and in the early years, of this decade is to relate the past. This side of the early thirties is the present, and the present is a new world at Hartsville.

James L. Coker, Jr., and his brother Charles died within a month of each other in early winter, 1931. David R. Coker was in poor health, a semi-invalid, during much of the decade, and he died in 1938. J. J. Lawton, the Major's son-in-law, lived until 1941, the longest of his generation in Hartsville.

These men were survived by more than a dozen children. Yet in practical effect their place in affairs and in carrying the family name and unity has been taken by a small number of sons; the succession has been

James Lide Coker, Jr., in the Carolina Fiber Company, by his son Richard Gay Coker;

D. R. Coker, in the Pedigreed Seed Company, by his son Robert R. Coker;

Charles W. Coker, in Sonoco Products Company, by his sons James Lide Coker III, and Charles W. Coker, Jr.;

J. J. Lawton, in the Hartsville Oil Mill, by his son Edgar H. Lawton.

Four sets of parents bore and trained these five young men in the Hartsville setting. There were, therefore, as many clear cut units of the larger family, and consequently multiple potentials for, if not disunity, then a weakening of the earlier family working together. Yet these young men also grew up in the emergence of the family's achievements at Hartsville, knowing the Major in varying degrees, and forever conscious of the spirit and presence of the family. They had lived and seen the family in cooperation, and disagreement as well. Had nothing else done so, the Hartsville community made them aware of the family situation, imposing quite subtly on them expectations that they would preserve much of the earlier unity.

All had their work cut out for them as they reached maturity, and in this they differed from their fathers. Perhaps this is the most pervasive characteristic of the present generation. Theirs has been the job of maintenance and expansion, a hard one, for if they have been spared some of the rigors of pioneering, to step into larger shoes has its own exacting requirements.

The times were changing. Sometimes to say this is platitudinous, but not in this situation. The year 1930 is a major milepost in the life of the South. Ahead for agriculture were fundamental changes. Ahead, also, were great efforts, largely successful, to decrease tenancy, improve health, and remove illiteracy. By 1930 the region-wide effect of industry was cumulating, and ahead was an expansion of startling proportions. Once the worst of the Depression was past, the southern rural people were to leave the farms in constantly increasing rates, and towns, cities, and metropolitan centers were to grow in the same way; through all of this—in war and peace during the next decades—were to swirl a hundred currents of changing social relations and attitudes and aspirations.

All of this was already a part of the new world at Hartsville, and would become more so, as the new generation met the somewhat belated arrival of the twentieth century in the South. By 1930 Hartsville's effective population was approaching 10,000,[1] which is to say that these young men had grown up

1. U. S. Bureau of the Census, *Fifteenth Census of the United States: 1930, Popula-*

THIRD GENERATION AT HARTSVILLE. *Upper left*, Charles W. Coker, Jr. (Dorothy Wilding, New York). *Upper right*, Richard G. Coker. *Lower left*, James L. Coker III (Bachrach, New York). *Lower center*, Edgar H. Lawton (Quarles, Florence). *Lower right*, Robert R. Coker (Bachrach, New York).

Above, Sonoco Products Company plant at Hartsville (McLaughlin Air Service). *Below*, Breeding plots for grains at Coker's Pedigreed Seed Company, George Wilds at left (courtesy of Coker's Pedigreed Seed Company).

in a town setting, while their fathers had known Hartsville in their early years as almost open country. By 1950 Hartsville approached 15,000 in population. Enterprises other than those of the Cokers, employing many people, have been established. In war and peace the people of Hartsville have taken in and have seen more of the larger world, in the common tendency of the towns of the South, and they have become less local in interest and development. All in all, this change has diminished significantly the ratio of personal contacts between members of the family and the people of Hartsville.

While the succession of this relatively small group of male Cokers has been unequivocal, it has been in part mediated by a number of people, some members of the family and some not, who stand in age and outlook as an intermediate generation. This is a varied group.

There is Mrs. D. R. Coker, whom D. R. Coker married in 1915, several years after the death of his first wife. This gracious lady was the former May Roper, daughter of Daniel C. Roper. There is no doubt that she contributed much to Mr. D. R.'s outward growth into public affairs and the larger dimensions of the agricultural situation after their marriage. Twenty years younger than her husband, Mrs. Coker has survived him vigorously, though without ostentation in the execution of the trusts which he left her in his will. A special interest with her has been to endeavor to continue the Pedigreed Seed Company largely along the lines of service originally laid down by Mr. D. R. One of the Coker men presently active has characterized her as "the best Coker of us all."[2] Astute as well as charming, she has been a strong arch between the past and the present.

There was George Wilds, who came as a growing boy to work for Mr. D. R. in 1908 in the breeding work. He was the first full-time helper in the work, and it was he who cared for

---

tion, I (Washington: U. S. Government Printing Office, 1933), p. 989; *Sixteenth Census of the United States: 1940, Population*, I (Washington: U. S. Government Printing Office, 1942), p. 979.

2. Conversation with James Lide Coker III.

the first increase plot of the Hartsville long staple cotton.[3] With Mr. D. R.'s encouragement he took subsequent leaves from his work to complete his education in scientific breeding, and despite attractive offers elsewhere, remained as head breeder of the Pedigreed Seed Company, where Mr. D. R. credited him with a large share of the success of the Company. Mr. D. R., in fact, looked upon Wilds essentially as a son. George Wilds married Ruth Lawton, daughter of J. J. Lawton and the Major's eldest child, Margaret. At Mr. D. R.'s death in 1938 George Wilds became President of the Pedigreed Seed Company.

In 1913, Dr. W. C. Coker, who was teaching at the University of North Carolina, sent A. L. M. Wiggins to Hartsville, to begin work as secretary to his brother D. R. Coker.[4] Young Wiggins soon made himself invaluable, and by 1921 he was general manager of the store and vice president of the Bank of Hartsville. Wiggins married Pauline Lawton, another daughter of J. J. and Margaret Lawton. He went on to become President of the American Bankers' Association, Undersecretary of the Treasury, and is at present Chairman of the Board of The Atlantic Coast Line Railway.

C. G. Timberlake married Anna Lee Lawton, a sister of Ruth and Pauline Lawton. Although Timberlake worked for a while with the Cotton Oil Company, he struck out on his own in several enterprises, with considerable success. He has, however, been a figure in many family affairs, and is therefore to be considered in this intermediate generation.

It is proper, also, to include in the intermediate generation a group of men who have no kinship with the Cokers. Now in their late fifties and sixties, they came as young men to work for the preceding generation, and stayed on because of their ability. When the present generation came to maturity and responsibility, these men were already experienced in their work, and even then held very responsible positions. They have been, therefore, extremely useful to the present generation.

3. Conversation with George Wilds.
4. Conversation with A. L. M. Wiggins.

While they work for the Cokers, these men have wrought out positions of their own in the Coker activities and in the community. They tend to some extent to stand between the Cokers and the community.

Most of these men work at Sonoco Products Company. They are such men as C. K. Dunlap, the engineering genius who is vice president in charge of engineering; C. H. Campbell, vice president in charge of sales; J. B. Gilbert, treasurer; J. H. Martin, general production manager; P. L. McCall, superintendent of paper making at Sonoco. All of these men are on the board of directors at Sonoco. To this list must be added J. F. Wilmeth, a lawyer who came to Hartsville at D. R. Coker's suggestion just after the First World War, and who is the Cokers' legal adviser.[5]

II

As has been previously noted, Charles Westfield Coker, president of Sonoco Products Company, died in 1931, at the relatively early age of fifty-two, and his son, James Lide Coker, III, succeeded him as president of the company. James was then twenty-eight. He had graduated from the University of North Carolina and had then gone on to the Harvard School of Business Administration, where he had received his Master's degree in 1928. He had then gone to work in various jobs in the Sonoco plant at Hartsville, becoming in 1930 assistant treasurer.[6] His father's early death imposed a heavy responsibility upon him and upon his younger brother, Charles Westfield Coker, Jr., who became vice president of Sonoco Products Company at the same time. Stock in Sonoco was widely held in the family, though C. W. Coker had held the controlling amounts. The board of directors was composed of family members of the older generation. It was something of a family matter, then, that the young men moved directly into the major positions at Sonoco. The older and intermediate generations were not averse to giving advice; D. R. Coker, who had been

5. Conversation with J. F. Wilmeth.
6. Conversation with James L. Coker III.

and continued to be a vice president, tended to mediate between the old and the new and the changeover was made successfully.

Sonoco at this time was beginning to reap the benefits of its leadership in developing a cone to carry rayon yarn, as well as of the other technical developments of the twenties. Thus despite the fact that the Depression was in full development, Sonoco was able to operate with a minimum of curtailment. As a matter of fact, the young men and their associates were beginning a period of enormous growth and expansion of Sonoco, a period of growth in which the company would move from the position of being one of several cone producers in the country to the position of the pre-eminent producer of cones.

Young James and Charles Coker both are always quick to point out, in discussing the growth of Sonoco under their management, that they have consciously followed the principles of development laid down by their father. The main principle, aside from that of fair dealing, is that of being ahead of the game with respect to technical development. They learned this lesson well and have put increasing amounts of interest and money into technical development. In doing so they have been able to meet, and in some cases to anticipate, the various demands of the textile spinning industry during the past twenty years. C. K. Dunlap's laboratory facilities were enlarged, and in 1934 the distinguished chemist, Dr. J. E. Mills, was brought in to organize and conduct specialized chemical research. Sonoco successfully provided cones for carrying nylon. In 1948, for instance, when Du Pont began to build a large plant for the manufacture of orlon yarn at nearby Camden, Sonoco was given the problem by Du Pont engineers of making a tube to carry the new orlon fabric. After some work, such a tube was successfully developed.[7]

There are several measures of the growth of Sonoco which, since the early thirties, has become by far the largest of the Coker enterprises in Hartsville. There is first the expansion of plant units outside of Hartsville. There are now plants in Garwood, New Jersey; Mystic, Connecticut; Lowell, Massa-

7. Conversation with Charles W. Coker, Jr.

chusetts; Akron, Indiana; Longview, Texas; Los Angeles, California; Mexico City, Mexico; and in Brantford, Ontario and Cranby, Quebec.[8] The building and acquisition of these plants is also a measure of Sonoco's ascendancy in the field. Some four thousand people are employed at these plants, while no more than five hundred were employed in the early thirties.

The most significant measure of growth is to be found in the Hartsville plant, for this is the home plant and the largest by far. In 1930 three hundred people were employed at Hartsville. Since that time there has been a steady rise: six hundred in 1935, one thousand in 1940,[9] and about fifteen hundred currently.[10] A great building for cone making was finished in 1937; a new spiral tube building in 1947; a new paper machine was installed in 1948. In addition to these developments there have been other minor enlargements, notably a building to house engineers and machine tool craftsmen who conceive and build most of the machines used at Sonoco.

An expansion of these dimensions of people employed and size of plant has brought about certain fundamental changes in the nature of operations at Sonoco. When there were but two hundred people employed in the Hartsville plant, as was the case in 1920, or even the three hundred in 1930, operations were conducted mainly on a personal basis. The superintendents of the various departments did their own hiring and firing for the most part, with only informal reference to backgrounds of the employees or to higher authority. On occasion foremen would authorize credit advances to employees, and C. W. Coker often did this type of thing himself.[11] In fact, Mr. Coker's personal acquaintance with all the employees of more than transient occupation at Sonoco, and his close interest in many of them, typifies this earlier way of doing things.

Expansion in size, and the coming in of the new generation of management, have, it seems, caused a change in the

---

8. Catalogue (Sonoco Products Company), and correspondence with R. G. Coker.
9. "Your Company and Your Job," pamphlet issued to employees, p. 8 (Sonoco Products Company).
10. From personnel records (Sonoco Products Company).
11. Conversation with J. H. Martin.

type of operations at Sonoco. The most significant development along these lines has been the establishment of a rationalized system of work standards and job evaluation, this being a substitution of a generally depersonalized system for the older, more informal, and personal arrangements. The George S. May Company was called in in the middle thirties to install an efficiency system, and this, with modifications, is the system that is in use at the present time.[12] Each job in the plant is evaluated in relation to other jobs. In job evaluation, consideration is given to the ". . . knowledge, skill, physical effort and responsibility . . ."[13] required to do the job satisfactorily.

Standards of performance at each job are established by a Standards Department, whose main tool is that of time studies. "Time study records the time taken to complete the different parts of a job; from these figures is fixed the time it should take an average trained operator working at an average pace to complete the job. Allowances are made in the time study for unavoidable delays."[14] On most jobs in the mill it is possible for employees to earn bonuses by performance over and above the standard set for the job. Daily production records are kept on each employee's time card.

Developments of this type may, of course, be partially attributed to sheer growth in size of the operations at Hartsville, and the consequent inability to handle them on the old informal and personal basis. Rationalization of production has also been a tendency of the times and perhaps is necessary in order to remain competitive. So far as the Cokers who moved into charge of Sonoco in the early thirties are concerned, this development seems to have been a natural outgrowth of their inexperience, wherein they felt the need for measurable and objective facts and figures on plant operations. They did not have the "feel of things" which comes only from long experience and from being present when all which exists was wrought out.

12. *Ibid.*
13. "Your Company and Your Job," p. 24 (Sonoco Products Company).
14. *Ibid.*

The three factors mentioned above have served also to raise in importance a number of executives at Sonoco. Generally, these are the men previously mentioned who constitute part of the intermediate generation, though included also are several young men on their way up. Because of their ability, and because the increasing size of the plant required it, a good deal of responsibility has been delegated to these men. A steering committee of top executives meets twice weekly with James and Charles Coker for discussion of important plant matters. When Charles W. Coker died in 1931, the board of directors of Sonoco was composed entirely of members of the family. Now men prominent in the operations of the company outnumber family members by almost two to one.

Sonoco, since the early thirties, in addition to the rationalization of production just described, has gone along with other general developments in the field of industrial management. There have been established a group insurance program, including health and accident provisions; a retirement plan, along with special recognition of long service by employees; an advisory committee composed of employees that meets regularly and effectively with management; suggestion boxes; a lunch room; a plant newspaper; a system whereby employees can begin to pay ahead on the education of their children at Coker College in Hartsville; safety programs; and recreational facilities on Prestwood Lake.[15]

So far, it seems, the union question has not seriously presented itself at Sonoco, though several other industries at Hartsville are organized. Primarily this seems to be because there has been little incentive for organization, inasmuch as wages at Sonoco have consistently been higher than in the surrounding area. In addition to the higher base rates that have prevailed, management at Sonoco generally has complied with the several rounds of postwar wage increases. Perhaps a contributing factor also has been the fact that a high proportion of Sonoco employees live outside of Hartsville in rural or rural non-farm areas, and for this reason are not particularly in-

15. *Ibid.;* these are all explained in the pamphlet.

clined to join in a union. Sonoco has always been considered a good place to work. Sonoco employees generally feel that the Cokers intend to give fair treatment. For the Cokers themselves, the situation remains unclear. All things being equal, they prefer not to have a union. On the other hand, Charles Coker, who handles personnel matters, has stated that management is willing to provide a meeting hall and other facilities for organization, so long as only the truth is dealt in and so long as management may also state its case.[16] The Cokers would be very unlikely to put on a violent, bitter-end fight to prevent unionization; on the other hand they probably will pursue their present course of staying ahead of union demands.

It will be recalled that the Coker industries were built in the open countryside, amid the tall pine trees on the banks of Black Creek. Almost exclusively, the people who have worked at Sonoco have also come from this countryside. Of the 1,413 people on whom records were available at Sonoco during the course of this study, 52.6 per cent were born in Darlington County: 16.0 per cent in Hartsville, 8.2 per cent in the town of Darlington, and 28.4 per cent in the rural areas of the county. Another 26.7 per cent of these employees were born in the several counties that immediately surround Darlington County. Only 7.8 per cent of these employees were born outside of the state of South Carolina, virtually none outside of the Southeastern region.

While Hartsville has grown, these Sonoco employees have by no means flocked to Hartsville to live. Of 1,550 employees on whom residence information was available, only 34.9 per cent lived within the city limits of Hartsville. Since, however, the city limit radii of Hartsville are very modest, a somewhat larger percentage actually lives in the Hartsville community, in the good-sized housing developments that have grown up just outside the city limits. A conservative estimate would, however, be that no more than 50 per cent of the Sonoco employees live in the Hartsville community. For the

---

16. Conversation with C. W. Coker, Jr.

remainder, no more than 5 per cent live in incorporated places within driving distance of Hartsville. The remaining 45 per cent live in rural areas, either actually on farms or in rural non-farm situations. This state of affairs squares pretty well with the background of the people working at Sonoco. Information was available on 1,368 employees as to their last previous employment. Of this number, 26.2 per cent listed farming as their last previous occupation, while 21.9 per cent listed their work at Sonoco as their first employment. Somewhat less reliable are the figures on the usual occupation of the fathers of the Sonoco employees. Information was available on only 495 of approximately fifteen hundred workers. Of this small number, 67.3 per cent listed farming as the usual occupation of their fathers.[17]

The Carolina Fiber Company and Sonoco Products Company were originally built side by side along Black Creek. By 1941 it seemed desirable to convert this physical proximity into actual merger of the two companies. There were several reasons. In the first place, the Carolina Fiber Company had not been so successful during the thirties as had been hoped, following the shift to the semi-chemical process of pulping in the late twenties. Paper making in the South had during these years became a large-scale, bulk business, and the more modest Fiber Company had found the going rather hard. Expansion beyond the resources of the company seemed necessary. On the other hand, with the uncertain war years ahead, Sonoco was anxious to make its paper supply more secure by taking in the paper making machinery and personnel of the Fiber Company. More compelling than this, perhaps, was the desire at Sonoco for diversification. This had been a concern of Mr. Charles Coker, and had been taken up by his sons. So long as the dependence of the company was preponderantly on cone and tube making, then there was considerable risk from the many ups and downs of the textile industry, and from competitors in the cone and tube field. All these factors

---

17. These figures were taken by the author from personnel records at Sonoco.

worked together to cause the two industries to merge in 1941.[18]

This merger presents the most concrete family situation available in the present generation. Richard Coker, son of James Lide Coker, Jr., had become vice-president of the Carolina Fiber Company on his father's death in 1931; P. H. Rogers, who had handled the business affairs for some years, became president at that time. When Mr. Rogers retired in 1939, Richard became president of the company. Richard, like his father, was an engineer. His main interest was in this type of work, for which he was well fitted. James and Charles Coker at Sonoco, on the other hand, had made general business administration their specialties, for which they in turn were well fitted. As part of the merger, Richard came into Sonoco in an engineering capacity, and this capacity has had more scope in the larger company. He is now Secretary and Chief Engineer of Sonoco. Whatever personal adjustments were required in this merger appear to have been worked out successfully. The success of the whole operation would seem to be evidence of a continuing viable family life in the present generation. It represents, again, expansion and more formal rationalization of activities, as well as of family capacities. Materially, the move has been amply justified. A great new paper machine was installed, on the basis of the paper making know-how taken over from the Fiber Company. The entire output of this machine has been sold for many years in advance, and Sonoco seems to have another reliable and remunerative string to its bow.

III

On Mr. D. R. Coker's death in 1938, George Wilds became president of the Pedigreed Seed Company, and remained there until his death in 1951. Howard Blakeslee, Science Editor for the Associated Press, described George Wilds in 1943 as "... a six-foot, square-jawed, ruddy faced South Carolinian. ..." George Wilds, actually, was several inches over six feet, and this description does not convey the single-minded enthusiasm

---

18. Conversation with J. L. Coker III and R. G. Coker.

that he had poured into the breeding work since 1908, when he came as Mr. D. R.'s first full-time helper. He would talk seed breeding without any provocation whatsoever, with anybody, anywhere. Mr. D. R.'s son, Robert, who had been sales manager several years prior to his father's death, became vice president and continued in charge of sales, until he succeeded George Wilds as president in 1951.

It will be recalled that a significant new development in a "bread and butter" cotton—Coker 100—had been introduced in 1937, a little over a year before Mr. D. R.'s death. This cotton supplanted the older Cleveland Five cotton and moved very rapidly into the cotton fields, especially in the upper South. Within a few years it was being planted almost exclusively in North and South Carolina. Wilt disease had continued to be an important factor in cotton growing in many areas of the eastern South, however, and breeding had been going on all along to place wilt resistance into the developing Coker 100. This was finally achieved, and in 1942 Coker 100 Wilt was placed on the market.

It proved to have more good characteristics than any cotton that we have ever worked with.... It has high production; a wide degree of uniformity; high manufacturing value and a high degree of wilt resistance. It can be planted on either wilt infested or non-wilt infested soils without any sacrifice in yield. It is the one cotton we have and can conscientiously offer for one-variety planting.[19]

The successful breeding of the Coker 100 Wilt cotton as a magnificent climax to the breeding of bread and butter cottons begun in 1915 requires a pause to note, generally, the cumulative effect of these cottons, and specifically, the success of Mr. D. R. Coker's long range, but very tight, planning. The unit of measure used here is South Carolina, where for the last thirty years the great bulk of cotton has been grown from Coker's pedigreed seed. In general Mr. D. R. bred seed for what he often called the eastern South—lower Virginia, the two Carolinas, Georgia, upper Florida and Alabama. For

---

19. George J. Wilds, "Commercial Cotton Breeding."

various reasons, the full force of his influence was felt in South Carolina. From South Carolina widening circles mark the diminishing specific influence of his work, though the decrease is not uniform in every direction. The influence of the Seed Company, for instance, has been greater in North Carolina than in Georgia.

Mr. D. R.'s original aim in breeding a bread and butter cotton was several fold. He desired to increase the yield per acre, the general measure being a substantial reduction of acreage without any necessary reduction in total yield. He desired, also, to increase the average staple length from less than an inch to between an inch and an inch and one-eighth. The end results of these two developments, as he saw it, would be a release of many acres for other crops and a more profitable cotton crop for the individual farmer.

The success or failure of these plans are to be checked in several ways. A good check is the survey of the cotton situation in South Carolina written by H. E. Shiver in 1949.[20] So far as yield per acre was concerned, Shiver found that

> At the turn of the century, in 1901, we were planting two million acres to cotton, securing an average yield of 159 pounds of lint per acre, and making a total of 692,000 bales. In 1943 our former giant, cotton, had shared half of his previous acreage with other crops, and on the remaining half came up with a yield of 373 pounds per acre, and a total production of some 845,000 bales. One-fourth more bales on one-half the former acreage achieved by a 135% increase in yield per acre.[21]

Staple length moved up also, "... from practically no inch cotton in 1901, to over 93% of it that length or better in 1943."[22]

As for the end results, acreage has been released for planting to other crops and this has been done substantially in South Carolina. Beyond this, Shiver found that "apparently it has

---

20. H. E. Shiver, B. F. Buie and Inman F. Eldredge, *South Carolina Raw Materials* (Columbia: University of South Carolina Press, 1949), p. 16.
21. *Ibid.*
22. *Ibid.*

been much more profitable to grow cotton in South Carolina than in most other cotton states."[23]

For the period 1930-35, the average farm price received in South Carolina was 9.2c per pound, and the average cost of production, after credit for cottonseed, was 9.4c inclusive of land rent, and 8.0c exclusive thereof. This is to be compared with an average price of 8.9c, and cost of 10.9c including rent, and 8.7c excluding same, for the cotton belt as a whole. For the period 1936-40, these figures become, for South Carolina, respectively 10.3c, 9.5c, and 7.6c; for the cotton belt, 9.9c, 9.6c and 8.0c. Finally, for the years 1941-43, the figures for South Carolina are 15.3c, 10.8c, and 8.8c.[24]

Shiver concluded that "this advantage, in the normal years, is very real, and undoubtedly is due in largest measure to premium prices for our greater average staple length and higher quality."[25] Now, of course, all of this development cannot be attributed to the Pedigreed Seed Company. Many other changes have come about in southern agriculture in the past two decades, notably the Federal farm programs, without which these developments could not have been accomplished. Two things stand out, however. First, Mr. D. R.'s long range planning, in accordance with which he bred his seed, was realistic. Second, it is his seed that is being grown in South Carolina, and the characteristics of high yield and staple length must be in the seed, or even perfect cultivation will not produce such a crop as is now being produced.

The ultimate fate of cotton growing in South Carolina and in the South as a whole is, at least, questionable. Suffice it to say that the increased yields and staple lengths have enabled South Carolina to overcome fundamental disadvantages with respect to the better situated cotton growing states of the deep South and Southwest. South Carolina's disadvantage in this respect, and the way in which it might be overcome, had been outlined by Mr. D. R. as early as 1927, when the bread and butter cottons were just beginning to come to climax.

23. *Ibid.*, p. 17.
24. *Ibid.*, pp. 16-17.
25. *Ibid.*, p. 17.

It is a well known fact that the new cotton territory in Texas and Oklahoma has during the past few years been able to produce cotton at a much lower per acre cost than has prevailed in South Carolina. . . .

In my opinion we can meet the situation and the way has recently been made clear. . . .

The production of more per acre of varieties of cotton which will bring 10 per cent or more premium over short cotton will allow South Carolina farmers to grow cotton profitably in competition with any other section, provided prices do not remain below the average level of the last crop. To do this, cotton should not be grown on poor or worn out land and not less than 600 pounds of a balanced fertilizer, plus 100 pounds of nitrate of soda or sulphate of ammonia should be used. In addition, mixed or run out seed and all varieties which will not produce inch cotton under average conditions and 1-1/16" cotton under favorable conditions should be discarded and in their place varieties of recent pedigree and proved productiveness should be substituted as quickly as possible.[26]

Similarly, the whole of cotton growing in the South is in the artificial situation of being maintained at or above parity prices. This makes southern cotton non-competitive with that grown in other parts of the world. The situation today remains about the same as when Mr. D. R. stated it in 1935:

My view is that the country cannot afford to allow the South to produce cotton at much less than the present level, and might well insist on both a higher level of prices and educational measures which will lead to a general increase in acre yields. Poverty and ignorance, wherever they occur, are a menace to the economic, social and political welfare of the nation and, by and large, they accompany 5 and 8c cotton. At these levels the cotton laborers of the south must be paid wages comparable with those paid the coolie of India and the fellah of Egypt, and the capital invested in lands and equipment receive scant, if any, return.[27]

He would not deny a stone wall when he faced it, saying that "if the price of cotton cannot be maintained somewhere

---

26. D. R. Coker to Alfred Scarborough, March 16, 1927 (Mrs. D. R. Coker).
27. D. R. Coker to Editor, *Wall Street Journal*, February 27, 1935 (Mrs. D. R. Coker).

around its present figure I should be in favor of the gradual abandonment of the crop and the substitution of other crops upon the sale of which the south could build and maintain a decent civilization." He thought that there was a chance, however, that the South could ". . . continue to grow cotton profitably and in some quantity by specializing in varieties scientifically bred and maintained which will produce greater acre yields and a higher price per pound than the average of the varieties now planted."[28] He bred, therefore, in this direction, hopeful that southern cotton could remain competitive; but if not, the abandonment could, on the basis of better varieties, be more gradual than abrupt, and less shocking to the people involved. These, of course, he never forgot, having written as early as 1915, that "of course our country cannot abandon cotton suddenly and there will probably always be a place for it in our agriculture or as long as we have an abundance of cheap labor that needs employment."[29]

Since Mr. D. R.'s death the Pedigreed Seed Company has worked in the new state of affairs that began to emerge with the coming in of the New Deal, and with the shift from almost complete one-crop emphasis in the eastern South. The effects of this new state of affairs have been somewhat contradictory, so far as the Seed Company is concerned.

The upsurge in agricultural prosperity since the black days of the late twenties and early thirties virtually saved the Seed Company from bankruptcy. Yet, on the other hand, the increasing interest of the government—state and Federal—in the agricultural situation has presented the Seed Company with a new set of problems in the shape of competition from Federal and state seed breeding agencies. The people at the Seed Company do not complain much about this, since it is all to the farmer's good. They do object, however, to those instances wherein the agency involved is at once an interested party at court and the jury. Such a situation as this has occurred rather

28. D. R. Coker to E. W. Montgomery, November 27, 1934 (Mrs. D. R. Coker).
29. D. R. Coker to Bright Williamson, June 2, 1915 (Mrs. D. R. Coker).

frequently: an experiment station will develop a new variety of crop; then the station will conduct variety tests, pitting its own variety against those of other breeders. The results then become official advice to the farmers. All this may be proper enough, but somehow the people at the Seed Company do not feel that it is quite cricket. It is not the easiest thing to pay taxes to support your competitor, who might well have begun his breedings from stock that you have worked on for many years. On the other hand, it is undeniable that the various farm agencies have spread the gospel well of the value of good seed. And the Seed Company itself secures good seed stocks on occasion from government agencies; a notable example is a stock of corn turned over to the Seed Company by the U. S. Department of Agriculture for further hybridization under South Carolina conditions. The Company also benefits greatly from testing equipment and other technical services made available by various government agencies.

On the whole, George Wilds felt, and Robert Coker concurs, that the situation is generally healthy. So far, the Seed Company has more than held its own, its seeds generally surpassing other seeds in objective tests, and sales bear out this conclusion. Robert Coker feels that the Company has one long-run advantage over the government work, that advantage being the continuing, organic interest of himself and others at Hartsville in seed breeding, both as a business and as a service to southern agriculture. Seed breeding takes time, and the continual movement in the government service of men going either up or out tends to break the continuity of interest and work that often is essential to good results.

The relation of the Seed Company to the agriculture of its area has been somewhat changed, of course, by the developments of the past two decades. While in scope its work is larger, and perhaps better also in quality, it is no longer in as unique a position as before. Many of the services that it formerly rendered to farmers are now generally available through official government channels. Many of Mr. D. R.'s older direct, personal ways are no longer possible in an agricultural world somewhat bureaucratized. This, along with the expanded operations, has tended to increase the importance of bulk business, of stepped-up advertising, and of a general meeting of the apparent new demands of the times.

Robert Coker came into the sales end of the Company in the early thirties, and, while he has a close interest in the breeding operations, he is quite sensitive to the fact that the Seed Company must stand or fall under the new conditions of competition. He conceives it to be one of his main functions to maintain the Seed Company on a throughly businesslike basis.

Along this line, Robert has moved in a somewhat different direction from his father with regard to action in public farm policies. While Mr. D. R. was not active in the general farm organizations, Robert had a leading part in the formation of the South Carolina State Farm Bureau, and has since been quite active in its affairs. Like his father, however, he finds himself in something of a dilemma over the present Federal farm program. He is inclined to view the continued support of farm prices by the Federal government with skepticism from an over-all point of view; on the other hand, he is quite certain that if any segment of the economy has as its due help from the Federal government, it is the farm segment.

Both George Wilds and Robert Coker continued to breed grains, expanding this work continuously as an extension of the program begun many years ago and to meet the changing needs of southern agriculture. The excellent Fulgrain oat that was introduced in the middle thirties lacked resistance to crown rust, a disease of increasing prevalence in the South. "Upon request to Washington we were promptly furnished with seed of Victoria, Capa, Pampa, Alber and Bond, all types having high crown rust resistance and some good yield factors."[30] It was found that two strains coming from ". . . a cross of Victoria x Fulgrain were so outstanding in type and yield that the seed were stretched to the limit. . . ."[31] From this resulted the Victorgrain oat, which was introduced in 1940, ". . . only

30. George J. Wilds, "Commercial Oat Breeding."
31. *Ibid.*

four years removed from a single head selection."[32] Problems never end, however, in the breeding of oats. Two new diseases, mosaic and helminthosporium blight, have appeared recently, the latter being particularly hard on all Victoria derivatives. Breeding work is going on now to work out resistance to these diseases.[33] George Wilds' statement of the guiding principle of this work squares pretty well with the history of the Pedigreed Seed Company: "We find that the commercial oat breeder's success depends upon his ability to find and rapidly increase for sale new and superior oats, in the meantime being able to offer at regular intervals improved strains of the already established varieties. Better still if these improved strains are of varieties originated by the seedsman."[34]

The staple cotton breeding is concentrated on the Coker 100 staple. The boll weevil of the twenties, and the increasing staple lengths of the bread and butter cottons, operated to curtail long staple planting in the upper South. The Coker 100 staple cotton is bred primarily for the deep South, and the largest-buying state is Mississippi.

The success in oat and cotton breeding has not been duplicated with regard to wheat and corn. Throughout its history the Seed Company has offered varieties of wheat, but none has been in the class of the Cleveland or Coker 100 cottons, or the Fulgrain and Victorgrain oats. Efforts have continued to develop a fully effective hybrid corn for the eastern South. The introduction of Coker 811 in the early 1950's was a forward step, though not the climax hoped for. Under average conditions, this corn, disease resistant, increases yield about one-fourth over open pollinated types of corn.

A major and striking development was made in the early 1950's in tobacco, when the Coker 139 was introduced. A high yielding tobacco, the 139 has great resistance to the Black Shank disease, that had spread widely throughout the tobacco growing area. Under these conditions, Coker 139 added on the average an extra yield of $100.00 per acre.

32. *Ibid.* 33. *Ibid.*
34. *Ibid.*

IV

In the present generation, it appears that Coker College is the activity around which the most consciously common interest and work is centered. It may well be that the future course of the College will be the best superficial measure of continuing family life. As has been noted, natural extension and the succession of generations has tended to make the family a more loosely organized group of individual units, with a somewhat less degree of cross-interest in each other's activities. In this situation, then, Coker College, as a neutral and mutual responsibility, has remained as the activity able to attract the greatest amount of common interest. Not only do the present Cokers look on the College as something of a trust handed down by the two preceding generations, but a decline in the College would be an obvious and public decline in family life. Coker College has needed the help of all the family, for, as an endowed institution, it has shared the fate of such institutions in a period of rising costs of operations.

Nor does the present generation show any disposition not to maintain the College. A little story that Mrs. D. R. Coker tells is to the point. One of her daughters had occasion to take out an insurance policy, and indicated that she intended to make her mother the beneficiary. Mrs. Coker demurred, and suggested Coker College as beneficiary. Whereupon the daughter declined, saying, "I know you wouldn't kill me to get the money for yourself, but I'm not so sure what you would do for the College." More concretely, full control of the College is now in the process of gradually passing to a self-perpetuating Board of Trustees, the Baptist Associations no longer selecting any members. As throughout the history of the College, a member of the family continues as Chairman of the Board, and all of the other active members of the family are represented on the board. During the course of this study a campaign for funds was conducted. Not only the Coker family, but the whole town of Hartsville was mobilized, A. L. M.

Wiggins being general chairman and virtually all of the top men at Sonoco taking active parts.

V

It is probably true that the beginning and ending question with regard to the present generation at Hartsville concerns the continuation of family life in the present and future. Now, despite surface appearances, this question does not find an answer easily. There are elements of both disunity and cohesion in the present situation at Hartsville. Natural growth in family size, immersion in growing activities, the growth of Hartsville—these and other factors might be expected to lower the degree of family unity gradually; yet common interests remain, and a sense of the family. If achievement is to be equated with continuing family life, then this generation has served family continuity well. It may be that achievement is incidental to family life, and may, in fact, be a hazard.

The truth is that there is no objective measure known for this situation. For instance, how to count the generations? The present is the fourth generation from Caleb, but perhaps it is more realistic to count it as the third from the Major. Yet, so far as the general folk tradition is concerned, the well-educated Major had considerably more behind him than the usual horny-handed founder of a dynasty.

Two things seem apparent. First, that some perspective is required. Two, it may well be that the important factor in the family situation is what the Cokers have thought and done about it. Lacking others, their measures may be the best. The next chaper will attempt to provide some perspective. To close this one there is given below a letter which D. R. Coker wrote to the various members of the family in 1935, three years before his death. This letter is the most formal statement by any member of the family with regard to family unity. It is not perfect for purposes here, for Mr. Coker was of the preceding generation. Yet he wrote it for the present generation primarily, in a going situation, and in an attempt, it seems, to remind the present generation that the family was important. Beyond doubt, he was somewhat disturbed over signs of disunity, though to what degree is not known. The letter is a partial measure, then, of what the Cokers tend to expect of themselves in the family.

The businesses of J. L. Coker and Co., Carolina Fiber Company, Hartsville Oil Mill, Sonoco Products Company, Bank of Hartsville and Pedigreed Seed Company are substantially owned by the same stock holders.

J. L. Coker and Company may be termed the parent corporation of all the others, as it can be truthfully said that without the financial contribution and management of the partners and stockholders of J. L. Coker and Company none of these corporations would have existed. At times every one of these corporations has received major financial assistance from the parent corporation or some of its largest stockholders. Today not one of them stands in need from any source, but it is undoubtedly true that the solidity and strength of all of these corporations are and always have been due to the solidarity and cooperative spirit of the stockholders and employees of these businesses.

Let us remember in the future, as most of us have in the past, that "in union there is strength." Let each of us, of the management, stockholders and employees, remember that if all of us at all times consider the best interests of all of our corporations and will contribute what he reasonably can to the business of all, it will contribute measurably to the interests of our group of stockholders as a whole and will also add to the safety of our general situation and to the satisfaction of management.

We have here a most unique unit, outstanding in many respects. None other that I know of so well weathered the recent financial storm. None other that I know of came through with heightened reputation for faithful performance of its duties to the public.

Times of stress may come again within the lives of most of you as they have continually occurred in the past, and I would have each of you remember that during such periods he who has a cash or realizable surplus is an asset to the general situation, while he who is in debt is a liability. Also, remember that an active friendly interest in the problems of all of our businesses by each of us will encourage management and, to some extent, add to profits and general prosperity.

It will probably occur to most of you that I am saying these things because of my long connection with all of our businesses, because of my intimate knowledge of the principles, policies and life of our founder and because in all human probability none of my generation will be here a few years hence. To say some of these things which, however trite and axiomatic they may sound, should be recalled periodically in order that the sound policies and principles which have guided our businesses in the past may be continually transmitted to those who come after us.[35]

35. Copy in D. R. Coker papers, under Address file, 1935 (Mrs. D. R. Coker).

13

The Family Perspective

I

IN 1897, sixty-seven years after Caleb Coker married Hannah Lide, the family situation stood as follows. At Hartsville, the Major was very nearly broke, and the chances were excellent that the Carolina Fiber Company would be a total loss. James' visionary plan, apparently, had failed; and James himself was sick a good deal from the strain. David, also, was sick enough to quit work, and his puttering around the garden and cotton fields had no particular purpose. Will, having decided that banking was not for him, was beginning graduate work, and there are those perhaps who might have thought that this direction did not hold all of the promise in the world. Young Charles was sick a great deal, and would not, as a matter of fact, finish college. Not long before this time Captain Coker's oldest son, Allen, had decided that he must forego graduate work to run the store at Society Hill because of economic necessity, his younger brothers were in various stages of their education, and the Captain's affairs were not in good order.

This situation of 1897 reflects nothing but the lack of promise of outstanding achievement. There was nothing dishonorable involved; there were no moral problems. The family was going on as before. The situation of 1897 had not been anticipated in, say, 1865, by the Major and his wife in terms of outstanding achievement, nor by Caleb and Hannah in any of the earlier years. The vital factors in this situation were, actually, the existence and strength of the family, and those things that the family had taught the children.

The Coker family has continued to exist as a way of survival, without pretensions or prior design to establishing a dynasty. The teaching of the children has been of this sort. However sympathetic the parents have been toward their children, however much strength the family has tendered specific individuals, the teaching of the children has been utterly realistic. Something more modest, but perhaps harder to attain, than great achievement has been the goal.

On February 24, 1853, Hannah Coker wrote her sixteen year old son James, who was then at school in Columbia, these soul-searching words: "Nothing can give us more heartfelt satisfaction & comfort or cause us deeper grief & woe than the conduct of our children. They are our hopes & expectations. For their good we are willing to make many sacrifices of comfort & pleasure, hoping to be repaid by seeing them grow up to be good, useful & respectable citizens. If, on the contrary, they should become idle immoral profligates, we would rather follow them to their graves or be carried there ourselves than live to endure such sorrow & disgrace."[1] Hannah was not often this overpoweringly solemn in her letters to her children, and in this letter she softened the lecture with trivial news and humor. Nevertheless, she meant what she said, and James and the other children apparently realized it. James may well have had this in mind when he told his friend Cadet Law during the difficulties at The Citadel that "he was ready to do almost anything just for the folks at home."[2]

Now there is no reason to think that Hannah did not possess the normal amount of hope that her sons would distinguish themselves. But before this, she knew that they must "grow up to be good, useful & respectable citizens." She was utterly realistic and powerfully simple: later, in September of 1853, she quoted to James in a letter the Biblical, "My son, if sinness

---

1. Hannah Coker to James Lide Coker, February 24, 1853 (R. E. Coker).
2. Tom Law, *Citadel Cadets, the Journal of Cadet Tom Law* (Clinton, S.C.: Presbyterian College Press, 1941), p. 52.

entice thee, consent thou not."³ In Hannah this was a massive force, this drive toward doing right and being useful. She would lay down her life, perhaps, for this in her children, but not for mere outstanding achievement.

The vitality of this teaching across the generations appears time and again. Very close to it is the closing paragraph of the Major's letter to his son James, quoted earlier: "Altogether we have much to be thankful for and my earnest wish is that you may all live happy and useful lives." Now the Major would not likely recur to Biblical admonition, but he meant something of the same thing as had Hannah when he sent his son David off to college with, " 'Son, always remember that you are a gentleman.' "⁴ Nor is there any reason to assume that the Major was thinking only of manners and the surface niceties. Since Will was away from home, the Major wrote a good deal to him, and many of the letters contain thankfulness that all is well, meaning the absence of difficulties and troubles. The Major dwelt upon prosaic problems, as proud as he was of, say, David's progress in breeding, and he always applied the old stipulations to the outstanding achievements. In 1908, for instance, Will received an attractive offer from the University of Texas. There was some raise in pay, but more important was the offer of much larger facilities for research and teaching. Will was not inclined to accept, and did not. The Major, though he was loath for Will to go so far from home, thought otherwise. "I am gratified that your worth and attainments are so widely known. To use them in this wider field seems to me to be your duty."⁵

Well toward the end of his life, the Major spoke at Father's Day exercises in the Baptist Church in Hartsville.

He addressed his remarks to the normal family, told of high, honorable and responsible position of the father, of his duties and opportunities, the training of children, the duty of helping mother with household affairs. He emphasized the importance of the

---

3. Hannah Coker to James Lide Coker, September 9, 1853 (R. E. Coker).
4. D. R. Coker, "Major James Lide Coker: A Son's Tribute," typewritten copy of talk made by D. R. Coker at Coker College, January 5, 1937 (Mrs. D. R. Coker).
5. Major Coker to W. C. Coker, October 13, 1908 (W. C. Coker).

control of children by love and affection on the part of the father and leaving the sterner punishments, application of the rod, etc., to the mother.[6]

In October of 1906 Captain Coker was suffering markedly from the after effects of a stroke, and his handwriting was almost illegible. But this, in part, is what he wrote his son Robert, who was then working in Peru: "After all it does not matter so much in what part of the world we are as does the way in which we come up to the measure of true manhood in dealing with what comes to us."[7] Later, in December of the same year, he wrote Robert, "but give good consideration for all that they pay you and see that they get full consideration for all they pay you."[8]

These themes moved across to the next generation. In 1919, the Major's daughter Jenny Coker, who had married Duncan Gay, died, leaving her husband and one child, a girl. David wrote his brother-in-law his conception of the main elements of the equipment that ought to be given a child:

... Such equipment, besides the purely cultural will include,

A courteous and democratic consideration of the views and rights of others and especially of older people,

A sense of responsibility to environment and the world at large (i.e. well developed ideas of the duties of citizenship),

A due appreciation of the value of money, the proper uses of money, and the responsibility which goes with wealth,

A respect for character and useful attainments as the things which overweigh all others,

A broad and unselfish view of life and its contacts.[9]

To his children, in his will, D. R. Coker conveyed the main hope that they would all live a "useful and constructive life." He advised them pointedly not to put their reliance in the possession of wealth.

Of the Cokers, C. W. Coker contributed the most lengthy

6. The *Hartsville Messenger*, June 10, 1915.
7. Captain Coker to R. E. Coker, October 26, 1906 (R. E. Coker).
8. Captain Coker to R. E. Coker, December 29, 1906 (R. E. Coker).
9. D. R. Coker to Duncan Gay (Mrs. D. R. Coker).

statement of child rearing and parent-child relationships. He felt that only as the child ". . . contributes to the success of his social order and in proportion to that success is the parent achieving his responsibilities of inculcating into the child all of those things that will permit the opportunity of being a happy and useful member of the great world community." C. W. Coker was also quite sensitive to the emerging problems of raising children in the modern world: "Not only is the child's physical and mental development an evolutionary process in the child itself, but the adjustment to a constantly changing social order increases the problem for the child, parent, and teacher."

. . . parents must realize these fundamental principles: First, the child must be taught respect for authority; first the authority of his parents, then the authority of his teachers. If this principle is taught early in the child's life, his respect for law will have already been achieved long before he gets away from the influences of his parents and teachers. Next, he should be taught respect for truth, and I am not speaking so much of truth as opposed to deception, but the recognition of truth in the physical world, and having a mind open and receptive to scientific facts . . . .

I think the all important business of being a parent is the business of being a parent; the proper training of the child; the close contacts; the establishment of confidences; the giving unstintedly of their love, directed and restrained only by an appreciation of the child's welfare; the establishment of a home in which the child may live securely and be happy in his contacts, where bitterness and ugliness, unkindness and inconsideration, and ingratitude are suppressed to the point of non-existence.

The principal thought that I want to leave with you today is that you appreciate that childhood is merely a period of life in which an individual is trained to fit himself into society, and to subject his personality to the social order in which he is to live.[10]

It is the word "useful" that most nearly and accurately characterizes the consistent theme running through the relations of parents and children of the Coker family. It occurs

---

10. Untitled manuscript in C. W. Coker papers (Sonoco Products Company). Apparently this was a talk delivered before a parent-teachers group.

time and again as that quality around which other good qualities will be grouped. It implies a high sense of responsibility for membership in the human race, and particularly in the local community.

Yet it is also true that the Cokers have not hesitated to define for themselves what is useful. Anxious as they have been to meet the requirements of responsible social participation, they have never doubted seriously their own minds, once the facts were in. Thus the Major, among other things, felt that "good influences gain strength as they move into the currents of society."[11] But he had a way of deciding in his own mind what were good influences, and he cautioned a friend not to despair of criticism for "there will always be persons to take up wrong impressions without reason or investigation. To keep them right would require all of a good man's time for an indefinite period."[12]

The Cokers have been rather hard on themselves with regard to local day by day events. Speaking most figuratively, no member of the family would ever have been turned out for failure to make an outstanding achievement; one might, however, have been turned out for failure to work when physically able, and for failure to feel that that which lay about him to do was eminently worth doing. It will, as a matter of fact, have to be accounted as one of the most significant facts about the members of the present generation that, having been raised as the third (or fourth) generation of a distinguished line and in relative wealth, each works hard and regularly at Hartsville.

The members of the present Hartsville generation show a considerable interest in the teaching of their children, and there is no evident tendency to run away from this most important responsibility. Schooling is looked into carefully and there is hope that this schooling will be more than a mere passage through a required number of years. In any family gathering the children are always the subject of a large part

---

11. Fragment of speech or letter (Watson collection).
12. Major Coker to Rev. C. C. Brown, October 12, 1912 (Watson collection).

of the conversation, and there is considerable intimacy among cousins of appropriate ages.

II

The realism of the Cokers in their preoccupation with making satisfactory and successful individuals before thinking of special achievements cannot be emphasized too much. Yet a family, as a growing thing, is formed of many interrelated and often opposite seeming parts. Thus, it certainly would be going against the facts to assume that being a Coker has not been important both to the rearing of the children and to the nature of the family. The Cokers are aware of who and what they are, and have been for some time.

As a matter of fact they have had no choice. When Caleb and Hannah moved to Society Hill, their family was the important unit in an intimate village-community where there was no anonymity whatsoever. The young couple and their growing family were nothing special in the eyes of the community, perhaps, but they were a well-identified family.

The same was true at Hartsville, and as the town grew up around the Major and his children, and as wealth and achievement tended more and more to set them apart, self-realization "as Cokers" increased. The Cokers have not dealt much in coats of arms and, in fact, have not had much curiosity about their genealogy. Yet, particularly at Hartsville, where they have been responsible for the conduct of so many affairs and where they have exercised such leadership largely as a family, they have been aware of themselves.

This awareness has not been grandiose. It does not appear in the Major's papers, for instance, but Lee Wiggins remembers one example. Wiggins, at the time the Pedigreed Seed Company was incorporated, drew up a trademark for the new company. The name Coker was prominently displayed in connection with a large red heart, and the motto "Blood Will Tell" was part of the whole. Wiggins took it to show the Major, who remarked that it seemed very well, and then added,

"Young man, you've got the Coker name on that. Don't ever sell anything but the best under that name."[13] In 1936, D. R. Coker wrote the official of a large bank, thanking him for ". . . the confidence and courtesies that your institution has constantly extended to all of the Hartsville corporations in which I am interested." He then went on to say that

> I have felt at times, and I hope I am right, that in consideration of our requests you were taking into account that for more than one hundred years the Coker name has been present on the mercantile and financial directories (if any existed one hundred years ago) and that during that entire time every obligation whether legal or moral has been met promptly and cheerfully by the institutions which Caleb Coker, his son J. L. Coker and the latter's sons and grandsons have been responsible for.[14]

In an earlier letter, D. R. Coker had written to the son of George Norwood, the Major's old Charleston partner: "Of course I am very small financially as compared with you and your statement to the Reserve Bank shows your ability to take care of the situation. It will do no harm to remind you, however, that I have inherited the financial friendships and relations of my father and will respond to your call on a moment's notice to the extent of my ability."[15]

At the present time, of course, the sense of the existence and presence of the family in Hartsville can almost be cut with a knife. The present Cokers are more aware of the family as something special than have been preceding generations. Expectations of family unity and of performance according to family standard tend to keep the several units of the family together and to exact expected performance from the individual members. Particularly are the Cokers drawn together in Hartsville, as being somewhat apart from the remainder of the community. Many business and other matters are yet settled in living rooms, around dining room tables, and in other informal situations. Certainly, also, family con-

13. Conversation with A. L. M. Wiggins.
14. D. R. Coker to T. E. Hemby, January 27, 1936 (Mrs. D. R. Coker).
15. D. R. Coker to J. W. Norwood, December 13, 1920 (Mrs. D. R. Coker).

siderations sometimes override purely impersonal considerations in business and other affairs.

However much of the older organic unity and feeling of the family remains in Hartsville, it is clear that there is also present the new and somewhat artificial element of being "The Cokers," of being something special and set apart. The present generation grew up as the family at Hartsville was assuming this quality; it has been a part of their lives, and it is a main element with which they must contend. It is likely that some naturalness has been removed, and also that there may well be some burden in having great jobs and responsibilities laid out. Charles Coker, Jr., feels that the people of Hartsville are probably tired of hearing about the Cokers. It may be, also, that the Cokers on occasion get tired of hearing about the Cokers.

More fundamental than personal feelings, of course, is a possible loss of naturalness in individual development. A main strength of the family has been the joining together of opposite tendencies in the individuals. James was an engineer who began industry at Hartsville. He had the Major's business and organizational help, and later it was Charles, the business executive, who consolidated the Cokers' position in industrial activity. Will was the botanical scientist who brought home the scientific information on seed breeding; David was the agriculturist, business man and man of public affairs who could take over and develop the scientific fact into public consciousness. There is something of the same relation in the present generation. James and Charles, confronted early with a large enterprise to run, have become business executives; Richard has tended to the engineering side. George Wilds, almost a family member, became the seed breeder and Robert Coker the salesman and promoter. Edgar Lawton has been a constructive, conservative voice in all affairs.

With regard to the individuals, these more or less opposite interests developed almost altogether from individual inclination in the preceding generation; somewhat less so in the present generation. The growth of enterprises at Hartsville may well impose responsibilities on the coming generations that will stifle the development of individual inclinations and capabilities, largely by requiring a disproportionate number to become business executives. Coker achievements have resulted largely from the fact that the Cokers have been able to do things themselves. It is likely that each generation should be generously leavened with those individuals who do not set policy and order things done.

The Cokers have not had much facility for foundering themselves on public questions. They have been people of principle, outstandingly so with regard to personal affairs; they have not hesitated to go down politically rather than take expediency by the hand. The Major was not, as he put it, a "Bryan or Tillman Democrat," yet he did not make a career of being "against" during the years when there was little choice. Rather, he went about his business, all the while taking an intelligent interest in public affairs, but never attempting the impossible. Dr. W. C. Coker remembered that once, when he and David were young men, they sat on the piazza of the Major's house, deploring the state of Darlington County administration. The Major agreed that things might be improved, but he advised the boys with some asperity not to be so free with their criticism until they were a little older and had tried their own hands. This was a quality of Caleb's, and it appeared in the Major's sons. To the point are D. R. Coker's relations with the New Deal. The Cokers have been notable for their lack of excess in all things, unless one might think that they have been excessively bold in planning on occasion.

The present being a world of transition, and the modern South being pre-eminently involved in change, this generation of Cokers finds itself confronted with a number of rather fundamental matters. They have been raised in relative wealth. In the case of the Cokers a general characterization is not worth much, but if one is made it labels them as generally conservative. The questions of changing labor relations and of the Federal farm program have already been dealt with.

Beyond these, the members of the present generation are seriously and genuinely concerned about the tendency toward centralization of power in Washington and the spread of governmental functions. The Cokers are registered Democrats. James Coker in 1944 was an elector on the Southern Democratic ticket in the presidential election of that year. In 1948, however, there was little if any public display by any of the Cokers of sentiment for Governor Thurmond and the States' Rights ticket. The Cokers were fairly close to Governor Byrnes, and generally endorsed his policies.

This general statement of their position applies only to general issues, such as states' rights as opposed to centralization, gradual civil rights as opposed to sudden civil rights for the Negro. On specific matters, this present generation has some of the older tendency to decide primarily on the merits of the case. A fairly vivid example of this has appeared with regard to Federal aid to education. The Cokers generally were in favor of this aid, and several took active steps in its behalf. J. H. Martin, general production manager at Sonoco, appeared before a committee of the House of Representatives, and was commended for his very able presentation of the case for Federal aid. At almost the same time, C. H. Campbell, vice president in charge of sales at Sonoco, made a speech denouncing all Federal expenditures of this nature, including those for the farm program. The Cokers have no objection to this type of disagreement. With regard to the insistent question of race relations, the Cokers are probably somewhere in the middle. They are for gradual change. During the course of the study James Coker, almost singlehanded, levied tribute on himself, various other members of the family and certain townspeople in order to build a Negro recreation building and park on the banks of Sonoco's Prestwood Lake. The Cokers are unlikely, however, to forsake their southern heritage suddenly.

III

Society Hill has changed little in size, and not a great deal in appearance, since Hannah and Caleb Coker began to establish themselves there in 1830. And, though the weight of family numbers and activities has shifted elsewhere, Camp Marion remains intact and in the hands of descendants. Caleb's store stands to this day. It, also, has never been out of the family hands.

The persistence of this store in the family has, in the twentieth century, been largely the work of two grandsons of Caleb and Hannah Coker—Allen Coker and Arthur H. Rogers. It will be recalled that Allen Coker entered the store with his father, Captain Coker, at a time when the store affairs were at low ebb, and when his younger brothers and sisters had yet to be educated. In due course the condition of the store was improved. Allen Coker remained at Society Hill, taking up rather large farming operations as well as continuing his work at the store. The only one of Captain Coker's sons who remained in Darlington County, he played a prominent part in business and public affairs. He became president of the Bank of Darlington, a post previously held by both Major and Captain Coker.

In recent years Arthur H. Rogers (son of Paul H. Rogers and Emma Coker Rogers) has figured in the management of the store, and the firm is now known as Coker and Rogers. After attending Furman University, Arthur Rogers went to work for the Major in Hartsville in 1898. In 1910 he returned to Society Hill to give his full time to farming operations. A quiet, industrious man, he has been both County Commissioner and a member of the County Board of Education.

IV

The family that has descended from Caleb and Hannah Coker has been traced in the great ongoing of American society, from Revolutionary America to the middle of the twentieth century.

For all of the family's achievements, the thing that stands out in the tracery is the continuity of identity—an identity that has maintained itself through change. Yet change is never enough to preserve identity; there is always an ultimate affirmation, an ultimate stopping place beyond which physical movement, hard circumstance, or even rationality may well cause an irreparable break.

Such an affirmation of life as it is found has not, by American society, been made the main prerogative of the family. Rather, it has been the prerogative of the individual, following his own dream and finding his own level, or of the corporate organization, strangely and impersonally persisting. This is characteristic of a shifting, changeful, dynamic, yet highly organized society.

The South, achieving most decisively of all the regions the set patterns and maturity of rural, agricultural societies, provided a congenial context for family continuity. This southern context became, in the setting of the total of American society, artificial and marginal in many ways. At home, then, the Cokers have had to overcome factors of poverty, inversion, and self-pity. Yet a family affirms not only itself, but the place and time in which it lives and has its being—friends, community, and cultural values. Here, then, the family has not been swept away in the ceaseless change of the larger society.

In the South, where once poverty and lack of opportunity were the major obstacles to family continuity and identity in place, increases of industry and urban living have now superseded. So now the region presents itself with somewhat the same situation as earlier prevailed in other parts of the nation. In this sense, therefore, affirmation of family life and continuity may well be more difficult in the future than in the past. So, even as the family has set an example, it finds a new challenge. And still again the paradox. For the sort of affirmation of life that a family makes becomes every day more relevant to an American society seeking maturity and stability.

Bibliography

FOR THE MOST PART this study is based upon original materials or fugitive published pamphlets dealing with the Cokers and their local area in Darlington County, South Carolina. These materials, particularly the original materials, are in no sense collected, and are, in fact, scattered over a wide area.

There are probably several thousand individual pieces of these materials. They have not been inventoried and it was not within the scope of this study to make an inventory, even had the circumstances of their use permitted it. In view of this, it seems advisable to note briefly the main points at which these materials are to be found.

1. The Watson collection: The name Watson collection has been given by the author to a large group of papers, letters, and published materials in the possession at the time of this work of Mrs. R. F. Watson, Greenville, South Carolina. Mrs. Watson is Major Coker's daughter, and these papers came to her on his death. The bulk of them were found in twenty-five letter files. These materials are of several sorts. There is a good deal of the Major's business correspondence for the years between 1900 and his death. There are also a number of personal letters to family members.

2. The D. R. Coker papers are in the possession of Mrs. D. R. Coker. These are Mr. Coker's day-by-day files, from 1919 until his death in 1938. These papers are of considerable bulk, running to about six filing cabinets. They, like the

papers in the Watson collection, have not been edited in any way. Here are Mr. Coker's business letters, most if not all of his speeches and articles, and the published pamphlets. The files are not altogether complete for the years 1919-38, several years being missing. Included in these papers are some earlier letters and papers on Mr. Coker's work during World War I.

3. Dr. R. E. Coker of Chapel Hill has collected a good many historical materials relating to the Coker family. He has, in the original, a large number of letters from and to Caleb and Hannah Coker, and but for him these undoubtedly would have been lost. He has, in addition, letters and other materials on his father, Captain W. C. Coker.

4. A number of Coker materials are to be found in the South Caroliniana Library of the University of South Carolina. Dr. R. E. Coker has turned over to this library the store books of the store at Society Hill. These are various ledger, cash, and receipt books. The first is dated 1832 and the last 1895. There are, however, a good many missing years. Also in this library are Caleb Coker's farm journal for 1856-61, Captain W. C. Coker's farm journal 1868-69, a short diary kept by Caleb Coker on a northern trip, and a photostat of Major Coker's letter to his mother at the time of Charles' death in 1862.

5. Mrs. J. L. Coker, Jr., of Hartsville (who died in 1953), had a number of miscellaneous papers of Major Coker's including both business correspondence and historical materials.

6. R. G. Coker of Hartsville has a letter book, loose letters and other materials pertaining to the early days of the Carolina Fiber Company.

7. The legal affairs of the Cokers, including deeds and wills, are recorded in the office of Clerk of Court, Register of Deeds, and Judge of Probate in Darlington, S.C.

8. Dr. W. C. Coker (who died on June 27, 1955) had among his papers in his home at Chapel Hill, N.C., a number of letters relative to Major Coker, as well as the Major's farm journal.

9. The relatively few materials pertaining to C. W. Coker are at the Sonoco Products Company, Hartsville, S.C.

BIBLIOGRAPHY

Ames, J. S. *The Williams Family of Society Hill.* Columbia: The State Co., Printers, 1910, for the Pee Dee Historical Society.

Atherton, Lewis E. "The Problem of Credit Rating in the Ante-Bellum South," *The Journal of Southern History,* XII, No. 4 (November, 1946), 534-56.

Babcock, Ernest Brown and Roy Elwood Clausen. *Genetics in Relation to Agriculture.* New York: McGraw-Hill Book Company, Inc., 1918.

Bacot, D. Huger. "The South Carolina Up Country at the End of of the Eighteenth Century," *American Historical Review,* XXVIII (July, 1923), 682-98.

Baker, O. E. "A Graphic Summary of Farm Machinery, Facilities, Roads and Expenditures," U. S. Department of Agriculture, Miscellaneous Publication 264, Washington: 1937.

Ball, W. W. *The State That Forgot.* Indianapolis: The Bobbs-Merrill Company, 1932.

Ballagh, James Curtis. *The South in the Building of the Nation.* Vol. III. Richmond: The Southern Historical Publication Society, 1909.

Bonner, J. C. "Genesis of Agricultural Reform in the Cotton Belt," *The Journal of Southern History,* IX, No. 4 (November, 1943), 475-500.

Bossard, J. H. S. and Eleanor S. Boll. "Ritual in Family Living," *American Sociological Review,* XIV (August, 1949), 463-68.

Boucher, C. S. *The Nullification Controversy in South Carolina.* Chicago: The University of Chicago Press, 1916.

Brewster, L. F. *Summer Migrations and Resorts of South Carolina Low Country Planters.* In Historical Papers of the Trinity College Historical Society, Series XXVI. Durham: Duke University Press, 1947.

Brunson, W. A. *Memories of Old Darlington.* Hartsville: Hartsville Publishing Company, 1909, for the Pee Dee Historical Society.

———. *Reminiscences of Reconstruction in Darlington.* Hartsville: Hartsville Publishing Company, 1910, for the Pee Dee Historical Society.

Buck, Paul H. "The Poor Whites of the Ante-Bellum South," *American Historical Review,* XXXI (October, 1925), 41-53.

Bullock, W. B. *The Romance of Paper.* Boston: R. G. Badger, 1933.

Burgess, Ernest Watson and Harvey J. Locke. *The Family from Institution to Companionship*. New York: American Book Co., 1945.

Calhoun, Arthur Wallace. *A Social History of the American Family*. (Rev. ed.). New York: Barnes and Noble, Inc., 1945.

Carson, William J. (ed.). "The Coming of Industry to the South," *Annals of the American Academy of Political and Social Science*, Vol. 153 (January, 1931).

Cavan, Ruth (Shonle). *The Family*. New York: T. Y. Crowell, 1945.

Charge Book of the Society Hill Library Society, in the library at Society Hill.

Church Book of the Gum Branch Baptist Church, Darlington County, S.C.

Church Book of the New Providence Baptist Church, Darlington County, S.C.

Clapperton, Robert H. and William Henderson. *Modern Paper Making*. Oxford: Basil Blackwell, 1941.

Clark, Thomas D. *Pills, Petticoats and Plows*. New York: The Bobbs-Merrill Company, 1944.

———. "The Furnishing and Supply System in Southern Agriculture since 1865," *The Journal of Southern History*, XII (February, 1946), 24-44.

Coggeshall, Mrs. Emma Edwards. "A Sketch of Hannah L. Coker." Manuscript in possession of Annie L. Edwards, Darlington, S.C.

Coker, Caleb. Plantation Journal. This is an irregularly kept journal for parts of several years preceding the Civil War.

Coker College. *Quarterly Bulletin*. Series XIV, No. 2 (February, 1937).

Coker, D. R. "The New Upland Staple Varieties—Shall We Plant Them?" Pamphlet dated January 1, 1912, in possession of Dr. W. C. Coker.

Coker, E. C. "Sketch of the Early History of Society Hill and Brief Notes on Some of Its Noteworthy Natives." In Records and Papers of the Darlington County Historical Society.

Coker, F. W. "American Traditions Concerning Liberty and Property," *American Political Science Review*, Vol. XXX, No. 1 (February, 1936), 1-23.

———. (ed.). *Democracy, Liberty and Property*. New York: The Macmillan Company, 1942.

———. "Income Stabilization and the American Political Tradition," in Max Millikan (ed.), *Income Stabilization in a Developing Democracy*. New Haven: Yale University Press, 1953, 77-110.

———. "Property Rights as Obstacles to Progress," *Annals of the American Academy of Political and Social Science*, Vol. 185 (May, 1935), 133-44.

———. *Recent Political Thought*. New York: D. Appleton-Century Company, 1934.

Coker, Hannah Lide. *A Story of the Late War*. Published privately.

Coker, James Lide. Farm Journal. In possession of Dr. W. C. Coker, Chapel Hill, N.C.

———. *Hartsville, Its Early Settlers*. Hartsville: published by the Pee Dee Historical Society, 1911.

———. *History of Co. E. 6th S.C.V. Inf. Co. G. 9th S.C.V. Inf. C. S. A.* Charleston: Press of Walker, Evans & Cogswell Co., 1899.

———. "History of the Railroads in the Pee-Dee Section," typed manuscript in the Watson collection, written in 1910.

———. Plantation Journal. In possession of Dr. W. C. Coker, Chapel Hill, N.C.

———. "Schools," typewritten manuscript in the Watson collection.

———. "Short Sketch of the Coker Family of Darlington District, South Carolina," typewritten manuscript in Watson collection.

Coker, James Lide, Jr. and H. C. Ferris. "The Sulphite Process of Manufacture of Cellulose for Paper Making," senior thesis submitted in 1888 at Stevens Institute of Technology, Hoboken, New Jersey. In library of Stevens Institute.

Coker, Lois. "History of Hartsville," typewritten manuscript in Hartsville library.

Coker, Robert Ervin. "Coker Forebears," typewritten manuscript.

———. "The Department of Zoology, University of North Carolina," *Bios*, XVIII, No. 4 (December, 1949), 220-21.

———. "Establishment of the Institute of Fisheries Research," mimeographed manuscript in the University of North Carolina Library.

———. *Experiments in Oyster Culture in Pamlico Sound, North Carolina.* North Carolina Geological and Economic Survey, Bulletin No. 15 (Raleigh: E. M. Uzzel and Co., 1907), 70.

———. "Functions of an Ecological Society," *Science,* Vol. 87, No. 2258 (April 8, 1938), 309-15.

———. *Oyster Culture in North Carolina.* The North Carolina Geological Survey, Economic Paper No. 10 (Raleigh: E. M. Uzzel and Co., 1905).

———. "Regarding the Future of the Guano Industry and the Guano Producing Birds of Peru," *Science,* XXVIII (July 10, 1908), 58-64.

———. "Some Philosophical Reflections of a Biologist," *The Scientific Monthly,* Vol. 48 (January and February, 1939), 61-68.

———. "Springville: A Summer Village of the Old Darlington District," *South Carolina Historical Magazine,* LIII (October, 1952).

———. *This Great and Wide Sea.* Chapel Hill: The University of North Carolina Press, 1947.

———. "William Caleb Coker," typewritten manuscript.

Coker, William Caleb. "Partial History of Companies F and M, 8th Regiment of South Carolina Volunteers," typewritten manuscript in possession of Dr. R. E. Coker, Chapel Hill, N.C.

———. "Remunerative Farming," *The Southern Cultivator,* XXIX, No. 5 (May, 1871), 174-76.

Coker Family Bible. This was the Bible of Caleb Coker, Sr., and his family; the flyleaf contains birthdates of the children of Caleb and Nancy Coker.

Coker's Pedigreed Seed Company Catalogues, 1914-51.

Cook, H. T. "The Coker Family," a manuscript in possession of R. G. Coker, Hartsville, S.C.

———. *The Life Work of James Clement Furman.* Greenville: 1926, copyright by Alester G. Furman.

———. *The Life and Legacy of David Rogerson Williams.* New York: The Garden City Press, 1916.

———. *Rambles in the Peedee Basin of South Carolina.* Published privately.

Copenhaver, J. E. "The History of Chemistry in South Carolina," *Journal of Chemical Education,* XXIX (November, 1942), 505-7.

Cornell, J. F. *The Pulp and Paper Industry.* Boston: Bellman Publishing Company, Inc., 1941.

Couch, John N. and Velma D. Matthews. "William Chambers Coker," *Mycologia,* XLVI, No. 3 (May-June, 1954), 374.

Cross, C. F. and E. J. Bevan. *A Text-Book of Paper Making.* London: E. F. N. Spon Ltd., 1936.

Damrin, Dora E. "Family Size and Sibling Age, Sex and Position as Related to Certain Aspects of Adjustment," *Journal of Social Psychology,* XXIX (February, 1949), 93-102.

Dargan, Edwin Charles. *Harmony Hall, Recollections of an Old Southern Home, 1852-1882.* Columbia: The State Company, for the Pee Dee Historical Society.

Darlington Press, April 25, 1907, in possession of F. W. Coker, New Haven, Conn.

Dowd, Clement. *Life of Zebulon Baird Vance.* Charlotte, N.C.: Observer Printing and Publishing House, 1897.

DuBose, John Witherspoon. *The Witherspoons of Society Hill.* Hartsville: The Hartsville Publishing Company, 1910, for the Pee Dee Historical Society.

Edwards, E. F. "Historical Background of the Present Situation in Southern Agriculture," *Southern Economic Association Proceedings,* III (1930), 78-93.

Folsom, Joseph Kirk. *The Family and Democratic Society.* New York: Wiley and Sons, 1943.

Freeman, Douglas Southall. *Lee's Lieutenants.* 3 vols. New York: Charles Scribner's Sons, 1942.

———. *R. E. Lee.* 4 vols. New York: Charles Scribner's Sons, 1934.

Gee, Wilson and Edward Allison Terry. *The Cotton Cooperatives in the Southeast.* New York: D. Appleton-Century Company, 1933.

Genealogical Chart of descendants of Abel Kolb, constructed by T. E. Wilson, C.E., Darlington, S.C.

Gregg, Alexander. *History of the Old Cheraws.* New York: Richardson and Company, 1868.

Green, Fletcher M. *The Lides Go South . . . And West: The Record of a Planter Migration in 1835.* Columbia: The University of South Carolina Press, 1952.

Groves, Ernest R. *The Family and Its Social Functions.* Chicago: Lippincott, 1940.

Guthrie, J. A. *The Newsprint Paper Industry.* Cambridge: Harvard University Press, 1941.

Hartsville Messenger. Files 1907-1951.

Hill, Reuben. *Families Under Stress.* New York: Harpers, 1949.

―――― and Howard Becker (eds.). *Family, Marriage and Parenthood.* Boston: Heath and Co., 1948.

Holley, W. C. and L. E. Arnold. "Changes in Technology and Labor Requirements in Crop Production." W. P. A., National Research Project. Report A-7.

Hunter, David. *Papermaking: The History and Technique of an Ancient Craft.* New York: Alfred A. Knopf, 1943.

Johnson, Thomas Carey. *Scientific Interests in the Old South.* New York: 1936.

Journals of the South Carolina Senate, in South Caroliniana Library, Columbia, S.C.

Kendrick, B. B. "The Colonial Status of the South," *Journal of Southern History,* VIII (1942), 3-22.

Key, V. O., Jr. (with the assistance of Alexander Heard). *Southern Politics.* New York: Alfred A. Knopf, 1949.

Koos, Earl L. "Class Differences in Family Reactions to Crisis," *Marriage and Family Living,* XII (Summer, 1950), 77-78.

――――. *Families in Trouble.* New York: King's Crown, 1946.

Law, Tom. *Citadel Cadets, the Journal of Cadet Tom Law.* Clinton, S.C.: Presbyterian College Press, 1941.

Lewis, Oscar. "An Anthropological Approach to Family Studies," *American Journal of Sociology,* LV (March, 1950), 468-75.

Lord, Russell. *The Wallaces of Iowa.* Boston: Houghton Mifflin, 1947.

Lynch, William O. "The Westward Flow of Southern Colonists Before 1861," *The Journal of Southern History,* IX (August, 1943), 303-27.

McCormick, T. C. "Major Trends in Rural Life in the United States," *American Journal of Sociology,* XXVI (March, 1931), 721-34.

McGrane, R. C. *The Economic Development of the American Nation.* Boston: Ginn and Co., 1942.

Malone, Dumas. *Edwin A. Alderman.* New York: Doubleday, Doran and Company, 1940.

Mead, Margaret. "What Is Happening to the American Family?" *Journal of Social Casework,* XXVIII (November, 1947), 323-30.

Meriwether, R. L. *The Expansion of South Carolina, 1729-1765.* Kingsport, Tennessee: Southern Publishers, Inc., 1940.

BIBLIOGRAPHY 317

Mills, Robert. *Atlas. A New Facsimile of the Original Published in 1825.* Columbia: Lucy Hampton Bostick and Fant H. Thornley, 1938.

——. *Statistics of South Carolina.* Charleston: Hurlbut and Lloyd, 1826.

Mims, Edwin. "The South Realizing Itself. Hartsville and Its Lesson," *World's Work,* Vol. 22, No. 5 (October, 1911), 14972-87.

Minute Book of the Darlington County Agricultural Society, in possession of J. M. Napier, Darlington, S.C.

Minute Book of Stockholders' and Directors' Meetings of the Carolina Fiber Company, in possession of R. G. Coker, Hartsville, S.C.

Minutes of the St. David's Society, in possession of Mrs. A. M. Coker, Society Hill, S.C.

Mitchell, Broadus. *William Gregg.* Chapel Hill: The University of North Carolina Press, 1928.

Mouzon, O. T. "The Social and Economic Implications of Recent Developments Within the Wood Pulp and Paper Industry in the South." Unpublished Ph.D. dissertation, University of North Carolina, Chapel Hill, 1940.

Murdock, Harold R. "A Record of Progress," *Southern Pulp and Paper Journal* (June, 1940), pp. 8-9.

Napier, J. M. "Historical Sketch of the Darlington County Agricultural Society," privately published pamphlet, 1946.

——. "Society Hill and Some of Its Contributions to State and Nation."

Nimkoff, Meyer F. *Marriage and the Family.* Boston: Houghton Mifflin, 1947.

Nixon, Raymond B. *Henry W. Grady.* New York: Alfred A. Knopf, 1943.

Norment, R. M., Jr. "The Darlington Riot." In Records and Paper of the Darlington County Historical Society.

Norwood, J. W. Appendix I: "Major James Lide Coker" in *Rambles in the Pee Dee Basin of South Carolina,* by H. T. Cook, pp. 413-41.

Odum, Howard W. *Southern Regions of the United States.* Chapel Hill: The University of North Carolina Press, 1936.

Otken, Charles H. *The Ills of the South.* New York: G. P. Putnam's Sons, 1894.

Pearce, Haywood J. *Benjamin H. Hill, Secession and Reconstruction.* Chicago: The University of Chicago Press, 1928.

Petty, Julian J. *The Growth and Distribution of Population in South Carolina.* (Bulletin No. 11 of the South Carolina State Planning Board) Columbia, South Carolina: State Council for Defense, July, 1943.

Pike, James. *The Prostrate State.* New York: Loring and Mussey, 1935.

Proceedings of the Darlington County Historical Society, in Darlington County Library, Darlington, S.C.

Receipt book of Coker and Gregg store, in possession of R. G. Coker, Hartsville, S.C.

Report of the Historical Society of Delaware, XLII, *The Welsh Tract Baptist Meeting, Records of Pencader Hundred. New Castle County, Delaware, 1701-1828.* Pts. I and II. Wilmington: 1904.

Rogers, James Harvey. *America Weighs Her Gold.* New Haven: Yale University Press, 1931.

———. *Capitalism in Crisis.* New Haven: Yale University Press, 1938.

Roper, Daniel C. *Fifty Years of Public Life.* Durham: Duke University Press, 1941.

Schaper, W. A. "Sectionalism and Representation in South Carolina," in *American Historical Association Annual Report for the Year 1900,* I (Washington, 1901), 237-463.

Shiver, H. E., B. F. Buie, and Inman F. Eldredge. *South Carolina Raw Materials.* Columbia: The University of South Carolina Press, 1949.

Simkins, Francis B. *A History of the South.* New York: Alfred A. Knopf, 1953.

———. *Pitchfork Ben Tillman.* Baton Rouge: Louisiana State University Press, 1944.

———. *The Tillman Movement in South Carolina.* Durham: Duke University Press, 1926.

——— and Robert Hilliard Woody. *South Carolina During Reconstruction.* Chapel Hill: The University of North Carolina Press, 1932.

Skoogs, William H. *The Southern Oligarchy.* New York: The Devin-Adair Company, 1924.

Smith, W. Roy. *South Carolina as a Royal Province, 1719-1776.* New York: The Macmillan Company, 1903.

Smythe, Augustine T. *The Carolina Low Country.* New York: The Macmillan Company, 1931.

Snowden, Yates. *History of South Carolina.* 5 vols. Chicago and New York: 1920.

Society Hill Library Society. *A Catalogue of Books Belonging to the Society Hill Library Society.* Philadelphia: C. Sherman, Printer, 1850.

South Carolina Agricultural Experiment Station. "Varieties of Cotton," *South Carolina Agricultural Experiment Station Bulletin No. 42,* March, 1899.

South Carolina Land Settlement Commission. *Report of the South Carolina Land Settlement Commission, 1923.* Columbia: The State Company, 1923.

South Carolina State Planning Board. *Progress Report on State Planning in South Carolina, 1938.*

Stevenson, L. T. *The Background and Economics of American Papermaking.* New York: Harper Brothers, 1940.

Store Books of J. L. Coker and Company, in possession of Mrs. D. R. Coker. The important item here is a letter book for several years around 1905.

Stout, John (ed.). *Historical Sketch of the Welsh Neck Baptist Church.* Greenville, S.C.: Hoyt and Keys, 1889.

Studley, J. D. *United States Pulp and Paper Industry.* Washington: U.S. Government Printing Office, 1938.

Taylor, Rosser H. *Ante-Bellum South Carolina.* Vol. 25, No. 2, *The James Sprunt Studies in History and Political Science.* Chapel Hill: The University of North Carolina Press, 1942.

Thompson, Holland. "The Civil War and Social and Economic Changes," *Annals of the American Academy of Political and Social Science,* 153: 14 (January, 1931), 11-20.

Townsend, Leah. *South Carolina Baptists, 1670-1805.* Florence, S.C.: The Florence Printing Company, 1935.

"Tribute of Respect," a periodical clipping, probably from a Baptist publication, published in 1859 on the death of Nancy Coker, in possession of T. E. Goodson, Hartsville, South Carolina.

U.S. Bureau of the Census. *Fifteenth Census of the United States: 1930, Population,* I. Washington: U.S. Government Printing Office, 1933.

U.S. Bureau of the Census. *Sixteenth Census of the United States: 1940, Population,* I. Washington: U.S. Government Printing Office, 1942.

U.S. Department of Agriculture. *An Historical Survey of American Agriculture.* (Yearbook Separate No. 1783.) Washington: U.S. Government Printing Office, 1941.

U.S. Department of Agriculture. *Yearbook of Agriculture, 1940.* Washington: U.S. Government Printing Office, 1940.

U.S. Department of Agriculture. *Yearbook of Agriculture, 1936.* Washington: U.S. Government Printing Office, 1936.

University of South Carolina Publication. *South Carolina, Economic Social Conditions in 1944.* Columbia: University of South Carolina Press, 1945.

Vance, Rupert B. *All These People.* Chapel Hill: The University of North Carolina Press, 1946.

—— and Gordon W. Blackwell. *New Farm Homes for Old; a Study of Rural Public Housing in the South.* University: The University of Alabama Press, 1946.

Wade, John Donald. *Augustus Baldwin Longstreet.* New York: The Macmillan Company, 1924.

Wallace, D. D. *History of South Carolina.* 4 vols. New York: American Historical Society, Inc., 1934.

Watkins, J. L. *Consumption of Cotton in the Southern States.* Yearbook of Agriculture, 1903.

Webber, H. J. Article in the *Arkansas Gazette* (Little Rock), September 26, 1920. Clipping in D. R. Coker papers.

Wellman, Manly Wade. *Giant in Gray.* New York: Charles Scribner's Sons, 1949.

Wells, E. L. *Hampton and Reconstruction.* Columbia: The State Co., 1902.

The Welsh Neck Church Book, the Welsh Neck Baptist Church, Society Hill, S. C.

Wheelock, Mary E. *Paper, Its History and Development.* Chicago: American Library Association, 1928.

Wilds, George J. "Commercial Cotton Breeding." Address before Annual Meeting of Georgia Agronomists, January 23, 1947. Available in mimeographed form from Coker's Pedigreed Seed Company.

——. "Commercial Oat Breeding." Address before Annual Meeting of Georgia Agronomists, January 22, 1947. Available in mimeographed form from Coker's Pedigreed Seed Company.
Wilds, Ruth Lawton. "Biography of J. J. Lawton," typed MS, March 23, 1934, in the possession of E. H. Lawton.
Williams, A. B. *Hampton and His Red Shirts*. Charleston: Walker, Evans and Cogswell Company, 1935.
Williams, G. Croft. *A Social Interpretation of South Carolina*. Columbia: University of South Carolina Press, 1946.
Williams, T. Harry. "An Analysis of Some Reconstruction Attitudes," *The Journal of Southern History*, XII (November, 1946), 476-86.
Wilson, Mrs. Furman E. *Memories of Society Hill*. Hartsville, S. C.: The Hartsville Publishing Company, 1909-1910, for the Pee Dee Historical Society.
——. "Memories of Society Hill and Some of Its People. Home Life, Written for My Own Children and Brothers and Sisters Alone." This is a typewritten manuscript in the Watson collection of Major Coker's papers.
Winkler, John K. *Tobacco Tycoon*. New York: Random House, 1942.
Wolfers, Arnold, Edgar S. Furniss and Walt W. Rostow. *James Harvey Rogers, 1886-1939*. Stamford, Conn.: privately printed, 1940.
Woodward, C. Vann. *Tom Watson, Agrarian Rebel*. New York: The Macmillan Company, 1938.
Zeichner, Oscar. "The Transition from Slave to Free Agricultural Labor in the Southern States," *Agricultural History*, XIII, No. 1 (January, 1939), 22-32.

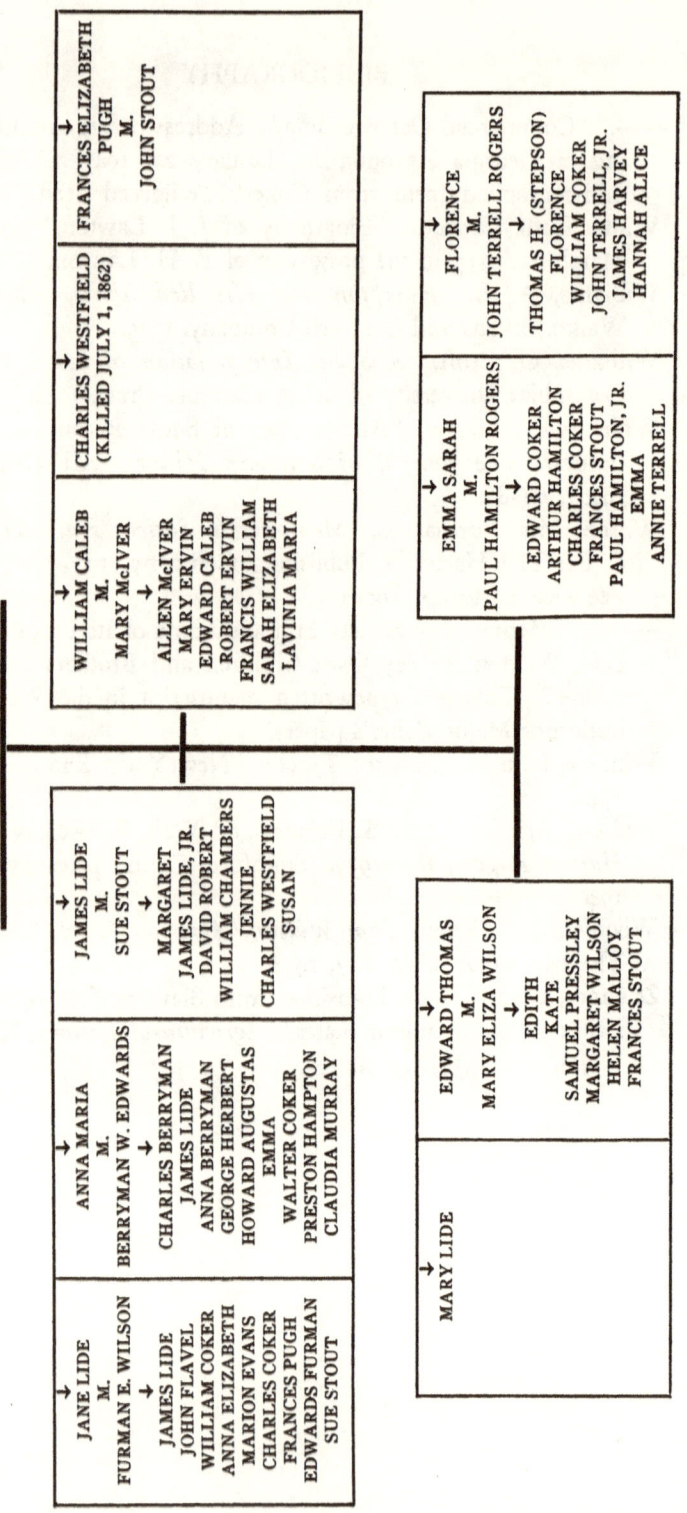

Index

Agriculture Adjustment Administration, 213-215
American Sulphite Pulp Company, 111
Atlantic Coast Line Railway, 116

Black Creek, 4
Bourbons, 99
"Bread and butter cotton," 167-168, 197-199

Campbell, C. H., 275, 305
Camp Marion, 36, 45-46, 79-80
Carolina Fiber Company, 236, 281
Cashaway Baptist Church, 20
Cheraw and Darlington Railroad, 107
Clemson College Experiment Station, 132
Coastal Plain, 3
Coker, Allen, 102, 295, 306
Coker, Anna Maria, 37, 38, 46-47
Coker, Ann McLendon (Nancy), 22-23, 42
Coker, Caleb, Sr., 21-22
Coker, Caleb, Jr., marriage, 3, 7; partnership with J. Eli Gregg, 7-8, 24-25, 31-32; arrival in Society Hill, 20; childhood in New Providence, 22-23; employed by Alexander Sparks, 23-24; builds new house, 25-26; concern for Hannah's health, 26-27; as merchant and businessman, 33-35; life at Camp Marion, 36, 45-46; and his children, 37, 43-45, 55-56; stewardship of family at New Providence, 42; member of Cooperation Party, 53-54; attitude toward secession, 53-55; farming operations, 1858, 54; pays northern creditors, 59; storekeeping after the war, 84; death, 90
Coker, Charles Westfield, 37, 57, 58, 65
Coker, Charles Westfield, Sr., 222; President of Southern Novelty Company, 223; and quantity production, 223-224; awareness of implications of science and industry, 224-226; technical developments at Sonoco, 227-229; as industrial executive, 230; concern for social welfare, 231-235; teaching of children, 298-299
Coker, Charles W., Jr., 271, 275
Coker, David R., 127; interest in agricultural experiments, 132-133; contact with Dr. H. J. Webber, 133-134; breeding of first long staple cotton, 134-136; efforts to sell staple cotton to mills, 136-140; growing of staple cotton in Hartsville, 140-144; interest in agricultural problems, 144-147; efforts to improve cotton marketing, 147-149; interest in crop diversification and specialization, 149-153; consideration of tenancy, 153-157; establishment of agricultural education in high schools, 157-158; interest in extension service, 158-159; incorporation of Coker's Pedigreed Seed Company, 159; responsibility of businessman and banker to farmer, 159-164; Class B Director of Richmond Branch Federal Reserve System, 165; concern for poverty of southern agriculture, 165-166; breeding of Webber Cotton, 167-168; "bread and butter" cotton, 168-169; breeding of corn, small grains,

INDEX

peas, velvet beans and sorghum, 169; seed catalogue, 169-170; State Food Administrator and Chairman of the State Council of Defense, 170; depression of 1920-1921, 190-196; breeding of Coker-Cleveland Cotton, 196-199; breeding of small grains, 199-200; rural poverty of the 1920's, 200-203; necessity of federal aid, 203; difficulties of Seed Company during the 1920's, 204-206; concern for state of American society, 206-209; support of Roosevelt, 209-210; advice on Federal farm program, 210-212; relations with A.A.A., 212-215; breeding of cold and smut resistant oats, 215-217; tribute to agricultural agents, 217-218; death, 218; letter on family unity, 292-293; teaching of children, 298

Coker, Mrs. David R., 273

Coker, Edward Caleb, 237-238

Coker, Edward Thomas, 37, 91

Coker, Emma Sarah, 37

Coker, Florence, 37

Coker, Frances Elizabeth Pugh, 37, 85

Coker, Francis William, 265-266, 268-270

Coker, Hannah Ann Frances Lide, marriage, 3; life in Springville, 3-7; arrival in Society Hill, 7-8; church membership, 17, 19; bad health, 26-31; trip to Springs, 29-30; instruction of children at home, 37-38, 43-45; behind enemy lines with James, 69-78; sends check to Baltimore, 84; leaves Camp Marion, 91; hopes for children, 296

Coker, James, 21

Coker, James Lide, 37; education, 38-39, 47-49; doctrine of special providence, 51-52; work on Hartsville plantation, 52-53; agricultural experiments, 53; enters war, 58; at First Manassas, 58-59; Battle of Fort Magrudger, 62; Battle of Seven Pines, 63; Seven Days Battle, 64; Battle of Fredericksburg, 68; wounded in Battle of Lookout Valley, 69; capture and journey home, 69-78; member, House of Representatives, 80-81; journey to Richmond, 81-82; new pattern of farm work, 85-86; opens store, 86-87; Union Reform Party, 89; discusses need for industry, 95-96; partnership with George Norwood, 96; establishment of bank, 98; establishment of Darlington Manufacturing Company, 98-99; turns main interest to Hartsville, 101-102; building of railroad, 107-108; decision to make paper pulp, 110-111; financial condition, 114; decision to make paper, 116; disagreement with Parsons, 117-121; relationship with James, Jr., 121-122; partner, Coker's Pedigreed Seed Company, 159; work at Carolina Fiber Company and Southern Novelty Company, 171; and his children, 172-173; proposed sale of Carolina Fiber Company stock, 173-174; interest in Welsh Neck High School, 174-175; establishment of Coker College, 175-178; interest in Coker College, 178-181; adherence to fundamentals, 183-188; conception of father, 297-298

Coker, James Lide, Jr., building of railroad, 107; attends Steven's Institute of Technology, 109; thesis on paper making, 109; attempts to make paper pulp from pine, 110-116; attempts to make paper, 116-127; difficulties with Parsons, 117-121; relationship with Major Coker, 121-123; develops new paper making processes, 122-125; solves resin problem, 126-127; cone and tube making, 128-130; death, 271

Coker, James Lide, III, 271, 275, 305

Coker, Jane Lide (Mrs. Furman E. Wilson), 26, 38, 46-47

Coker, Mary Lide, 37, 91

Coker, Richard Gay, 236, 271, 282

Coker, Robert Ervin, education, 247-249; early work on North Carolina coast, 247-249; work in Peru, 249; work for United States Bureau of Fisheries, 249-250; at University of North Carolina, 250-253; major research, 250-251; interest in ecology, 251-252; work in national scientific agencies, 252; chairman, Department of Zoology, 252-253; establishment of Institute of Fisheries Research, 253-255; later books, 255; philosophy of a biologist, 255-256

Coker, Robert R., 271, 283, 289

Coker, Sarah, 246-247

INDEX

Coker, Sue Stout, 56, 69, 94, 85; bad health and death, 172-173
Coker, Thomas, Sr., 20-21
Coker, William Caleb, 37; attends South Carolina College, 47; enters war, 57; at First Manassas, 58-59; Lt. in new company, 64; wounded in Battle of Malvern Hill, 64; wounded at Sharpsburg, 67; Battle of Fredericksburg, 68; wounded and captured at Gettysburg, 68; return home from war, 82-83; postwar health and work, 85; stewardship at Society Hill, 90-91; analysis of Southern agriculture, 91-95; race for State Senate, 96-97; career in State Senate, 97-98; governor's race, 1886, 99-101; management of mill, 102-103; death, 103; qualities of mind and spirit, 103-105; Darlington Riot, 105; conception of the law, 106-107; advice to son, 298
Coker, William Chambers, contact with Dr. Webber, 133; makes first field selections of long staple cotton, 134; education, 238-240; at University of North Carolina, 240-245; taxonomic works, 240-241; arboretum, 242-243; editor, *Journal* of the Elisha Mitchell Scientific Society, 243; establishment of the Department of Botany, 243; major research, 243-244; outstanding students, 244; as teacher, 245; interest in Coker College, 245; death, 245
Coker-Cleveland cotton, 197-199
Coker College, establishment of, 175-178; interest of family in, 291-292
Coker 100 cotton, 216
Coker family, 295-300, 302-303
Coker's Arboretum, 242-243
Coker 100 Wilt cotton, 283
Columbia State, 144
Cones, first made at Hartsville, 128-130
Cook, H. T., 183
Cooperative Cotton Marketing, views of D. R. Coker, 201
Cotton economy, and credit, 32, 35

Dargan, Edwin Charles, 183
Darlington County Agricultural Society, 87, 147, 154
Darlington Manufacturing Company, 98, 103

Darlington Riot, 105, 106
Deltatype Webber Long Staple Cotton, 217
Depression of 1920-21, 190, 194
D. M. Jones and Company, 138
Donaldson, Margaret, 84
Dossey, Reverend, 17-18
Dunlap, C. K., 226-229, 275

Edwards, Berryman, 85
Edwards, Howard, 112, 113, 173-174
Edwards, Walter, 173-174
Evans, Josiah, 14

Farmer's Alliance, 160
Farmer's Union, 160-161
Federal Reserve System, 165
Ferguson's Navarro oats, 200
Ferris, H. C., 109
Fulghum oats, 199
Fulgrain oats, 215
Furman, James Clement, 18, 29-30

Gandy, Henry, 113
Gilbert, J. B., 275
Grady, Henry, 184
Grange, 160
Gregg, J. Eli, 24
Griffin and Little, 125

Hall, A. J., 180
Hampton, Wade, 96, 97, 99
Hartsville, S. C., Caleb buys plantation at, 49; wreckage of Sherman, 82; growth of, 272-273
Hartsville Company, 182
Hartsville Messenger, 143, 146, 158
Hartsville Railroad, 107
Hoover, Herbert, 203
Houston, David F., 158

J. L. Coker and Company, 194, 203-204

Knapp, Dr. Bradford, 158
Kohn, August, 139

Lawton, Edward H., 271
Lawton, Joseph J., building of railroad, 107-108; as partner in J. L. Coker and Company, 130-131; partner in Coker's Pedigreed Seed Company, 159; interest in Welsh Neck High School, 175; death, 271

Lawton, Margaret Coker, 107
Lide, David, 28
Lide, James, 6, 27
Lide, Maria, 41-42
Lide, Major Robert, 5, 6
Lides, family of, 4, 28, 41
Long, Dr. W. W., 157
Long Bluff, 10, 12

MacRae, Hugh, 210
Martin, J. H., 275, 305
Middle Country, 3, 5-6
Mills, Dr. J. E., 218, 276
Mills, Robert, 8
Mims, Edwin, 164, 184
Moore, Andrew E., 140

Napier, J. M., 157, 217
New Providence, 20
New South, 184-185
Norton, J. B., 199
Norwood, George, 96, 115
Norwood, J. W., 174, 185

Page, Walter Hines, 164, 184
Pairpont Corporation, 221-222
Parker, Lewis W., 140
Parsons, W. H., Sr., agreement with Cokers, 111, 112, 113, 114, 116, 117-123
Parsons, W. H., Jr., 115
Pedigreed Seed Company, financial difficulties in 1920, 204-206; influence of cotton breeding, 284-286; relations with governmental agencies, 287-288; grain breeding, 289; hybrid corn breeding, 290; development of Coker 139 tobacco, 290
Pee Dee Historical Society, 183
Pee Dee Middle Country, 11, 13
Pee Dee River, 4, 5, 6, 7
Pine, for paper making, 110, 125-127
Poe, Clarence, 217
Pusey and Jones, 124

Radicals, 96, 97
Reconstruction in Darlington County, 87-90
Resin, obstacle to paper making, 125-127
Richardson, J. P., 100
Rogers, Arthur H., 306
Rogers, James Harvey, education, 257-258; academic work in monetary analysis, 258-260; economic analysis for national policy in depression, 260-263; adviser to President Roosevelt, 263; concern for democratic action in economics, 263-265; death, 264
Rogers, Paul, in Carolina Fiber Company, 174, 235, 236, 282
Roosevelt, Franklin, 209, 210
Roper, Daniel C., 210

St. David's Society, 12, 15, 39-40
Sheppard, J. C., 100
Shoemaker, Daniel N., 134
Smith, W. F., 128-130, 220-221, 223
Society Hill, 7; description of, in 1826, 8-9; Welsh settlement, 9-10; other settlers, 10-11; revolt in 1760's, 11; establishment of court and jail, 11; declaration of rights in 1774, 11-12; establishment of St. David's Society, 12; as religious, legal and educational center, 12-13; growth after 1800, 13; commerce, 13; leading families and public servants, 13-14; establishment of library, 16; summary of life in village, 16-19
Sonoco Products Company, expansion, 276-178; changes in organization, 276-279; unions, 279; merger with Carolina Fiber Company, 281
South Carolina Association of Cotton Manufactures, 139
South Carolina Council, "Report of the Committee on Agriculture, 1931," 211
South Carolina Experiment Station, 144-145
South Carolina State Farm Bureau, 289
Southern Cotton Association, 160-161
Southern Novelty Company, established, 128-130; capitalization, 129, 174; early developments in cone making, 220-222
Sparks, Alexander, 23
Springville, S. C., 3, 4, 5, 6, 7
Stevens Institute of Technology, 107, 109

Tiller, Bill, 217
Tillman, Benjamin R., 99, 100, 101, 105, 106
Timberlake, C. G., 274
Tubes, first made at Hartsville, 128-130

INDEX

Union Reform Party, 89

Victorgrain oats, 289-290

Wallace, Henry A., 212, 216
Webber, Dr. H. J., 133-134, 167-168
Welsh Baptists, 9
Welsh Neck, 10
Welsh Neck Baptist Association, 175
Welsh Neck Baptist Church, 10, 14, 40
Welsh Neck High School, 175
Whittemore, B. F., 96-97

Wiggins, A. L. M., 159, 274
Wilds, George, early work in Pedigreed Seed Company, 159, 217, 273-274; marriage, 274; president, Pedigreed Seed Company, 282-283
Wilds, Mrs. George, 274
Wilds Long Staple Cotton, 216
Williams, David Rogerson, 14-15, 17, 149
Williams, McIver, 150-151
Wilmith, J. F., 275
World Cotton Conference, 196
World's Work, 164, 184

www.ingramcontent.com/pod-product-compliance
Lightning Source LLC
Chambersburg PA
CBHW021352290426
44108CB00010B/215